بسم الله الرحمن الرحيم

Gibril Fouad Haddad

SUNNA NOTES

Studies in Ḥadīth and Doctrine

Volume III:

The Binding Proof of the Sunna

SUNNA NOTES
Studies in Hadith and Doctrine
Volume 3:
The Binding Proof of the Sunna
Adapted from ʿAbd al-Ghanī ʿAbd al-Khāliq's
Ḥujjiyyat al-Sunna
Foreword by Dr. Muḥammad Saʿīd Ramaḍān al-Būṭī

ISBN: 978-1-938058-80-6

Reprint: Institute for Spiritual & Cultural Understanding, Fenton, MI USA
First edition: AQSA Publications, UK & WARDA Publications, Germany

Published in the US by Institute for Spiritual & Cultural Understanding 17195 Silver Parkway #401, Fenton, MI 48430 USA
Tel: (810) 593-1222
Email: info@sufilive.com
Web:
http://www.sufilive.com
Purchase online at: http://www.isn1.net

Typesetting by Abd al-Hafidh Wentzel
Cover Calligraphy by Moncef Elh

Cataloging-in-Publication Data
A CIP catalogue record for this book is available from the British Library

بسم الله الرحمن الرحيم

﴿فَلَا وَرَبِّكَ لَا يُؤْمِنُونَ حَتَّىٰ يُحَكِّمُوكَ فِيمَا شَجَرَ بَيْنَهُمْ
ثُمَّ لَا يَجِدُوا فِي أَنفُسِهِمْ حَرَجاً مِّمَّا قَضَيْتَ وَيُسَلِّمُوا تَسْلِيماً﴾

(٤:٦٥)

{*But nay, by your Lord! They shall not believe in truth until they make you judge of what is in dispute between them and find within themselves no dislike of that which you decide, and submit with full submission.*}(4:65)

Some people came and said: “Messenger of Allah, verily we love Allah!” whereupon Allah revealed {*Say: If you love Allah, follow me; Allah will love you and forgive you your sins. Allah is forgiving, merciful*} (3:31). Al-Ḥasan said: “Thereafter, the mark of their love for Him was their adherence to the Sunna.”

CONTENTS

THE BINDING PROOF OF THE SUNNA

Abbreviations 10
Chains of Transmission – Dedication 11

Foreword: The Proofs of the Sunna
by Muḥammad Saʿīd Ramaḍān al-Būṭī 13
The Sources of the Law 14
The Meanings of Sunna 15
Fiqh Levels of the Sunna 16
Neither Disregard Nor Exaggerate 19
Muslims Who Denigrate the Sunna 19
Muslims Who Denigrate Prophetic Medicine 20
The Inferiority Complex 23
Anti-Sunna Infiltrators 27
Ways to Undermine the Sunna 28
The "Qur'ān-Only" Fraud 29
Assault on Ḥadīth Science Targeting Islam 32

The Binding Proof of the Sunna
adapted from ʿAbd al-Ghanī ʿAbd al-Khāliq's *Ḥujjiyyat al-Sunna* 35
Preliminaries 37
{*The Decision Rests with Allah Only*} 37
{*And Obey the Prophet*} 37
Conditions for Using Ḥadīth as Proof 39
Differences in Relying upon Ḥadīth Transmission 39
The General Evidentiary Force of the Sunna 40
Chapter 1: The Prophet's Immune State Dictates that Ḥadīth is Revelation 45
Chapter 2: Divine Approval of the Companions' Conformity with the Sunna 51
Chapter 3: Proofs from the Noble Qur'ān for the Sunna as Evidence 61
a) Verses that Indicate the Obligatoriness of Believing in the Prophet ﷺ 61

b) Verses that indicate that the Prophet ﷺ elucidates the Book and explains its wisdom in a manner that carries authority on the part of Allah ﷻ 69
c) Verses that indicate the obligatoriness of obeying the Prophet ﷺ in absolute terms 72
d) Verses that indicate the obligatoriness of following and imitating him ﷺ in whatsoever issues from him 80
e) Verses indicating that Allah ﷻ has tasked the Prophet ﷺ with following and conveying what is revealed to him 82
Chapter 4: Proofs from the Noble Sunna for the Sunna as Evidence 87
THE CONVEYANCE FROM THE ONE WHO NEVER LIES ﷺ THAT: 87
1. Allah ﷻ has revealed to him ﷺ the Qur'ān and other than it 90
2. Whatever legal rulings he ﷺ has expounded and stipulated are the expositions and stipulations of Allah Himself 92
3. It is impossible to understand the laws and ordinances of Islam from the Qur'ān alone 93
4. Sunna-based practice is Qur'ān-based 95
5. The *Umma* in its entirety and without exception has been ordered to accept his ﷺ words, obey his commands and prohibitions, and follow his Sunna 96
6. Whoever obeys him ﷺ and holds fast to his Sunna obeys Allah ﷻ and follows guidance 96
7. Whoever disobeys him ﷺ and rejects his sayings has disobeyed Allah, followed misguidance, and perished 98
8. Faith and belief remains incomplete until one follows all that he ﷺ brought 101
9. Nothing but truth comes out of his ﷺ blessed mouth 104
10. The best guidance of all is his ﷺ guidance 104
The ḥadīth "I have left among you two matters…" 107
11. Anything that he ﷺ did not himself bring but which people innovate after him according to their whims and caprice, or to serve their lusts, is an innovation 117
HIS ﷺ ORDER TO HOLD FAST TO HIS SUNNA AND HIS PROHIBITION TO FOLLOW OR PRACTICE ONLY WHAT IS FOUND IN THE QUR'ĀN IN ABANDONMENT OF THE SUNNA 125

HIS ﷺ COMMAND TO LISTEN TO HIS HADITH, MEMORIZE IT, AND CONVEY IT TO WHOEVER DID NOT HEAR IT 128
Chapter 5: It is Unfeasible to Act Solely on the Basis of the Qur'ān 133

Ibn Ḥajar's Commentary on the Ḥadīth of *Islām, Īmān, Iḥsān* 151
1. Al-Bukhārī's Chapter-Title and First Narration: Book of *Īmān* 154
2. Al-Bukhārī's Second Narration: Book of *Tafsīr* 155
3. Muslim's First Set of Narrations 156
4. Muslim's Second Set of Narrations 159
5. Muslim's Third Narration 160
6. **Ibn Ḥajar's Commentary** on al-Bukhārī's Chapter-Title and First Narration as well as the Variants 162
The Difference Between *Islām* and *Īmān* 163
The Complementariness of *Islām* and *Īmān* 165
Muslim's Chains and the Variance of Their Texts 168
The Reason This Ḥadīth Took Place 172
A Note of Benefit on the Qadariyya Heresy 178
A Warning: Confirmation vs. Mere Belief 180
A Warning: There is No Sight of Allah ﷻ in the World 184
Critique of Ibn ʿArabī's Interpretation 185
A Note of Benefit: The Questioner Already Knew 186
A Note of Benefit: ʿĪsā ﷺ Asked Gibril ﷺ about the Hour 189
Two Warnings: Child-Bearing Slaves – The Word "Lord" 194
A Warning: Knowledge of the Unseen 197
A Note of Benefit: Cognizance and Knowledge 198
Warnings: Gibril's Form–Didacticism– "Mother of the Sunna" 201

Indexes 203
Index of Qur'ānic Verses 205
Index of Narrations 207
Bibliography 215

ABBREVIATIONS

ʿAbd al-Razzāq = his *Muṣannaf*

Abū Dāwūd = his *Sunan*

Abū Yaʿlā = his *Musnad*

Aḥmad = his *Musnad*

Al-Bazzār = his *Musnad*

Al-Bukhārī = his *Ṣaḥīḥ*

Al-Dārimī = his *Musnad*, also known as the *Sunan*

Al-Ḥākim = his *Mustadrak ʿalā al-Ṣaḥīḥayn*

Al-Haythamī = his *Majmaʿ al-Zawā'id*

Ibn Abī Shayba = his *Muṣannaf*

Ibn ʿAdī = his *Kāmil*

Ibn ʿAsākir = his *Tārīkh Dimashq*

Ibn Ḥibbān = his *Ṣaḥīḥ*

Ibn Khuzayma = his *Ṣaḥīḥ*

Ibn Mājah = his *Sunan*

Ibn Saʿd = his *Ṭabaqāt al-Kubrā*

Mālik = his *Muwaṭṭa'*

Al-Munāwī = his *Fayḍ al-Qadīr*

Muslim = his *Ṣaḥīḥ*

Al-Nasā'ī = his minor *Sunan* known as *al-Mujtabā*

Al-Ṭayālisī = his *Musnad*

Al-Tirmidhī = his *Sunan*

بسم الله الرحمن الرحيم

The pauper in need of his Lord's mercy and compiler of this book, Gibrīl ibn Fouād, is graced to narrate "Ḥujjiyyat al-Sunna" by specific permission (ijāza khāṣṣa) from the two Shāfiʿī Masters of Damascus Shaykh Muḥammad Saʿīd ibn Mullā Ramaḍān al-Būṭī and Shaykh Muṣṭafā ibn Saʿīd al-Khinn, both of them from Shaykh Muṣṭafā ibn ʿAbd al-Khāliq, from his brother Shaykh ʿAbd al-Ghanī ibn ʿAbd al-Khāliq; and by general permission (ijāza ʿāmma) from Shaykh Wahbī ibn Sulaymān Ghāwjī al-Albānī al-Ḥanafī, from Shaykh ʿAbd al-Fattāḥ Abū Ghudda (1336-1417), from Shaykh ʿAbd al-Ghanī ibn ʿAbd al-Khāliq al-Shāfiʿī al-Miṣrī (1326-1402).

This book is dedicated to the blessed memory of our Shaykh, the Sharīf and Murshid Sayyidī Muḥammad al-Muṣṭafā Baṣīr ibn Sayyidī Ibrāhīm ibn Sayyidī Imbārak al-Baṣīrī al-Ḥasanī al-Idrīsī al-Maghribī al-Sūsī al-Muqri' al-Faqīh al-Mālikī al-Ṣūfī al-Shādhilī al-Darqāwī (Ramaḍān 1360 – Night of mid-Shaʿbān 1427), my Allah thank and reward him on behalf of the Umma, and grant him the Highest Paradise, Āmīn!

Foreword

Shaykh Muḥammad Saʿīd Ramaḍān al-Būṭī on
The Proofs of the Sunna
from his Commentary on al-Nawawī's *Riyaḍ al-Ṣāliḥīn*[1]

In the Name of Allah All-Beneficent Most Merciful

This is the seven hundred and twenty-sixth lesson on Imām al-Nawawī's book *Riyāḍ al-Ṣāliḥīn* – may Allah Almighty have mercy on him and benefit us with his learning.

[Imām al-Nawawī said – Allah Most High have mercy on him and benefit us with his wisdom:] Book of the Etiquette of Travel (*ādāb al-safar*); Chapter on the desirability of setting forth on the fifth day of the week (*al-khamīs* = "Thursday") and the desirability of doing so at the beginning of the day.

It is narrated from Kaʿb ibn Mālik ﷺ that the Prophet ﷺ went out on the campaign of Tabūk on the day of Thursday, and he liked to set forth on Thursday. The ḥadīth is agreed upon [by al-Bukhārī and Muslim].

In another narration in the two *Ṣaḥīḥs*: "Very rarely indeed did the Messenger of Allah ﷺ set forth – meaning: for travel, or military campaign, or the like – other than on the day of Thursday."

And it is narrated from Ṣakhr ibn Wadāʿ al-Ghāmidī ﷺ the Companion that the Messenger of Allah ﷺ said: "O Allah! Bless my Community in its mornings" and that whenever he sent out a military detachment or an army, he would send them out at the beginning of the day. Ṣakhr was a trader and he would send out his wares at the beginning of the day; thereafter he became wealthy and his property abundant. Abū Dāwūd and al-Tirmidhī narrated it and the latter said: "It is a fair (*ḥasan*) narration."

[1] Unpublished lectures delivered in Damascus through the nineties.

This is what Imām al-Nawawī mentioned in the chapter of the desirability of setting forth on the day of Thursday and the desirability of doing so at the beginning of the day.

The Sources of the Law

We know that the sources of Islamic Law (*maṣādir al-sharī ʿa al-Islamiyya*) are summed up in the Qur'ān first of all, then the Sunna, then scholarly Consensus (*al-ijmāʿ*), then Analogy (*al-qiyās*) to what the Qur'ān and the Sunna have explicitly stipulated. This is what the masses of the scholars have agreed upon.

The foundation of these four sources is, of course, the Qur'ān. For by the Qur'ān we know the probative force of the Sunna; and by the Qur'ān we know the probative force of Consensus; and by the Qur'ān we know the probative force of Analogy.[2]

If the Qur'ān had not ordered us to obey the Messenger of Allah ﷺ we would not have obeyed him.[3] But Allah said: {*Whosoever obeys the Messenger obeys Allah, and whosoever turns away: We have not sent you as a warder over them*} (4:80); {*We sent no Messenger save that he should be obeyed by the leave of Allah*} (4:64); {*And We have revealed unto you the Remembrance that you may explain to mankind that which has been revealed for them*} (16:44). Because of this, and because the Qur'ān is the principal source and the first source of legislation, the acceptance of the book of Allah dictates the acceptance of the Sunna of the Messenger of Allah ﷺ.

[2] "Probative: adj. providing proof or evidence."—*Webster's*.

[3] Cf. ʿAbd al-Khāliq's comments: "The meaning of {*And obey the Prophet*} is therefore "Know that whatever the Prophet ﷺ commands or forbids you to do, it is I Who commands and forbids you" as explicited in the verse {*And whatsoever the Messenger gives you, take it, and whatsoever he forbids, abstain from it*} (59:7). Without such an order, the Prophet's ﷺ command would not have been binding upon us." See below (p. 37-38).

The Meanings of Sunna

When we say that the Sunna of the Messenger of Allah ﷺ is the second source [of the Law], branching out of the Qur'ān, many among the uneducated public become confused. To them, the meaning of the term sunna is whatever stands opposite to *farḍ*. They know that there are obligations (*furūḍ*), non-obligatory practices (*sunan*), merely permissible practices (*mubāḥāt*), forbidden practices (*muḥarramāt*), and offensive practices (*makrūhāt*).[4] So the meaning of sunna [in this context] is: "The act for which, if you do it, Allah ﷻ will reward you for it and, if you do it not, He will not take you to task for leaving it."

Thus, if we say "the Sunna is the second source of legislation," some of the uneducated public think that the meaning of the Sunna is what stands opposite to *farḍ*. This is incorrect. What is meant by Sunna here, when we enumerate the sources of the Law, is not what is the opposite of *farḍ* but the rulings indicated by the life (*sīra*) of the Messenger of Allah ﷺ, his sayings, and his deeds whether these deeds are obligatory, or addressing the forbidden, or desirable, or merely permissible. Each and every one of these categories is addressed by the actual states, statements, or deeds of the Messenger of Allah ﷺ. This is what we call "Sunna" here.

So "Sunna" has two meanings. In *fiqh* we say: "This is *masnūn*, while this is *wājib*." It means that if you leave the latter, Allah ﷻ shall take you to task – this is *wājib*; while if you leave the former, He shall not take you to task – this is sunna.[5] We apply these distinctions in *fiqh*. However, when we speak of the principles of legislation (*uṣūl al-tashrīʿ*) and its sources, and we say that the first source is the Qur'ān while the second source is the Sunna,

[4] See "The Meaning of Sunna and *Bidʿa*" in volume 2 of this series, *The Excellent Innovation*.

[5] Al-Būṭī uses the words *farḍ* and *wājib* interchangeably according to the usage of the Shāfiʿī *madhhab*, which sees no difference between them except in matters pertaining to *Ḥajj*.

the word "Sunna" here does not mean what stands opposed to *farḍ*. Rather, we mean by it all the rulings without exception – whether obligatory, desirable, merely permissible, forbidden, or offensive – which the Sira of the Messenger of Allah ﷺ points to, whether in his deeds, words, or tacit approvals. We should know this well.

We are now using the second type of terminology. We say: The original source of the Law is one – the Qur'ān. Branching out of this original first source, there is a second source – the Sunna. The latter means: all that which the Messenger of Allah ﷺ taught us and mentioned to us. This second source contains rulings that pertain to the obligatory, which the Sunna indicates; it contains rulings that pertain to the forbidden, which the Sunna indicates; it contains rulings that pertain to the praiseworthy, rulings that pertain to the offensive, and rulings that pertain to the merely permissible, all of which the Sunna indicates.

I said these words as preliminaries in order to prevent from the beginning some of the confusion that may exist in the minds of some of the listeners.

Fiqh Levels of the Sunna

A second point. We say: "The Sunna of the Messenger of Allah ﷺ indicates this." Now the Prophet's ﷺ Sunna is one of the sources of the Law, and this is categorical knowledge. There is no dispute nor discussion about this. However, the level of followership dictated by the Sunna in some cases is that of the obligatory (*wājib*). In other cases the level of followership in such-and-such a Sunna is praiseworthy (*mandūb*). In other cases it is merely allowed (*ma'dhūn bihi*), meaning permissible (*mubāḥ*). And in other cases yet, the Prophet ﷺ is warning us, in his Sunna, of prohibited or offensive matters.

Therefore, what the Sunna shows us has different levels. For example: the Prophet ﷺ said: "Do not sit in the roadways."[6] This is a ruling which the Sunna has indicated, but it is part of the forbidden matters. The Prophet ﷺ made exceptions [to this] after it was said to him: "We have necessities in our roadways" saying: "If you must have your gatherings, then give the road its right." We have mentioned this ḥadīth in a previous session. When the road is given its right, sitting in it becomes permissible. So the Sunna showed us two rulings here: one that is forbidden and one that is permissible.

I shall give another example. There are, among the rulings of the Sunna, those that are obligatory. The Qur'ān said: {*Establish prayer* (*ṣalāt*) *and pay the poor-due* (*zakāt*)} (2:43, 2:83, 2:110, 4:77, 24:56, 73:20). But the Qur'ān did not expound to us the modality of *zakāt*.[7] Meaning: What is the number of head of cattle upon which *zakāt* becomes due? Twenty, or forty, or fifty, or a hundred? The Qur'ān did not mention the least number for which *zakāt* becomes due. Where is this mentioned? In the Sunna. The Messenger of Allah ﷺ said: "For every forty sheep or goats, one head."[8] So then the due payment of one sheep or goat for every forty was indicated by the Sunna; however, is this ruling obligatory or praiseworthy? It is obligatory.

[6] It is narrated from Abū Sa'īd ؓ that the Messenger of Allāh ﷺ said: "Beware of sitting in the roadways." They said: "Messenger of Allāh, we have necessities which we address in our gatherings." He replied: "If you must have your gatherings, then give the road its right." They said: "Messenger of Allāh, and what is the right of the road?" He said: "[1.] Lowering the gaze; [2.] Refraining from harm; [3.] Returning the salām; [4.] Commanding good and forbidding evil." Narrated by the Two Shaykhs. It is also narrated by Abū Dāwūd whose narration adds: "And giving directions." Al-Ṭabarānī's version adds: "And rescuing the one in distress."

[7] Cf. 'Abd al-Khāliq and Ibn Ḥazm below (p. 40-44 and p. 133-140).

[8] Narrated from Ibn 'Umar in the Four *Sunan* and Aḥmad's *Musnad* as well as from 'Alī by Abū Dāwūd and Aḥmad, and from other Companions. Al-Tirmidhī said: "Ibn 'Umar's ḥadīth is fair (*ḥasan*), and it is used by the totality of the jurists."

There are other rulings which the Sunna indicated but which do not rise to the level of the obligatory. Instead, they are only at the level of the "sunna". For example, we pray two *rak'as* of Sunna prayers after the obligatory *maghrib* prayer. Were these two *rak'as* stipulated by the Qur'ān or the Sunna? They were stipulated by the Sunna. Are these two *rak'as* obligatory or non-obligatory? They are non-obligatory. They are sunna in the juristic sense. That is: if you pray them, Allah ﷻ shall record for you a reward; and if you do not pray them, He shall not record for you an offense. These two *rak'as* were shown to us by the Sunna, which is the second source of legislation, and at the same time the ruling pertaining to them is "praiseworthy" (*mandūb*).

Does the eclipse prayer (*ṣalāt al-khusūf*) – indicated by the Sunna – rise to the level of "obligatory" or "praiseworthy"? Praiseworthy.

Even among the praiseworthy matters indicated by the Sunna, there are those matters that rise to the level of "emphasized Sunna" (*sunna mu'akkada*) and those that do not quite reach that level but are only "Sunna."

Now, in what category does the Prophetic ḥadīth agreed upon by al-Bukhārī and Muslim and narrated by Ka'b ibn Mālik ؓ fit, whereby the Prophet ﷺ "liked to set forth on the day of Thursday?" Is this ruling indicated by the Qur'ān or the Sunna? The latter. Does this Sunna-based ruling rise to the level of obligatoriness? No. It remains at the level of what is sunna. Is it an "emphasized Sunna?" Again, no. But it is sunna. We must know this well.

To recapitulate: The Sunna is the first subsidiary source (*al-maṣdar al-far'ī al-awwal*) after the Qur'ān among the sources of Islamic Law. We describe it as a subsidiary source because it is the Qur'ān that actually indicated that it is a source, and the basis of everything is the Qur'ān. The Qur'ān commanded us to follow the Messenger of Allah ﷺ: therefore we follow the Messenger of Allah ﷺ.

Neither Disregard Nor Exaggerate

I clarified this matter for two reasons. First, in order to give this ruling the place that the *Sharīʿa* gave it: It is praiseworthy (*yundab*) that your setting forth on a trip take place on a Thursday, because the Prophet ﷺ used to do it and would prefer it thus. Does this mean that if you were to travel on the day of *jumuʿa* – Friday – or the fourth day of the week – Wednesday – you would commit a forbidden act? No.

Neither disregard nor exaggerate. Do not neglect this Sunna. Try to travel on a Thursday if you can, when you have to travel; but do not impose on yourself something which Allah ﷻ did not impose on you, and say: "If I do not travel on Thursday I shall not travel" as if the matter were an obligation. By keeping a middle path between the two we would steer clear of both excess (*al-ifrāṭ*) and neglect (*al-tafrīṭ*).

Muslims Who Denigrate the Sunna

The second reason I clarified this matter is that some people in our time – and by the words "some people" I mean: among the Muslims – indeed, some of those who have studied the Law (*al-mutafaqqihīn*), who speak in the name of Islam, and who are renowned among people for making *daʿwa* to Islam and being concerned with Islam, pay no attention (*yuhmilūn*) to that kind of Sunna. They avert their eyes from it!

For example, the fifth day of the week – Thursday – is the day on which the Messenger of Allah ﷺ used to like to set forth on a trip. If he wanted to begin a project he would begin it on the fourth day – Wednesday – saying: "Nothing is begun on a

Wednesday except it is completed"[9] and other similar matters. You will find people in our time, among the Muslims, who not only pay no attention to these matters but even advise, in public functions, against paying attention to them!

If someone such as myself proposed to a group of people, for example, to set forth on a trip or a picnic on a certain day, and I said to them: "Try to make your trip fall on a Thursday," perhaps someone would scoff and philosophize, saying: "Whether we travel on Thursday or Wednesday, or Friday, what is the difference between this day and that? These are among the matters in which the Prophet ﷺ acted as a human being, not as a prophet." They will say this and they will toss these narrations behind their backs.

This attitude exists. Unfortunately, there are many similar types who will dismiss, scoff at, and belittle the Muslims' conformity to that matter – which we never said was on the level of obligation, but only on the level of praiseworthiness. Yet they deprecate any conformity with it.

Muslims Who Denigrate Prophetic Medicine

This is a very grave matter. There are other related aspects to this question. For example, the Prophet ﷺ spoke about many kinds of food and warned that they contained abundant remedies for many diseases. Prophetic medicine (*al-ṭibb al-nabawī*) is well-known, and many are those who have authored books on this subject. Yet we find today, among the Muslims, those who belittle following the Prophet ﷺ in these matters. They will claim that to treat them seriously contradicts science and civilization.

[9] *Mā budi'a bi-shay'in yawma al-arbiʿā'i illā tamma.* Al-ʿAjlūnī said in *Kashf al-Khafā'* (2:237) that al-Sakhāwī said in *al-Maqāṣid al-Ḥasana* that he had found no basis (*aṣl*) for the actual attribution of this ḥadīth to the Prophet, although al-Marghinānī – the author of *al-Hidāya* – used to narrate it with a *marfūʿ* chain. See more in al-Qārī's *Asrār.*

Of course, when I see that those who say these things are actually immoral people (*fasaqa*), I pay no heed to them whatsoever. A corrupt person is nothing but a corrupt person. But I notice that some of those who pray, and those who speak and write about Islam, take this position.

For example, it is related in the *Ṣaḥīḥ* that the Prophet ﷺ said: "The black seed is a remedy or cure for every disease except death."[10] These are authentic words, yet I find those who, when they pass by such a narration, fold it up and put it aside without speaking about it; and when they hear those who mention it or read it aloud, they will dispute it, pay no attention to it, and say: "This falls under the chapter of Arab customs that prevailed in the Arabian peninsula at the time. It was known among them that the black seed contained a remedy, and the Prophet ﷺ merely conveyed whatever word of mouth the Arabs conveyed at the time on the topic." Meaning: [they claim] there is no relation to Divine revelation in these words whatsoever.

I shall give another example. The Prophet ﷺ said, according to the narration of the two Shaykhs [al-Bukhārī and Muslim], Imām Aḥmad, al-Tirmidhī, and others, as narrated by Saʿd ibn Abī Waqqāṣ: "Whoever eats seven *ʿujwa* dates in the morning, no poison nor magic will harm him on that day." That is: from the *ʿujwa* dates that grow in Madīna until our day, not from any *ʿujwa* date. This ḥadīth is agreed upon in its authenticity and there is no problem concerning it. Yet you will find some Muslims who speak and write about Islam, and who display ardent zeal for Islam, not acknowledging the least authority of this ḥadīth over them. If you tell them it is a sound ḥadīth they

[10] Narrated from ʿĀʾisha and Abū Hurayra by al-Bukhārī, Muslim, al-Tirmidhī, Ibn Mājah, and Aḥmad through nineteen chains. Al-Zuhrī said: "The black seed is black cumin (*al-shūnīz*)." It is also named the seed of blessing (*ḥabbat al-baraka*), Indian cumin, fennel-flower, corn cockle, and wild savager. Latin name: *nigella sativa*.

will not argue with you but will say: "The Prophet ﷺ said these words only as part of the custom current at the time among the people of the Arabian peninsula and not as part of Divine revelation. So the statement is possibly right and possibly wrong."

Did the Companions of the Messenger of Allah ﷺ understand these ḥadīths – some of which I just mentioned by way of illustration – in the same way as some Muslims do today? Our refuge is in Allah! Did the Successors understand that the Prophet ﷺ was saying these words merely by way of conveying whatever the Arabs customarily said in the Time of Ignorance, and that they were words that were "possibly right, and possibly wrong?" Is this the way the Successors understood these ḥadīths? What about their successors (*tābiʿū al-tābiʿīn*), is this the way they understood them? Or those who came after them?

All the generations that came after the Messenger of Allah ﷺ until our own time understood that these words spoken by our master, the Messenger of Allah ﷺ, are words consisting of "non-recited revelation" (*waḥyun ghayru matluwwin*). Meaning that the wording came from the Messenger of Allah ﷺ but the meaning came from Allah ﷻ. These meanings are among the gifts which Allah ﷻ has lavished upon his Messenger Muḥammad ﷺ.

These are some of the problems – or rather, the tragedies – from which Muslims suffer within their own sphere. Would that these were merely the type of problems caused by corrupt people or transgressors or individuals who went astray from the Law, but no: they are caused by Muslims who speak out in the name of Islam.

The Inferiority Complex

The Prophet ﷺ said "the black seed is a remedy for every illness." If we went back to medical science and honest, fair-minded physicians, we would see that all of them bow their heads in approval of this authentic Prophetic saying. You will find that this takes place among foreigners before Arabs and Muslims. Whereas the Muslims – and I could name names if I wanted – pay no attention to those ḥadīths. Why? Because of their inferiority complex.

The inferiority complex is our bane. Those people think:[11] I am a Muslim, so I need to show those foreigners that I am civilized. They must see that I talk science, that I am just like them, that I understand civilization. I have to impress them. But if I say that the Prophet ﷺ said this, and tell them that we Muslims believe that in the black seed there is a cure for every disease, how then will those foreigners look at me? They are going to scorn me. In order to impress them, I have to say to them: "Oh, no! The Prophet ﷺ only said these words as one who passed on the customs of the Arabs in their time, in whose milieu this black seed was available, and after which it disappeared together with the customs of those folks. As for us, these words do not carry any weight! We do not follow the Prophet ﷺ in these matters!" This way I shall impress them.

I have to know that in such a scenario I only make myself smaller in the eyes of foreigners. For the latter will instantly feel that I suffer from this inferiority complex. When they feel this, I will fall from grace in their sight. I am speaking in colloquial terms so that we understand our ills without ambiguity.

Days ago I was in Germany, where a friend – a practicing, pious, believing Muslim – said to me: "Many Muslims come to

[11] At this point Dr. al-Būṭī began speaking in colloquial Arabic until the end of the following paragraph.

my clinic for some treatment or other. I know full well that their remedy consists of what the Messenger of Allah ﷺ prescribed. I tell them: 'Take four or five capsules of black seed compound for two or three weeks and you will be cured.' They have no trust in this prescription. Each one of them will come to me and say: 'Doctor, just give me a prescription like respectable people. Give me real medication, what kind of prescription is this?' I answer them: 'But this is a real medication for you in my expert opinion!'"

He went on to say: "German patients come to me, and after examining them I find that the same prescription applies to them – meaning, that prescribed by the Messenger of Allah ﷺ. When I fill that prescription for them they accept it and take it. I do not reveal to them that the Messenger of Allah ﷺ said this, I only say: this is your medication. It is strange to say, but those non-Muslims, when I tell them that the black seed is the remedy for the disease they are suffering from, they have faith, do whatever is prescribed to them, and after a while come back cured; while the Muslims who are the most knowledgeable of people in the life of the Messenger of Allah ﷺ and know of his Prophethood – they have no faith in such a prescription!" And of course there are those in Europe who prepare those blackseed concoctions in far greater abundance, unfortunately, than in our Muslim countries!

I am recounting this in order to show you the problems of Muslims today and how they enfeeble their Islamic personalities and feel ashamed of following their Prophet Muḥammad ﷺ in these matters. I heard someone with my own ears say to me: "It is imperative that anything by the name of Prophetic medicine (*al-ṭibb al-nabawī*) be removed far from any suggestion of applicability, for it causes too many problems!"

To remove Prophetic medicine after fourteen centuries? Are the spineless Muslims of today more knowledgeable in these matters than the Muslims of old, from the time of the Companions until our time? Now our spineless contemporary Muslims raise their heads as the would-be judges of the Muslims of the past, saying to them: "You were all in error when you considered Prophetic medicine a type of science Divinely revealed to the Messenger of Allah ﷺ!" So this is one of the greatest problems we are facing today.

When the Prophet ﷺ says to us: "Whoever eats seven *ʿujwa* dates in the morning, no poison nor magic will harm him on that day," he either tells the truth or lies. If this is not revelation from Allah ﷻ then what makes him sure of this? (Consider well what I am saying now, for I am speaking in terms of pure logic.) If this did not come to him as a Divine revelation, then how did he know it? In that case he should not be declaring such words. For when there is no Divine inspiration and revelation from Allah ﷻ, then it is something unseen. So how did he know? This would mean that I am imputing a lie to the Messenger of Allah ﷺ as long as I claim that such words do not come from Allah the Almighty. Do you see the danger of such positions?

When you claim – O Muslim, mosque-goer, writer about Islam! – that "the Prophet ﷺ merely transmitted this material from the custom of the Arabs in his time" we know that in your view this "custom of the Arabs in his time" is not accurate nor true; for you consider that, today, we should cover it up and not mention it in scholarly conversation. Fine. So, when the Prophet ﷺ transmits such words, he is in fact confirming them. This means that – in your view – he is confirming material that is neither accurate nor true! So he has become a liar – and we seek refuge in Allah from uttering such an enormity. You have now attributed a lie to the Messenger of Allah ﷺ, and Allah knows best whether you have done this unwittingly or wittingly.

Yes, this is a very grave matter indeed. This is the situation among us Muslims, particularly among those who write about Islam, displaying concern about Islam and Muslims. Of course, I do not say that this applies to all of them. However, this disease is present and growing worse. Once more, I say to you: it is the disease of an inferiority complex. When X speaks and writes about Islam then sees that Muslims are behind the West in civilization and technology and so forth, what will he do? He will constantly try to dust himself off from this film of backwardness lest it deposit on him. He will try to polish his act so as to appear "modern just like you, scientific just like you." One who feels inferior will always try to remedy his predicament in this way, so that "they" will not belittle him. And among the ways in which he wants to do this, is that when he feels like saying: "Every day I take a spoonful of honey with the seed of blessing (*ḥabbat al-baraka*) according to the Prophet's prescription," he immediately fears that "they" will consider him backward. A daily spoonful of honey with black seed, in the age of science? The age of technology? The age of the atom? The age of I know not what else? Busy with a fifteen-century-old thing that was publicized by the Arabs?! No-no. I should not talk of such things so that I will not be accused of backwardness. And this is the great disease of feeling inferior.

When I free myself of this disease and know full well the truthfulness of the Messenger of Allah ﷺ, putting my trust in my dearest Beloved, the Beloved of Allah ﷺ, at that time I shall put the criteria of all these people under my feet. I shall not ask a single one of them for his opinion. Let them scoff at me or not scoff at me – I have no concern whatsoever. My protecting friend is my Lord, and my examiner is His Beloved ﷺ! He is the one I follow and the authority upon whom I rely. *In shā Allah*, whatever they wish to say, let them say.

Idhā ṣaḥḥa minka al-wuddu fal-kullu hayyinu
Wa-kullul-ladhī fawqa al-turābi turābu.

If Your love is true then all is fine and easy,
And all those that walk upon the dust are dust!

When I free myself of all feelings of inferiority that is what I shall say. When I take this position I shall, on the contrary, gain magnitude in the eyes of those people. The Arabic proverb says: *al-mar'u ḥaythu yaḍa'u nafsah* – "One is wherever one places oneself." If you belittle yourself and see yourself as one who forever needs to cleanse himself, then – by Allah! – this is exactly how people will look upon you. But when you find yourself trusting in the words of the Messenger of Allah ﷺ such as this doctor who lives in the West, in the heartland of that world that lives far from Islam – yet in the midst of that furnace he prides himself in his Islam and precisely in these matters. Did the sciences scoff at him, or did he, on the contrary, acquire the respect of people? The latter, for he told me that he later reveals to the cured patient that this medicine comes from Muḥammad ﷺ and that he, the doctor, was only the mailman delivering it.

Anti-Sunna Infiltrators

The gravest and greatest of ills, however, is other than that. We are now speaking about a matter which is part of the Sunna of the Messenger of Allah ﷺ in its technical sense as the second source of Divine legislation. We have said that this is part of the straightforward matters which are considered praiseworthy. So many are the *Sunan* which we take from this second source of legislation and which enter into the category of common everyday matters! If you apply them, there is no objection, rather, you will get reward. For example: how the Prophet ﷺ ate with three fingers, how he drank, how he slept and placed his right hand under his right cheek when he slept, etc.

There are people today – a fifth or sixth column, I do not know – who are paid to tear up this second source of the Law which is the Sunna, and to alienate the Muslims from the Sunna. I am speaking in full knowledge of what I say.

Ways to Undermine the Sunna

What is the way to tear up the Sunna? There are many ways. One of them is to create doubt in the authenticity of the ḥadīths of the Messenger of Allah ﷺ that have come down to us. Another way is to clamor to weigh such ḥadīths "in the light of the criteria of the twentieth century" or "positivism" (*al-waḍʿiyya*) or "the march of civilization" (*al-tayyār al-ḥaḍārī*). Then they deride the ḥadīth and ask "What is this, to prefer travel on the day of Thursday? Can someone actually state such a thing?!" And so they fight the Sunna with words such as these. They will also mention the ḥadīth of the Prophet ﷺ that states: "If a fly falls into one of your containers [of food or drink], immerse it completely then remove it, for under one of its wings there is venom and under another there is its antidote."[12] They try to instill doubt about the Sunna by quoting such ḥadīths together with the comment: "This is the twentieth century, what are these fantasies?" I already cited to you the excerpts quoted in our newspapers from a Chinese periodical named Shanghai in which expert doctors stated that the fly contains proteins that neutralize the harmful germs it carries if only these proteins could be obtained. I have this article and I have publicized it in our own periodical *Ṭabībak.*[13]

[12] Narrated from Abū Hurayra and Abū Saʿīd al-Khudrī by al-Bukhārī, Ibn Mājah, Abū Dāwūd, al-Nasāʾī, Aḥmad, Ibn Ḥibbān, and al-Ḥākim.

[13] Only in modern times was it discovered that the common fly carried parasitic pathogens for many diseases including malaria, typhoid fever, cholera, bubonic plague, and others. It was also discovered that the fly carried parasitic bacteriophagic fungus capable of fighting the germs of all these diseases. See our article at: http://mac.abc.se/home/onesr/h/hof.html.

The "Qur'ān-Only" Fraud

We should know that it is on the basis of such discoveries that science falls prostrate before the Sunna. What is more important is that this Fifth Column is concerned with driving a wedge between Muslims and the Prophetic Sunna. They will say: "Fourteen hundred years separate us from the Prophetic Sunna, so how on earth can we tell the true from the false? And then it is replete, my friend, with narrations that contradict science, contradict civilization, etc." So what is the solution? They answer: "The Qur'ān, my brother, the Qur'ān! It contains everything! Take the Qur'ān and leave everything else!"

What is the purpose behind this? To enable the enemy to isolate the Muslims after bringing them out from their fortress – the Sunna – then they will pounce on them and evaporate their Religion until nothing remains.

In one of the colloquia I attended I heard the report of a certain William Clifford, chairman of the criminology department in one of the universities of Australia, which he submitted to the United Nations toward the end of the seventies, as part of a series of talks sponsored by the Arab University on the theme of the fight against crime in Arab societies. During those conferences the idea of applying the *Sharī'a* in order to fight crime was proposed. This was the original reason for William Clifford's presence in the United Nations at the time. After the conclusion of these talks, that man prepared a thirty-page report which he submitted to the United Nations, copies of which he surreptitiously sent to various research or think-tank organizations tasked with the observation and analysis of the Islamic world, its advances and backwardness in various fields, etc.

It was the will of Allah that a copy of this report fell into my hands. What did it say? It said: "There are among the Arabs aspirations to return to Islam in such a way as to bring out the

Muslims from a formalistic relationship (*ʿilāqa taqlīdiyya*) to a living relationship (*ʿilāqa ḥayya*) with Islam." This was in the introduction of the report. It went on to say: "If the Muslims succeed in their planning to return to this living relationship with Islam as I have observed it – in the context of the present empowerment of Arabs through their oil reserves – then the combination of the material power of oil and the ideological power of Islam, if they are used to the full, means that the West will find itself facing a formidable power. It may not be long until the West itself is brought to decline both materially and ideologically in the face of such a power."

Then he proceeds to present proposed solutions. His plan goes as follows:

1. It is imperative that the Arabs do not remain alone in control of this resource. The West must help itself to it to whatever extent is possible.

2. It is imperative to stem the rise of the Islamic expansion that shifts the Muslims from a purely formal relationship to a potent, living relationship with Islam. The way to do this is as follows:

a) To suggest that the Qur'ān alone is the source of Islam. Muslims must be alienated from the Sunna. This is found verbatim in William Clifford's report!

b) Muslims must be encouraged to apply complete independent scholarly striving (*al-ijtihād al-muṭlaq*) in the understanding of the Qur'ān. Let everyone explain it for themselves.

When this state is achieved what will happen? Religion will evaporate. Exactly in the same way as water when it is boiled and boiled and boiled over the fire, until nothing remains of it.

This report exists, dear brethren. It is available and I have discussed it on several occasions in Europe and elsewhere.

Today, when we find those among us who fight the Sunna, claiming that they fight it under the aegis of Islam and in the guise of Religion: these people are completely exposed and fool no one. They are known. How many books have been published recently, calling people to abandon the Sunna and follow only the Qur'ān? A letter even came to me from one of their authors whose name I shall not mention, stating: "It is asked of you that in your talks on television and elsewhere you tell people that the Qur'ān is the one and only source for the Law, because the Sunna is no longer in existence today and there is no such thing as the Sunna, and because it contains a mixture of truth and falsehood," and so on and so forth.

Fools speak and the wise take heed. The reports are present and available for all to see. All of these ask for Islam to disintegrate and form multifarious Islams opposed to one another and at great discrepancy. "Contemporary readings" all call to this.[14] What pre-school child will accept the inane claim that "Muḥammad ﷺ must not speak in explanation of the Qur'ān, he is only delivering a message which is the Qur'ān, but let someone else come today, not a specialist but a common person, and he will explain the Qur'ān?" Is there a sane mind that can validate such a claim? If I come and tell you the meaning of the verse

[14] A reference to such anti-Sunni works as the engineer Muḥammad Shaḥrūr's *Qirā'a Mu'aṣira lil-Qur'ān* ("A Contemporary Reading of the Qur'ān") and Mahmūd Abū Rayya's *Aḍwa' 'alā al-Sunna al-Nabawiyya* ("Spotlights on the Prophetic Sunna"). The first book was refuted by Muḥammad Māhir al-Munajjid in *al-Ishkāliyya al-Manhajiyya* ("The Method of Obscurantism"); Shawkī Abū Khalīl in *Qirā'a 'Ilmiyya līl-Qirā'āt al-Mu'āṣira* ("A Scientific Reading of the 'Contemporary Readings'"); and Yūsuf al-Ṣaydāwī in *Bayḍat al-Dīk* ("The Rooster's Egg") while the second book was refuted by Muḥammad 'Abd al-Razzāq Ḥamza in *Ẓulumāt Abī Rayya* ("Abū Rayya's Layers of Darkness") and al-Mu'allimī al-Yamānī's *al-Anwār al-Kāshifa* ("The Lights of Exposure").

{*This is the Scripture whereof there is no doubt*} (2:2) you have to accept it, but if Muḥammad ﷺ tells you its meaning, then you must not accept it? Is there a preschool child who can reasonably accept this statement? Our refuge is in Allah!

When I myself read the Qur'ān I find that it says {*But nay, by your Lord, they shall not believe until they make you judge of what is in dispute between them and find within themselves no dislike of that which you decide, and submit with full submission*} (4:65). What does this mean? Further, we know very well that this verse was revealed in relation to a matter which the Messenger of Allah ﷺ decided and for which there is no Qur'ānic text.[15] The Creator revealed this verse to show to us without ambiguity that the believer is not considered a believer until he is fully content with the judgment of the Messenger of Allah ﷺ – yet this [specific] judgment is not mentioned in the Qur'ān! Nevertheless Allah ﷻ stipulated the above and swore to it. These words cannot be glossed over.

Assault on Ḥadīth Science Targeting Islam

In the past, the conspiracies against Islam ran their course covertly. Nowadays they are all wide open and there are no more secrets. All of this is now exposed for all to see. Only the other day I read an article by someone who said: "The science of ḥadīth (*muṣṭalaḥ al-ḥadīth*) does not exist." This science which classifies ḥadīths into what is authentic or inauthentic, or into lone-narrated or mass-transmitted reports is all nonsense and does not exist according to that writer. What is his purpose? The bridge that links us to the ḥadīths of the Messenger of Allah ﷺ is the science of ḥadīth – the very science about which Western historians have acknowledged that "If Western civilization had lived on for thousands of years it would not have been able to rise to the level

[15] See below, p. 67-69.

of inventing something like the science of ḥadīth among the Arabs." But now here is X ascending the pulpit of Islam and asking that we all fall silent so that he can impart to us his message that ḥadīth is all poppycock, the science of ḥadīth does not exist and – the Qur'ān also is nonsense! For someone who makes such claims about ḥadīth, I swear by Allah ﷻ besides Whom there is no God, that he also holds the same belief about the Qur'ān. However, he does not want to expose himself. So he limits his statements to the ḥadīth.

Dear brethren, if we want to follow the Word of Allah, then we must take it completely and in all its parts. But if someone wants to abandon the Book of Allah, then he must announce it loud and clear so that we may know of his intention without hypocrisy nor deception.

People come to us asking: "It is true so-and-so wrote such-and-such? You must answer him and refute him!" First of all, the person whom you see speaking about Islam, examine his behavior. If you see that he has long been practicing Islam, fasting, praying, spending time in worship, then you can believe him in most of what he says and consider in fairness that may be right or wrong in the remainder, perhaps in his learning or otherwise. But if you see someone speaking out and attacking the ḥadīth, then you find out that he does not pray and that he spends his nights in activities that Allah ﷻ abhors – then how in the world can his words convince you? Even if you own only a small vegetable stand or a modest business you will never let such words affect you, for you can see that the actual state of that person belies his words.

In Europe I witnessed an incident that happens all too frequently. A young man was known to be hopping from club to club and from party to party when, all of a sudden, he began to go to the mosque, grew a long beard and wore a short robe, then little by little he entered among the Muslims and began to tell them: "This is a *bid*ʿ*a*! This is not a *bid*ʿ*a*! You have commited *kufr*! You have committed *shirk*! Do this! Don't do that! This robe is too long!" Etc. In brief, he began to cause dissension among people and unending quarrels and *fitna* where, before, the Muslims were all one and happy with their unified practice of Islam. Does any-one have any doubt about such a person? Where was he before? Only yesterday, he was a corrupt person. Any reasonable person can tell that he has been employed for a certain end. "What is your name?" we ask him. He replies: "Abū Ḥudhayfa." "Your real name?" "Abū Ḥudhayfa, Abū Ḥudhayfa." So here is this unknown, entering the mosque and manipulating his way to become imām, telling the people to do this and that and creating discord; and when the people of the mosque are asked what the name of their imām is they answer "Abū Ḥudhayfa" and have no idea of his real name. What if he is some non-Muslim passing for a Muslim? Abū Ḥudhayfa. No sooner than they began to research his background, he disappeared.

As our master ʿUmar said : "Neither am I a swindler, nor can a swindler deceive me." The believer is not a hypocrite, but neither must he let the hypocrites get the best of him. This is the reality of Muslims today. Hired hands are manipulating them from every side both in Europe and in Muslim countries. They are mobilized to destroy the Sunna and alienate the Muslims from it under the name of "developing Islam" on the fabricated claims that Islam is finished and needs reform. Beware of them.

{*Fain would they put out the light of Allah with their mouths, but Allah disdains (aught) save that He shall perfect His light, however much the disbelievers are averse*} (9:32). And praise belongs to Allah the Lord of the worlds.

The Binding Proof of the Sunna[16]

[16] Adapted and expanded from Dr. ʿAbd al-Ghanī ʿAbd al-Khāliq's *Ḥujjiyyat al-Sunna* (p. 243-252, 278-334).

Preliminaries

﴾*The Decision Rests with Allah Only*﴿

Allah Almighty ﷻ is the one and only judge and ruler according to the Qur'ānic texts {*The decision rests with Allah only*} (6:57, 12:40, 12:67) and {*Whoso judges not by that which Allah has revealed: such are disbelievers*} (5:44) and there is Consensus that obedience to His judgment is definitely binding upon all. However, the specifics of this judgment are not disclosed in these verses but in other verses of the Book as well as in the Sunna, Consensus, legal analogy, and other sources of the Law. The meaning of the expression "Sunna as evidence" is that the Sunna points to the judgment of Allah, either as definitive knowledge (*ʿilm*) or as probable knowledge (*ẓann*), bringing it out and disclosing it for us. We understand the Divine rulings by means of the Sunna and it becomes binding upon us to put its content into practice. The real meaning of the Sunna as evidence is therefore exposition (*iẓhār*) and proof-inference (*dilāla*) necessitating obligatory practice of their results because the latter is the Divine decision.

﴾*And Obey the Prophet*﴿

It would be incorrect to say, based on the preceding argument, that the probative nature of the Sunna creates laws external to the Qur'ān and legislated by the Prophet ﷺ. The meaning of the verse {*And obey the Prophet*} (4:59, 5:92, etc.) is not that the Prophet ﷺ is also a judge whose orders and prohibitions are law issuing from him rather than Allah ﷻ. Allah ﷻ declared the obligatoriness of obeying the Prophet ﷺ only in the sense that He made it obligatory for us to obey him in whatever he orders and makes obligatory for us to do. It is Allah ﷻ Who makes it obligatory for us both to obey and carry out, except that the orders for some of the acts are formulated by the Prophet ﷺ. Such formulation is only a proof or sign of the binding order of Allah Himself. The meaning of {And obey the Prophet} is therefore "Know that whatever the Prophet ﷺ commands or forbids you to do, it is I Who commands and forbids you" as explicited in the verse {And whatsoever the Messenger gives you, take it, and whatsoever he forbids, abstain from it} (59:7). Without such an order, the Prophet's ﷺ command would not have been binding upon us. Illustrating this principle is the following narration from ʿAlqama:

> ʿAbd Allah ibn Masʿūd ؓ said: "Allah ﷻ curses women who tattoo others, women who have tattoo applied to them, women who have their eyebrows clipped, and women artificially tooth-gapped, all for cosmetic purposes, changing the Divine fashioning." News of this reached a woman of Banū Asad called Umm Yaʿqūb. She came to him saying: "Abū ʿAbd al-Raḥmān! I heard that you cursed such-and-such." He replied: "Why should I not curse those whom the Messenger of Allah ﷺ cursed?" She said: "Lo! I certainly read all that is between the two covers [of the volume of Qurʾān], and I did not find this." He replied: "Had you read it you would have certainly found it. Did you not read {And whatsoever the Messenger gives you, take it, and whatsoever he forbids, abstain from it} (59:7)?" She said yes. He said: "the Messenger of Allah ﷺ forbade it."[17]

---

[17] Narrated by al-Bukhārī and Muslim, Abū Dāwūd, Ibn Mājah, Aḥmad, al-Dārimī, al-Bayhaqī in *al-Sunan al-Kubrā* (7:312) and *Shuʿab al-Īmān* (6:170), Ibn Ḥibbān (12:314), ʿAbd al-Razzāq (3:145 §5103), al-Ḥumaydī in his *Musnad* (1:53), and Ibn ʿAbd al-Barr in *Jāmiʿ Bayān al-ʿIlm* (2:1181-1182 §2336-2337). Ibn Ḥajar in *Fatḥ al-Bārī* (10:378) in commentary of this hadith said that al-Nawawī said: "An exception from the prohibition of plucking away facial hair is when a woman has a beard, mustache, or hair growing between her lower lip and chin, in which cases it is not unlawful for her to remove it, but rather is commendable (*mustaḥabb*)," the permissibility being on condition that her husband knows of it and gives his

Conditions for Using Ḥadīth as Proof

By Consensus, using a ḥadīth narrated from the Prophet ﷺ as proof for either doctrine or legal rulings hinges on two conditions:

a) Establishment of the principle that the Sunna is one of the proofs and foundations of legislation (*tashrī'*).

b) Establishment that such a ḥadīth actually issued from the Prophet ﷺ through a reliable narrative chain. This condition does not apply to the Companions who actually heard him say it.

Differences in Relying upon Ḥadīth Transmission

There have been differences among the Muslims in relying upon ḥadīth from the second of the two perspectives outlined above, that of transmission.

1. The *Khawārij*

The "Secessionists" or *Khawārij* said that there is no way to establish that a ḥadīth actually issued from the Prophet ﷺ whether as definitive or probable knowledge or whether by mass transmission or lone transmission. On this basis they rejected putting into practice anything and everything that was narrated from the Prophet ﷺ. They did this not because it issued from him, or because what issues from him is not a proof, but only because they deemed its transmission unreliable. Al-Suyūṭī describes their reasoning in the first pages of his book *Miftāḥ al-Janna fīl-I'tiṣām*[18] *bil-Sunna*:

permission, though it is prohibited if he does not, because of the deception it entails. Mufti Lajpūrī in his *Fatāwā Raḥīmiyya* declared it required (*wājib*) for her to pluck such hair from her face.

[18] "*Iḥtijāj*" in 'Abd al-Khāliq's text.

There are those who rejected using the Sunna as proof although they affirmed Prophethood for the Messenger of Allah ﷺ. They did this on the basis of their claim that the caliphate rightly belonged to ʿAlī ؓ and that when the Companions conferred it upon Abū Bakr ؓ, they all committed apostasy according to those lost souls – may Allah ﷻ curse them! They also declared ʿAlī an apostate – may Allah curse them! – for not demanding his right. On this basis they built the rejection of all ḥadīths because, they claimed, they are narrated by disbelievers. We belong to Allah and to Him is our return![19]

2. The *Muʿtazila*

The "Isolationists" or *Muʿtazila* said that a ḥadīth is reliably established to issue from the Prophet ﷺ only through mass transmissions. They rejected all lone-narrated ḥadīths.

3. *Ahl al-Sunna*

They accept both mass-transmitted and lone-narrated reports to establish the reliability of ḥadīth, but differ upon the conditions of acceptance.

4. The *Shīʿa*

They only accept the ḥadīths narrated through their Imāms or those that follow their creed, as they consider that whoever did not side with ʿAlī ؓ cannot be trusted.

The General Evidentiary Force of the Sunna

We now turn to the first of the two conditions stated for using ḥadīth as a proof, namely, the establishment of the principle that the Sunna is one of the proofs and foundations of Islamic legislation.

[19] Al-Suyūṭī, *Miftāḥ al-Janna* (p. 16 §7).

There is no doubt that some of the scholars of Islam have rejected the evidentiary nature of the Sunna with regard to specific issues and according to certain conditions. For example, some denied that the Sunna is independently probative of legislation apart from the Qur'ān. This is refuted by every single Companion who heard and applied the Sunna directly from the Prophet ﷺ either before Qur'ānic revelation or with only partial knowledge of it. It is also refuted in the case of ḥadīths of definite or specific meaning that apparently contradict – but in fact clarify – verses of assumed or general meaning. It is also refuted in the case of the Sunna for which no precedent is found in the Qur'ān, as in the ruling of the Prophet ﷺ in favor of al-Zubayr at the revelation of the verse {*But nay, by your Lord, they shall not believe until they make you judge of what is in dispute between them and find within themselves no dislike of that which you decide, and submit with full submission*} (4:65). Al-Shāfiʿī pointed out that this decision is stipulated in the Sunna, not the Qur'ān, and that had it been in the Qur'ān, there would have been no cause for specifying that by rejecting it they would not be believers.[20] Further, their belief is invalid until they submit specifically to that ruling, *i.e.* the Sunna, independently of the Qur'ān.

Others denied that the Sunna may abrogate the Qur'ān and there is disagreement concerning this point.

We are not addressing the above specifics here but only the establishment of the Sunna as a proof as a whole. Did any of the Ulema ever deny the latter or claim that the Sunna is in no way whatsoever probative? The answer is no.

In fact, it cannot be imagined that one may reject the entire evidentiary force of the Sunna and remain a Muslim. For the foundation of Islam is the Qur'ān, which cannot be described as

[20] In *al-Risāla* (p. 83).

the Word of Allah ﷻ when one unconditionally rejects the probativeness of the Sunna since the fact that the Qur'ān is the Word of Allah was established by none other than the Prophet's ﷺ explicit statement that this was the Word of Allah and His Book. That statement is obviously part of the Sunna. Therefore, to say that the Sunna is no proof is no different than a denial of an integral part of the Religion and an attempt to undermine the basis of the Religion.

As for the claim that the Qur'ān is established as the Word of Allah through its nature as an evidentiary miracle (*mu'jiza*) and not through the Sunna, the answer is that the Qur'ān does describe itself as an evidentiary miracle – and therefore the Word of Allah – as a whole, and also as one sūra, and also as three verses. This attribute, however, does not apply to single verses or pairs of verses. We know that single verses or pairs of verses are the Word of Allah only because the Prophet ﷺ said so. Yet we use single verses or even parts of single verses as proofs in doctrine and legal rulings. We could not do this without the Prophet's ﷺ assurance, meaning without the Sunna as evidence. Since the fact that a single verse or part of a verse must be necessarily known to be part of the Word of Allah, and the fact that their probative force must be necessarily known, both hinge on the probativeness of the Sunna, it follows that the latter must be necessarily known as well.

It is further inconceivable that the evidentiary nature of the Sunna not be necessarily known when so many of the issues around which the Consensus of jurists has formed, and which themselves are necessarily known – such as the number of prayer-cycles in obligatory prayers – hinge on it. How could the necessarily known hinge on something not necessarily known? As for the claim that those issues can be understood from the Book alone, it is an attempt to do the impossible. The Imāms of the past were much more capable than us, yet they admitted their inability to do it as indicated in the following report:

> Al-Ḥasan al-Baṣrī narrated that while the Companion ʿImrān ibn Ḥuṣayn was relating ḥadīths from the Prophet ﷺ, a man said to him: "Abū Nujayd! Talk to us from the Qur'ān." Whereupon ʿImrān said to him: "You and your friends all read the Qur'ān: can you tell me about the *ṣalāt*, what it contains specifically and what its features are? Can you tell me the rate of *zakāt* for gold? Camels? Cows? The different types of goods? No. But I witnessed it, and you were not there." Then he said: "The Messenger of Allah ﷺ imposed upon us such-and-such in the *zakāt* etc." The man said: "You have given me new life, may Allah ﷻ give you new life also!" Al-Ḥasan said: "This man did not die before he had become one of the authoritative jurists of the Muslims."[21]

If all the above necessary issues hinge on the evidentiary nature of the Sunna, then how can a believer come and argue against it, when such an argument targets those issues as well? And to argue against the necessity of those issues constitutes apostasy, since belief consists in confirming what the Prophet ﷺ brought regarding what must be necessarily known in the Religion. Ibn ʿAbd al-Barr said:

> The Sunna is divided into two types. The first is the Consensus transmitted from the masses to the masses. This is one of the proofs that leave no excuse for denial and there is no disagreement concerning them. Whoever rejects this Consensus has rejected one of the textual stipulations of Allah ﷻ and committed apostasy. The second type of Sunna consists in the

[21] Narrated by Ibn Ḥibbān cf. Ibn Ḥajar in *Lisān al-Mīzān* (1:3) and by al-Ḥākim (1:109-110) with a sound chain. Cf. al-Suyūṭī, *Miftāḥ al-Janna* (p. 73 §131, p. 23-25 §23).

reports of established, trustworthy lone narrators with uninterrupted chains. The congregation of the Ulema of the Community have said that this second type makes practice obligatory. Some of them said that it makes both knowledge and practice obligatory.[22]

[22] Ibn ʿAbd al-Barr, *Jāmiʿ Bayān al-ʿIlm* (2:33) cf. the chapter "Lone-Narrated Reports" in the first volume of our *Sunna Notes* entitled *Ḥadīth History and Principles.*

CHAPTER 1

The Prophet's ﷺ Immune State Dictates that Ḥadīth is Revelation

By Consensus, the evidentiary miracle of the Qur'ān is proof that the Prophet ﷺ is immune (*maʿṣūm*) from the deliberate commission of anything that might compromise his Message. In addition, the most correct position is that he is also immune from error in that regard, while those who hold the possibility of error for him concur that such possibility is conditional upon his immediate Divine appraisal and self-correction. It follows that every Divinely-sanctioned discourse on his part is, by Consensus, truthful and in conformity with what comes from Allah ﷻ, therefore it is obligatory to accept it and conform to it. This proof leads us to establish the evidentiary nature of the following:

- His saying about the Qur'ān that it is the Word of Allah ﷻ.
- His saying before every ḥadīth *qudsī*: "The Lord of Glory said..." or some similar wording.
- His narration from al-Miqdām ibn Maʿdīkarb: "I was given the Qur'ān and something very near it! Soon a man will say, leaning on his couch with his stomach full: 'Follow this Qur'ān, whatever you find in it to be [declared] permissible then declare it permissible, and whatever you find in it to be [declared] prohibited then declare it prohibited.' Truly whatever the Messenger of Allah has declared prohibited is just like what Allah ﷻ has declared prohibited. Lo! The meat of the domestic ass is prohibited to you. So is the meat of beasts of prey with fangs. So is a find belonging to the beneficiary of a treaty unless its owner does not want it. If one or more people arrive among some people the latter must receive them hospitably; if they do not, they must give them the amount equivalent to their hospitality."[23]

[23] See below, n. 93.

- His saying: "Here is Gibrīl, the Messenger of the Lord of the worlds, who has breathed into my innermost that no soul dies until it receives its sustenance in full, even if it is slow in coming. Therefore, beware of Allah ﷻ and ask Him gracefully. Let not the delay in obtaining sustenance drive you to apply it [once received] toward disobeying Allah. Lo! Allah ﷻ – one does not obtain what He has except through obedience."[24]

All these reports come from one who is exempt from lying and therefore constitute proofs showing that revelation is divided into two kinds:

a) The Book, which is the evidentiary miracle used to worship by means of recitation.

b) Everything else, namely: the ḥadīth *qudsī* and the Prophetic ḥadīth, whose meaning was revealed but whose wording was chosen by the Prophet ﷺ. If all this is from Allah ﷻ, then all this constitutes inescapable proofs for human beings until the Day of Resurrection.

Also established as probative on the basis of his exemption from lying in the course of delivering his Message are sayings such as the following:

[24] Narrated from Ḥudhayfa by al-Bazzār – cf. Ibn Ḥajar, *Mukhtaṣar* (1:506 §874) – with a chain of trustworthy narrators except Qudāma ibn Zā'ida who is unknown according to al-Haythamī (4:71), but the ḥadīth is strengthened by witness-narrations from Ibn Mas'ūd by al-Bayhaqī in *Shu'ab al-Īmān* (7:299), Ibn Abī Shayba (7:79), al-Quḍā'ī in *Musnad al-Shihāb* (2:185), and al-Dāraquṭnī in his *'Ilal* (5:273); from al-Muṭṭalib ibn Ḥanṭab by al-Shāfi'ī in his *Musnad* (p. 233) and al-Bayhaqī in *Shu'ab al-Īmān* (2:67); from Abū Umāma al-Bāhilī by Abū Nu'aym in *Ḥilyat al-Awliyā* (1985 ed. 10:26-27); and from Jābir by al-Daylamī as mentioned in *Kashf al-Khafā'* (1:155, 1:268).

– "The claimant must produce clear proof, and the disputant has to swear an oath." (*Al-bayyinatu ʿalā al-muddaʿī wal-yamīnu ʿalā man ankar.*)[25]

– "Islam is built on five things."[26]

– "People! Truly I do not command you anything except what Allah ﷻ has commanded you, and I do not prohibit for you anything except what Allah ﷻ has prohibited for you. Therefore be graceful in your requests from Him. By the One in Whose hand is Abū al-Qāsim's life, the sustenance of each one of you shall surely come to him just as his term of life shall surely come to pass. Therefore, if you find yourself in difficulty because of some need, ask for your sustenance through obedience to Allah ﷻ."[27]

– "Pray as you see me pray."[28] The establishment of this ḥadīth as probative means that all his prayer-related actions are established as probative.

[25] Narrated from Ibn ʿAbbās by al-Bayhaqī in *al-Sunan al-Kubrā* (10:252) with a sound chain according al-Ṣanʿānī in *Subul al-Salām* (4:132) and al-Nawawī as cited by al-Mubārakfūrī in *Tuḥfat al-Aḥwadhī* (4:475), while Ibn Ḥajar in *Fatḥ al-Bārī* (1959 ed. 5:283) considers it fair. Al-Bukhārī cites it without chain in his *Ṣaḥīḥ*. The second half is narrated from Ibn ʿAbbās by al-Bukhārī, Muslim and al-Tirmidhī who declares it *ḥasan ṣaḥīḥ*. This is a nearly mass-narrated, "famous" (*mashhūr*) ḥadīth narrated from eight Companions in all and counted by al-Kattānī in *Naẓm al-Mutanāthir* (p. 169-170) as "mass-narrated in meaning."

[26] Narrated from Ibn ʿUmar by al-Bukhārī, Muslim, al-Tirmidhī (*ḥasan ṣaḥīḥ*), al-Nasāʾī, and Aḥmad. Also narrated from Jarīr ibn ʿAbd Allah by Aḥmad.

[27] See below, n. 99.

[28] Narrated from Mālik ibn al-Ḥuwayrith by al-Bukhārī.

- "Take your pilgrimage rites [from me], for I may not perform pilgrimage again."[29] The probative force of this order and that of the acts and details of pilgrimage are similar to that of the previous report.

- "Satan has despaired of ever being worshipped in your land. However, he is satisfied to be obeyed in everything else among the deeds that you hold despicable. Therefore beware! Lo! I have left among you something which, if you cling to it, you shall never be led astray: the Book of Allah and the Sunna of His Prophet."[30]

- "Whoever innovates in this matter of ours something that does not belong to it, such innovation is rejected."[31] This and the previous report, since they come from one exempt from lying, indicate that our Prophet's ﷺ Sunna is probative in all aspects which we just mentioned and that there is no misguidance whatsoever in conforming to it. Rather, the misguidance lies in abandoning the Sunna or practicing what contravenes it.

Al-ʿIrbāḍ ibn Sāriya said:

> The Messenger of Allah ﷺ prayed among us that day then turned to face us and admonished us so intensely that eyes wept and hearts trembled. A man said: "Messenger of Allah! This sounds like the admonishment of one who bids farewell, therefore, what solemn promise do you require of us?" He replied: "I exhort you to beware of Allah ﷻ! I exhort you to hear and obey, even if your leader should be a black Ethiopian. Lo! Whoever of you lives shall live to see great divisions. You

[29] Narrated from Jābir by Muslim, al-Nasāʾī, Abū Dāwūd, and Aḥmad. Also by al-Bayhaqī in *al-Sunan al-Kubrā* (5:125) with the wording "Take your pilgrimage rites from me."
[30] See n. 149.
[31] See n. 202.

must follow my Sunna and the Sunna of the rightly-guided, upright successors after me. Hold on to it firmly, bite upon it with your very jaws! Beware of newfangled matters. Every newfangled matter is an innovation and every innovation is misguidance."[32]

Some versions have the wording cited by Ibn Mandah below, beginning with the words "I am leaving you on a path that is clear as day." Some versions add: *wa'innamā al-mu'minu kal-jamali al-anifi ḥaythu qīda inqāda*, "The believer is no different than the docile camel who lets himself be led wherever he is led."[33]

[32] Narrated from al-ʿIrbāḍ ibn Sāriya by al-Tirmidhī (*ḥasan ṣaḥīḥ*) with four chains, Abū Dāwūd [this is his wording], Ibn Mājah with two chains, Aḥmad – he declared it *ṣaḥīḥ* according to Ibn Rajab – with four chains (Arna'ūṭ ed. 28:367 -377 §17142-17147 *ṣaḥīḥ*=Zayn ed. 13:278-280 §17077-17080 *ṣaḥīḥ*), al-Dārimī, Ibn Ḥibbān (1:178-179 §5 *ṣaḥīḥ*), al-Ḥākim in *al-Mustadrak* with five chains (1:95-97=1990 ed. 1:174-177) – declaring it *ṣaḥīḥ* – and in *al-Madkhal ilā al-Ṣaḥīḥ* (p. 80-81), al-Ājurrī with four chains in *al-Sharīʿa* (p. 54-55 §79-82=p. 46 *ṣaḥīḥ*), Ibn Abī ʿĀṣim in *al-Sunna* (p. 29 §54 *ṣaḥīḥ*), al-Ṭaḥāwī in *Mushkil al-Āthār* (2:69= 3:221-224 §1185-1187 *ṣaḥīḥ*), Muḥammad ibn Naṣr al-Marwazī with four chains in *al-Sunna* (p. 26-27 §69-72 *ṣaḥīḥ*), al-Ḥārith ibn Abī Usāma in his *Musnad* (1:197-198), al-Rūyānī in his *Musnad* (1:439), Abū Nuʿaym who cited it "among the *ṣaḥīḥ* narrations of the people of Shām" in *Ḥilyat al-Awliyā'* (1985 ed. 5:220-221, 10:115), al-Ṭabarānī with several chains in *Musnad al-Shāmiyyīn* (1:254, 1:402, 1:446, 2:197, 2:298) and *al-Kabīr* (18:245-257), al-Bayhaqī in *al-Sunan al-Kubrā* (10:114), *al-Madkhal* (p. 115-116), *al-Iʿtiqād* (p. 229), and *Shuʿab al-Īmān* (6:67), al-Baghawī who declared it *ḥasan* in *Sharḥ al-Sunna* (1:205 §102 *isnād ṣaḥīḥ*), Ibn al-Athīr in *Jāmiʿ al-Uṣūl* (1:187, 1:279), Ibn ʿAsākir in *al-Arbaʿīn al-Buldāniyya* (p. 121), Ibn ʿAbd al-Barr in *al-Tamhīd* (21:278-279) and *Jāmiʿ Bayān al-ʿIlm* (2:924 §1758) where he declared it *ṣaḥīḥ*, and others. (See also, on this ḥadīth, Ibn Rajab's commentary in the second volume of our *Sunna Notes* entitled *The Excellent Innovation*).

[33] Narrated by Ibn Mājah, Aḥmad (28:367 §17142 *isnād ḥasan*), al-Ḥākim (1:96= 1:175), al-Ṭabarānī in *al-Kabīr* (18:247), al-Bayhaqī in *al-Madkhal* (p. 116), and al-Lālikā'ī, *Sharḥ Uṣūl* (1:74). This addition is also narrated as a stand-alone ḥadīth *mursal* from Makḥūl by Ibn al-Mubārak in *al-Zuhd* (p. 130) and al-Bayhaqī in *Shuʿab al-Īmān* (6:272 §8128).

The establishment of the order to follow the Prophet's ﷺ Sunna as evidence is tantamount to establishing as evidence all the different kinds of Sunna such as the verbal Sunna (*al-sunnatu al-qawliyya*), the active Sunna (*al-sunnatu al-fiʿliyya*), and the confirmative Sunna (*al-sunnatu al-taqrīriyya*) definitely and for all time.[34] Ibn Mandah said:

> When Allah ﷻ completed His Religion and consolidated it, opening up to His Prophet ﷺ what He had promised him and informing him of his impending death, He revealed to him the verse {*This day I have perfected your Religion for you and completed My favor unto you*} (5:3). At that time the Prophet ﷺ understood that his life was about to be taken and he asked his Companions [in his Farewell Pilgrimage]: "Have I conveyed the Message?" To which his Companions replied "Yes." Then he said: "O Allah! Bear witness."[35] And he said: "I am leaving you on a path that is clear as day whether by day or by night. None shall stray from it after me except one who is bound for destruction.[36] Whoever of you lives shall live to see great divisions, etc."[37]

[34] See the chapter "The Meaning of Sunna and *Bidʿa*" in our monograph *The Excellent Innovation*, *Sunna Notes*, volume II.

[35] Narrated from Jābir by Muslim, Abū Dāwūd, and Ibn Mājah. "He meant by this to take Allah as a witness over [the acknowledgment of] the people." Ibn al-Athīr, *al-Nihāya* (5:111). This is similar to the moving of the forefinger towards the *Kaʿba* in *tashahhud* in which the Muslim "proclaims *tawḥīd* with his hand, his tongue, and his heart" (al-Nawawī). Other versions from Abū Bakrah al-Thaqafī, Ibn ʿUmar, Abū Saʿīd al-Khudrī, Ibn Masʿūd, Jābir, Abū Ghādiya, and others in the *Ṣaḥiḥayn*, *Sunan*, and Aḥmad omit mention of the raising of the finger toward heaven.

[36] Narrated from al-ʿIrbāḍ by by Ibn Mājah, Aḥmad, etc. cf. n. 33.

[37] Ibn Mandah, *Faḍl al-Akhbār* (p. 25).

CHAPTER 2

Divine Approval of the Companions' Conformity with the Sunna

It is established that the Prophet ﷺ used to exhort his Community to hold on to his Sunna and warn them not to contravene it. It is further established that his Companions used to obey him faithfully in this and follow his sayings, deeds and tacit confirmations or disapprovals, considering that anything that issued from him in his capacity as a Prophet constitutes a proof to be followed, except in the following cases:

- In purely worldly matters, in which they felt free but not bound to consult him.
- In revealed matters foreign to their understanding, in which they sought explanations but which they held to be unquestionably true.
- In some acts of his considered restricted to him exclusively.
- In some commands of his which he did not himself enact, on the interpretive basis that such commands implied mere permissibility, not obligation.

In all the above exceptions the Companions may have refrained from following the Prophet's ﷺ order but not because they doubted that he must be followed nor because they doubted that disobeying him is forbidden.

We also know that the Companions were more capable than us in juridical exertion (*ijtihād*) and the inference of rulings from the Book. Yet they did not try to understand the Book autonomously and on their own in everyday situations. Rather, they consulted with the Prophet ﷺ as long as they were able to ask him. If he was absent when a Companion was involved in some important incident, the latter searched the Book first, then the Sunna, then, if he found nothing, he exerted his personal understanding. Later, he went over his decision with the Prophet ﷺ and the latter would either confirm it or rectify his error. Thus, these rulings issued from the Prophet ﷺ and the Companions, and Allah ﷻ approved of them without telling them that they were wrong, as revelation was going on at that time. If their practice were wrong, Allah ﷻ would have certainly corrected it. Not only did Allah ﷻ not correct them, on the contrary, He ordered them to follow and obey the Prophet ﷺ, cautioning them against disobeying him and contravening him.

Following are some of the proofs for the points we have just listed, namely:

a) The Companions' firm adherence to the Sunna of the Prophet ﷺ.

b) The fact that they considered the Sunna a proof from his very lifetime.

c) Their avoiding trying to understand the Book independently as long as they could consult with him first or later.

d) Their discarding of their own juridical conclusions reached in his absence if, after they asked him about them, he differed with them.

- The Prophet ﷺ began to wear a gold ring, whereupon people began to wear gold rings. Then he discarded it saying: "I shall never wear it again." So the people discarded their gold rings.[38]

- As the Prophet ﷺ was praying with his Companions he suddenly removed his sandals and placed them on his left. When the people saw this they all took off their sandals. After he

[38] Narrated from Ibn 'Umar by al-Bukhārī, Muslim, and others.

finished praying he asked: "What made you take off your sandals?" They said: "We saw you take off yours." He replied: "Gibrīl told me that there was dirt on them."[39]

- The Prophet ﷺ had prayed two *rak'as* of the noon prayer in his Mosque among the Muslims when he was ordered to face the Holy Sanctuary. He turned around, and the Muslims turned with him.[40]

- Ibn Mas'ūd ﷺ came to the mosque on the day of *Jumu'a* as the Prophet ﷺ was delivering his sermon and heard him say: "Sit all of you!" Whereupon Ibn Mas'ūd sat down at the door of the mosque. Seeing him the Prophet ﷺ said: "Come over, 'Abd Allah ibn Mas'ūd!"[41]

- 'Abd Allah ibn Rawaḥa heard the Prophet ﷺ say: "Sit!" Whereupon he sat in the middle of the road. The Prophet ﷺ passed by him and said: "What are you doing?" He replied: "I heard you say: 'Sit', so I sat." The Prophet ﷺ said: "May Allah ﷻ increase you in obedience."[42]

- A woman came to the Prophet ﷺ and said: "Messenger of Allah! The men have taken for themselves everything that you say. Set one day in which you will devote yourself to us so that we may come and hear you." He said: "Gather on such-and-such a day at such-and-such a place." They gathered and he came to them,

[39] A sound ḥadīth from Bakr ibn 'Abd Allah by Abū Dāwūd, Aḥmad, and al-Dārimī.
[40] Narrated by Ibn Sa'd (1:241-242), Ibn Abī Dāwūd, and al-Bazzār as cited by Ibn Ḥajar in *Fatḥ al-Bārī* (1959 ed. 1:503).
[41] Narrated from Jābir by Abū Dāwūd with a sound chain (§1091) and Ibn 'Abd al-Barr in *Jāmi' Bayān al-'Ilm* (2:867 §1633); from Ibn 'Abbās by Ibn Khuzayma (3:141); and *mursal* from 'Aṭā' ibn Abī Rabāḥ by 'Abd al-Razzāq (3:211) and in al-Haythamī's *Zawā'id Musnad al-Ḥārith* (2:923).
[42] Narrated by 'Abd al-Razzāq (3:211), Ibn 'Abd al-Barr in *Jāmi' Bayān al-'Ilm* (2:867 §1633), and al-Muttaqī al-Hindī in *Kanz al-'Ummāl* (§37170-37171).

teaching them what Allah ﷻ had taught him. Then he said: "There is not one woman among you that sends three of her children before her [to the hereafter] except that they shall block her from the Fire." One woman said: "Or two? Or two? Or two?" The Prophet ﷺ said: "Or two. Or two. Or two."[43]

- Muʿādh ibn Jabal said: "When the Messenger of Allah ﷺ sent me to Yemen he said: 'How will you pass judgment if a judgment is asked of you?' I replied: 'I shall pass judgment on the basis of the book of Allah.' He said: 'What if it is not in the book of Allah?' I replied: 'Then on the basis of the Sunna of the Messenger of Allah ﷺ.' He said: 'What if it is not in the Sunna of the Messenger of Allah?' I replied: 'Then I shall strive on my own and leave no stone unturned.' Whereupon the Prophet ﷺ slapped my chest and said: 'Praise to Allah ﷻ Who has graced the messenger of the Messenger of Allah with what pleases the Messenger of Allah.'"[44]

[43] Narrated from Abū Saʿīd al-Khudrī by al-Bukhārī and Muslim.

[44] This ḥadīth is not established from the perspective of *isnād* but considered nevertheless authentic and relied upon by the generality of the *Umma* and the massive majority of the Ulema. Narrated by Abū Dāwūd, al-Tirmidhī who said that a link of its chain was missing, Aḥmad, al-Dārimī, Ibn Abī Shayba (4:543, 6:13), al-Ṭayālisī (p. 76), ʿAbd ibn Ḥumayd in his *Musnad* (p. 72), al-Ṭabarānī in *al-Kabīr* (20:170), Ibn Saʿd (2:347-348, 3:584), al-Khaṭīb in his *Tārīkh* (13:77) and *al-Faqīh wal-Mutafaqqih* (1:188-189), al-Bayhaqī in *al-Sunan al-Kubrā* (10:114), *Maʿrifat al-Sunan* (1:173-174 §291) and *al-Madkhal* (p. 207), Ibn ʿAbd al-Barr in *Jāmiʿ Bayān al-ʿIlm* (2:844-846 §1592- 1594=2:56), al-Baghawī in *Sharḥ al-Sunna* (10:116), Ibn ʿAsākir, al-Qāḍī Wakīʿ in *Akhbār al-Quḍāt* (1:98), Ibn ʿAdī (2:613), and others. Al-Bukhārī in *al-Tārīkh al-Kabīr* (2:277) stated that it has no sound chain, as did ʿAbd al-Ḥaqq al-Ishbīlī, Ibn Ḥazm in *al-Iḥkām* (7:417=6:36), and Ibn al-Jawzī in *al-ʿIlal al-Mutanāhiya* (2:758-759 §1264) who conceded its meaning was true. However, because it is unanimously considered authentic by the jurists, it is considered *ṣaḥīḥ* as a ḥadīth as indicated by al-Khaṭīb, Abū Bakr al-Rāzī in *Aḥkām al-Qur'ān* (3:179), Ibn al-ʿArabī in *ʿĀriḍat al-Aḥwadhī*, Ibn Kathīr in his *Tafsīr* (1:4), Ibn al-Qayyim in *Iʿlām al-Muwaqqiʿīn* (1:202-203), Ibn Ḥajar in *Talkhīṣ al-Ḥabīr* (4:182-183 §2076), al-Tahānawī in *Muqaddimat Iʿlā' al-Sunan* (2/2:57-58), al-Arna'ūṭ in al-Ṭaḥāwī's *Sharḥ Mushkil al-Āthār* (9:213-214 §3584),

- The Prophet ﷺ called Abū Sa'īd ibn al-Mu'allā al-Anṣārī as the latter was praying. Abū Sa'īd turned his face to him but did not answer him. After Abū Sa'īd finished praying the Prophet ﷺ asked him: "What prevented you from answering me? Did Allah ﷻ not say {*O believers! Obey Allah and the Messenger when he calls you to what quickens you*} (8:24)?"[45]

- The Prophet ﷺ said [in Ramaḍān]: "Do not fast [two days] in succession without breaking your fast [in between]." They said: "But you do." He replied: "I am not like you. During the night my Lord feeds me and gives me drink." Yet they did not discontinue it. So the Prophet ﷺ did not break his fast with them for two days – or two nights – then they saw the new moon. He said to them: "Had it come later, I would have made you fast longer," as if he were punishing them.[46]

- A man kissed his wife while fasting and experienced great pleasure from it, so he sent out his wife to ask about it. She went to see Umm Salama who said to her: "The Prophet ﷺ kisses us even when he is fasting." She went back and told her husband, whereupon he said: "The Prophet is not like us, Allah ﷻ makes licit for His Messenger whatever He wishes." The woman went back to see Umm Salama and found the Prophet ﷺ with her. The Prophet ﷺ said: "What does this woman want?" Umm Salama told him. He said: "Why do you not tell her that I kiss

al-Zayn in *Musnad Aḥmad* (16:164 §21906), the author of *Nibrās al-'Uqūl* (1:82-83) as cited in *Ḥujjiyyat al-Sunna* (p. 287 n. 6), and Abū Ghudda in his edition of al-Lacknawī's *al-Ajwibat al-Fāḍila* (p. 228-238). For further discussion of this ḥadīth cf. n. 95 in the second volume of our *Sunna Notes* entitled *The Excellent Innovation.*

[45] Narrated by al-Bukhārī and Aḥmad. Also narrated from Ubay ibn Ka'b instead of Abū Sa'īd by al-Tirmidhī (*ḥasan ṣaḥīḥ*), al-Nasā'ī in *al-Sunan al-Kubrā*, Abū Dāwūd, Aḥmad, and others. Ibn 'Abd al-Barr cites both reports in *Jāmi' Bayān al-'Ilm* (2:864-865 §1630-1631).

[46] Narrated from Abū Hurayra by al-Bukhārī, Muslim, Aḥmad, and al-Dārimī.

even when I am fasting?" She said: "I did, then she went back to her husband and he said: 'The Prophet is not like us, Allah ﷻ makes licit for His Messenger whatever He wishes.'" Hearing this, the Prophet ﷺ became angry and said: "I am truly the most Godwary among you, and the most aware and knowledgeable of the limits set by Allah ﷻ."[47]

- ʿAlī said: "I used to pass pre-seminal fluid frequently but was ashamed to ask the Prophet ﷺ about it because of his daughter's position [as ʿAlī's wife]. So I told al-Miqdād to ask him. The Prophet ﷺ said: "Let him wash his organ and make ablution."[48]

- Ibn ʿUmar narrated: "I divorced my wife while she was in her menses. ʿUmar mentioned this to the Prophet ﷺ, whereupon the latter became upset. Then he said: "Let him take her back and keep her until after her menses have passed, then a second menstrual period, then, after the latter is over, if he still desires to divorce her let him divorce her while she is in her state of purity and before touching her. That is the waiting period (*ʿidda*) which Allah ﷻ has commanded."[49]

- Yaʿlā ibn Umayya said: "I said to ʿUmar ibn al-Khaṭṭāb: '[Concerning the verse] {*It is no sin for you to curtail worship if you fear that those who disbelieve may attack you*} (4:101). What if the people are safe?' He replied: 'I wonder just as you do.' So I asked the Prophet ﷺ and he said: 'It is a charity given to you by Allah ﷻ, so accept His charity.'"[50] Al-Suyūṭī said in commentary of this ḥadīth: "The scholars said that the Companions had understood the verse to mean that, short of a situation in which

[47] Narrated *mursal* from ʿAṭā' ibn Yasār by Mālik.
[48] Narrated by al-Bukhārī and Muslim.
[49] Narrated in the Nine Books.
[50] Narrated in the Nine Books except al-Bukhārī and Mālik.

there is fear, the command to shorten the prayer is reversed, until the Prophet ﷺ told them that the dispensation held in both cases."[51]

- The Prophet ﷺ gave instructions to a party of Companions on the Day of [the battle of] the Clans: "Let none pray *ʿaṣr* before you reach the Banū Qurayẓa." Another narration states *ẓuhr*. On the way, one or more of them remarked that *ʿaṣr* had entered. Some said: "We shall not pray until we reach it."[52] Others said: "On the contrary, we shall pray,[53] because that was not what was meant [*i.e.* to delay prayer beyond its time]." Later on the incident was mentioned to the Prophet ﷺ and he did not take to task either of the two groups.[54]

Imām al-Nawawī said in commenting on this ḥadīth that he considers that every *mujtahid* can be correct. He said:

> In this ḥadīth there is evidence supporting those who act upon their understanding and according to analogy while attending to the actual meaning of words, and also to those who stick to the external letter. There is also evidence that the *mujtahid* must not be taken to task in what he did through his *ijtihād* if he did his best. And it can be inferred from this that every *mujtahid* is correct (*wa-qad yustadallu bihi ʿalā an kulla mujtahidin muṣīb*). Those who take the opposite view can say that the Prophet ﷺ did not manifest which of the two sides was correct, but he did not take them to task. There is no disagreement that the *mujtahid* is not taken to task even if he was mistaken, as long as he did his utmost in striving. And Allah ﷻ knows best.[55]

[51] Al-Suyūṭī, *Miftāḥ al-Janna* (p. 89 §165). Cf al-Baghawī, *Sharḥ al-Sunna* (4:168).
[52] Or: "Let us not pray until we reach it."
[53] Or: "Let us pray."
[54] Narrated from Ibn ʿUmar by al-Bukhārī with the wording *ʿaṣr*, and by Muslim with that of *ẓuhr*.
[55] Al-Nawawī, *Sharḥ Ṣaḥīḥ Muslim* (*Kitāb al-Jihād*, Ch. 23, al-Mays ed. 11/12:341).

Ibn Ḥajar reiterates this position in his commentary on the same ḥadīth in al-Bukhārī:

> In this ḥadīth there is evidence that each of two *mujtahids* that differ in a matter of the branches, is correct" (*wa-fīhi anna kulla mukhtalifayni fīl-furūʿ min al-mujtahidīna muṣīb*).[56]

There is a superficial discrepancy concerning what prayer was actually mentioned, since it is related in al-Bukhārī as ʿ*aṣr* and in Muslim as *ẓuhr*. Both reports are authentic and confirmed by other sound chains. Al-Nawawī and Ibn Ḥajar said this discrepancy is resolved by the possibility that the travellers left in two groups, to each of whom was given a different order. The first group had not prayed *ẓuhr* yet; while the second had prayed *ẓuhr*, but not ʿ*aṣr*. Or, it is solved by the possibility that one single group left together, containing those who had already prayed *ẓuhr* and those who had not. The import of the ḥadīth was to make haste and not dismount to pray or do anything else.

- Abū Saʿīd al-Khudrī narrated that two men went on a trip and decided to pray but found no water. They made dry ablution (*tayammum*) then prayed. Thereafter, they found water and the time of prayer had not yet elapsed. One of them repeated his prayer, while the second one did not. The Prophet ﷺ said to the latter: "You have followed the Sunna faithfully, and your prayer is complete." He said to the one who repeated his prayer: "You have twice the reward."[57]

[56] Ibn Ḥajar, *Fatḥ al-Bārī* (*Kitāb al-Maghāzī*, ch. 31, 1989 ed. 7:520).

[57] Narrated by al-Nasāʾī, Abū Dāwūd, al-Dārimī, and al-Bayhaqī in *al-Sunan al-Kubrā* (1:231). Ibn Ḥajar in *Talkhīṣ al-Ḥabīr* (1:156 §2112), al-Ṣanʿānī in *Subul al-Salām* (1:98), al-Zaylaʿī in *Naṣb al-Rāya* (1:160) and al-Tahānawī in *Iʿlāʾ al-Sunan* (1:326) all indicated that it is sound (*ṣaḥīḥ*) as stated by al-Ḥākim (1:178-179 =1990 ed. 1:286) and Ibn al-Sakan in *al-Siḥāḥ*.

– A group of the Companions was traveling, ʿUmar and Muʿādh among them. The latter two woke up in need of major ablution (*ghusl*), but found no water. Each of them exercised his own juridical reasoning. Muʿādh made an analogy between purity by means of sand and that by means of water, whereupon he rubbed sand all over himself and prayed. ʿUmar did not consider it correct and he postponed his prayer. When they returned to the Prophet ﷺ he showed them that Muʿādh's reasoning was incorrect as he had applied it when a legal text was available to that effect, namely the saying of Allah {*Then go to high clean soil and rub your faces and your hands therewith*} (4:43). The Prophet ﷺ said to Muʿādh: "It would have been enough for you to do that." Then he turned to ʿUmar and explained to him that just as dry ablution eliminates the state of lesser impurity (*al-ḥadath al-aṣghar*), it also eliminated that of major impurity (*al-ḥadath al-akbar*). He also told him that the "touching of women" mentioned in the same verse – and because of which *tayammum* becomes permissible – does not refer to the preliminaries of intercourse but to intercourse itself.[58]

[58] I did not find a source for this report. However, the *Ṣaḥīḥayn* and *Sunan* mention something similar with ʿAmmār instead of Muʿādh.

CHAPTER 3

Proofs from the Noble Qur'ān for the Sunna as Evidence

The book of Allah is filled with verses that categorically denote the Sunna as evidence. These verses are of at least five types, although a single verse can be of more than one type.

a) Verses that indicate the obligatoriness of believing in the Prophet ﷺ.

b) Verses that indicate that the Prophet ﷺ elucidates the Book and explains its wisdom in a manner that carries authority on the part of Allah ﷻ.

c) Verses that indicate the obligatoriness of obeying the Prophet ﷺ in absolute terms in whatever he orders and whatever he prohibits.

d) Verses that indicate the obligatoriness of following and imitating him in all that issues from him as being exemplary so as to be loved by Allah.

e) Verses indicating that Allah has tasked him with following and conveying whatever is revealed to him whether in recited (*matlū*) or non-recited form.

a) Verses that Indicate the Obligatoriness of Believing in the Prophet ﷺ

The first type of verses denoting the probativeness of the Sunna are the verses that indicate the obligatoriness of believing in the Prophet ﷺ. "Belief" or *īmān* here signifies the confirmation of (*taṣdīq*) and compliance with (*idh'ān*) his message and with all that he brought from Allah whether it is mentioned in the Qur'ān or not. Of this type also are the verses that show that not following him and/or not accepting his judgment both contradict belief:

- Allah said: {*O you who believe! Believe in Allah and His Messenger and the Scripture which He has revealed unto His Messenger, and the Scripture which He revealed aforetime. Whosoever disbelieves in Allah and His angels and His scriptures and His messengers and the Last Day, he verily has wandered far astray*} (4:136).

- And He said: {*So believe in Allah and His Messenger and the light which We have revealed. And Allah is aware of what you do*} (64:8).

- And He said: {*Say (O Muḥammad): O mankind! Lo! I am the Messenger of Allah to you all, (the Messenger of) Him unto whom belongs the Sovereignty of the heavens and the earth. There is no God save Him. He quickens and He gives death. So believe in Allah and His Messenger, the unlettered Prophet, who believes in Allah and in His words and follow him that haply you may be led aright*} (7:158).

- Al-Qāḍī ʿIyāḍ said: "*Īmān* in the Prophet Muḥammad ﷺ is specifically obligatory, no īmān is complete except through it, and no Islam is correct except with it. Allah ﷻ said: {*And as for him who believes not in Allah and His Messenger Lo! We have prepared a flame for disbelievers*} (48:13)."[59]

- Allah ﷻ said: {*Lo! We have sent you (O Muḥammad) as a witness and a bearer of good tidings and a warner, that you (mankind) may believe in Allah and His Messenger, and may honor Him, and may revere Him, and may glorify Him at early dawn and at the close of day*} (48:8-9).

- And He said: {*The (true) believers are those only who believe in Allah and His Messenger and afterward doubt not, but strive with their wealth and their lives for the cause of Allah. Such are the sincere*} (49:15).

[59] Al-Qāḍī ʿIyāḍ, *al-Shifā'* (2:1).

- And He said: {*They only are the true believers who believe in Allah and His Messenger and, when they are with him on some common errand, go not away until they have asked leave of him. Lo! those who ask leave of you, those are they who believe in Allah and His Messenger. So, if they ask your leave for some affair of theirs, give leave to whom you will of them, and ask for them forgiveness of Allah. Lo! Allah is Forgiving, Merciful*} (24:62).

Concerning this verse al-Shāfiʿī said:

> "He has made the completion of the beginning of belief – to which everything else is subordinate – belief in Allah then in His Messenger. So if a human being believes in Him but does not believe in His Messenger, the designation (*ism*) denoting completion of belief in no way whatsoever applies to him, until he believes in His Messenger together with Him."[60]

Ibn al-Qayyim said:

> "The verse incorporates among the requisites of belief the fact that they not go anywhere – when they are with him – except with his permission. It is all the more fitting that they also not adopt any position nor enter any path of knowledge except after his permission. Such permission on his part can be known by the proof of what he brought establishing the permission."[61]

- Allah ﷻ said: {*Not unto the weak nor unto the sick nor unto those who can find naught to spend is any fault (to be imputed though they stay at home) if they are true (naṣaḥū) to Allah and His Messenger. Not unto the good is there any road (of blame). Allah is Forgiving, Merciful*} (9:91).

[60] Al-Shāfiʿī, *al-Risāla* (p. 75).
[61] Ibn al-Qayyim, *Iʿlām al-Muwaqqiʿīn* (1:58).

Abū Sulaymān al-Khaṭṭābī said:

> Being absolutely true (*naṣīḥa*) is a term that expresses the complete application of one's will to the good of the party to whom one is being true. It is impossible to come up with a synonym for it. Its lexical meaning is sincerity (*ikhlāṣ*) [...]. Thus one's being true (*naṣīḥa*) to Allah is one's correct belief in Him with unity (*al-waḥdāniyya*) and one's describing Him in terms appropriate to Him, declaring His Transcendence from what is impermissible to apply to Him, desiring what makes one beloved to Him, staying far away from what causes His wrath, and sincerity in worshipping Him. Being true to His Book consists in believing in it, putting into practice its contents, beautifying its recitation, being humble before it, magnifying its status, striving to understand it and acquire knowledge of it, and defending it from the interpretation of extremists and the attacks of atheists. As for being true to His Messenger, it consists of confirming his Prophethood, and doing one's utmost to obey his commands and prohibitions.[62]

Al-Ājurrī said about the meaning of being true to the Messenger of Allah ﷺ:

> "It consists in coming to his aid, supporting him, and protecting him both in life and death; in giving life to his Sunna by pursuing it, defending it, disseminating it; and in acquiring his noble manners and beautiful traits."[63]

- Allah ﷻ said: {*And when it is said unto them: Come unto that which Allah has revealed and unto the Messenger, you see the hypocrites turn from you with aversion*} (4:61).

[62] As quoted in ʿAbd al-Khāliq, *Ḥujjiyyat al-Sunna* (p. 293). See also al-Nawawī's magisterial commentary on the ḥadīth of *naṣīḥa*.
[63] *Ibid.*

Concerning this verse Ibn Ḥazm said:

> Let one therefore beware of Allah ﷻ to Whom is the return. Let his soul feel fear upon recitation of this verse and his anxiety increase in intensity that he might be meant by the epithet mentioned in that verse – that despicable, ruinous trait which necessitates hellfire. So whoever debates his opponent in a given matter of the Religion and its rulings – which we were commanded to learn and understand – calling him unto what Allah has revealed and what the Prophet ﷺ has said, but the other turns away and calls him unto analogy or to So-and-so's saying: let him know that Allah has named him a perfidious hypocrite [...]. And if someone were to say: "We do not take except what we found in the Qur'ān," such a person would be an apostate (*kāfir*) by Consensus of the Islamic Community, and would not thereby be obligated to pray more than one *rakʿa* between the going down of the sun and the dark of night, and another one at dawn [cf. 17:78]. For this is the least that has been called *ṣalāt*, and there is no limit (*ḥadd*) set for the most in that chapter. One who follows such a position is an idolatrous disbeliever (*kāfir mushrik*) whose life and property are licit. The only ones to go that path are some of the extremist *Rāfiḍīs* upon whose apostasy Consensus has formed in the Community. And success is from Allah ﷻ. Now, should someone follow only what the entire Community has agreed upon and nothing else, leaving all that they differed about with regard to what the texts mention: such a person is a transgressor (*fāsiq*) by Consensus of the Community. These two preliminaries make it obligatory to accept what is transmitted.[64]

[64] Ibn Ḥazm, *al-Iḥkām fī Uṣūl al-Aḥkām* (1:101, 2:80).

- Allah ﷻ said: {*And they say: We believe in Allah and the Messenger, and we obey; then after that a faction of them turn away. Such are not believers. But if right had been with them they would have come unto him willingly. Is there in their hearts a disease, or have they doubts, or fear lest Allah and His Messenger should wrong them in judgment? Nay, but such are evil doers. The saying of (all true) believers when they appeal unto Allah and His Messenger to judge between them is only that they say: We hear and we obey. And such are the successful. He who obeys Allah and His Messenger, and fears Allah, and keeps duty (unto Him): such indeed are the victorious. They swear by Allah solemnly that, if you order them, they will go forth. Say: Swear not; known obedience (is better). Lo! Allah is Informed of what you do. Say: Obey Allah and obey the Messenger. But if you turn away, then (it is) for him (to do) only that wherewith he has been charged, and for you (to do) only that wherewith you have been charged. If you obey him, you will go aright. But the Messenger has no other charge than to convey (the message), plainly*} (24:47-54).

Concerning these verses al-Shāfiʿī said:

> Allah ﷻ has informed human beings in this verse that their call unto the Messenger of Allah ﷺ that he judge between them is a call unto His own judgment. For the judge between them is the Messenger of Allah ﷺ, and if they surrender to the judgment of the Messenger of Allah, then they but surrender to His, as stipulated by Allah ﷻ Himself."[65]

- Allah ﷻ said: {*And it becomes not a believing man or a believing woman, when Allah and His Messenger have decided an affair (for them), that they should (after that) claim any say in their affair; and whosoever is rebellious to Allah and His Messenger, he verily goes astray in error manifest*} (33:36).

[65] Al-Shāfiʿī, *al-Risāla* (p. 84).

Concerning this verse Ibn al-Qayyim said:

> "Allah ﷻ has stated in this verse that there is no choice left for a believer after His judgment and the judgment of His Prophet. Whoever makes an alternative choice after this has strayed in manifest misguidance."[66]

– Allah ﷻ said: {*But nay, by your Lord! they will not believe (in truth) until they make you judge of what is in dispute between them and find within themselves no dislike of that which you decide, and submit with full submission*} (4:65).

Concerning this verse Ibn Ḥazm said:

> This verse suffices for whoever understands and shows caution, believing in Allah and the Last Day, and knowing with certainty that this covenant is his Almighty Lord's covenant with him and His will recorded against him. Therefore, let every human being examine his soul, and if he finds in it any reserve towards the Prophet's ﷺ judgment in any report he knows to be authentic among those reports that reached him; or if he finds his soul reticent to submit to what has reached him from the Messenger of Allah ﷺ, but leaning instead to so-and-so's saying, or to his analogies and preferences; or if he sees that his soul sets up, as judge over what he contends, someone other than the Messenger of Allah ﷺ – whether a Companion or anyone lesser: let him know that Allah ﷻ has sworn an oath – and His Word is the truth! – that he is not a believer, and Allah has spoken the truth. If he is not a believer, then he is an apostate, and there is no middle way![67]

Ibn al-Qayyim said concerning the same verse:

[66] Ibn al-Qayyim, *I'lām al-Muwaqqi'īn* (1:57).
[67] Ibn Ḥazm, *al-Iḥkām fī Uṣūl al-Aḥkām* (1:100).

> Allah ﷻ swore by Himself that belief was absent from people until they made His Prophet a judge between whatever is disputed between them, minute or major. Yet He did not consider their making such arbitration a sufficient factor of their belief until the least element of reservation or unease at his verdict and judgment had completely disappeared from their hearts. He did not even make the latter condition sufficient until they submitted with full submission and let themselves be led in complete followership.[68]

Al-Shāfiʿī explained thus the circumstances in which the verse was revealed:

> This verse [4:65] was revealed – according to what has reached us, and Allah knows best – in the matter of a man who contended with al-Zubayr over a piece of land, whereupon the Prophet ﷺ ruled in favor of al-Zubayr.[69] This judgment is a Sunna of the Messenger of Allah ﷺ and not a ruling stipulated in the Qurʾān. The Qurʾān shows – and Allah knows best – what I just described. If it had been a judgment based upon the Qurʾān, it would have been a ruling stipulated by the Book of Allah, in which case they, in refusing to submit to a stipulated ruling of the Book of Allah, would have been considered not to be believers without any difficulty, simply for rejecting the ruling that had been revealed and refusing to submit to it.[70]

Al-Shāfiʿī thus adduced the verse as a proof for the probativeness of the Sunna by showing that this ruling was not specifically or clearly stipulated in the book of Allah for, had this been the case, their lack of belief would have stemmed from their rejection of the ruling of the Book and their refusal to submit to it, not from

---

[68] Ibn al-Qayyim, *Iʿlām al-Muwaqqiʿīn* (1:57).
[69] It was a dispute over the use of a stream between al-Zubayr and one of the *Anṣār*. Narrated from ʿAbd Allah ibn al-Zubayr in the Six Books and Aḥmad.
[70] Al-Shāfiʿī, *al-Risāla* (p. 83).

failing to resort to the Prophet's ﷺ arbitration, nor from not submitting to the latter, nor from harboring reservations about it. In such a case it would have appeared more appropriate to say: "Nay, by your Lord! they will not believe until they accept the Book's ruling and submit to it fully." And Allah knows best.

b) Verses that indicate that the Prophet ﷺ elucidates the Book and explains its wisdom in a manner that carries authority on the part of Allah ﷻ

The second type of verses denoting the probativeness of the Sunna are the verses that indicate that the Prophet ﷺ elucidates the Book and explains its wisdom in a manner that carries authority on the part of Allah ﷻ. Among these verses are those that state that the Prophet ﷺ is teaching the Community the Book (*al-kitāb*) and the Wisdom (*al-ḥikma*). The latter is, as al-Shāfiʿī and others said, the Sunna. Muḥammad ibn Naṣr al-Marwazī (d. 294) said:

> Allah revealed two types of revelation, naming one Qur'ān and the other *ḥikma*, differentiating between them, both being from Him, and the *ḥikma* is whatever the Messenger ﷺ instituted (*sanna*) that is not mentioned in the Book. Otherwise it would be as if He said "Allah reveals unto you the Scripture and the Scripture" which is far-fetched. [...] No one denies this except one who is dim-witted."[71]

Even if we should concede that the Wisdom also means the Book, then the Prophet's ﷺ teaching of Wisdom to the Community means its explanation, the exposition of its generalities, and the elucidation of its difficulties. All this dictates the probative force of his explanation of the Book as contained in his sayings, his actions, and his tacit approval and disapproval. That is, his Sunna.

[71] In *al-Sunna* (p. 110 §401).

- Allah ﷻ said: {*And We have revealed unto you the Remembrance that you may explain to mankind that which has been revealed for them, and that haply they may reflect*} (16:44).
- And He said: {*And we have revealed the Scripture unto you only that you may explain unto them that wherein they differ, and* (*as*) *a guidance and a mercy for a people who believe*} (16:64).
- And He said: {*Even as We have sent unto you a Messenger from among you, who recites unto you Our revelations and causes you to grow, and teaches you the Scripture and wisdom, and teaches you that which you knew not*} (2:151).
- And He said: {*Allah verily has shown grace to the believers by sending unto them a Messenger of their own who recites unto them His revelations, and causes them to grow, and teaches them the Scripture and wisdom; although before* (*he came to them*) *they were in flagrant error*} (3:164).
- And He said: {*He it is Who has sent among the unlettered ones a Messenger of their own, to recite unto them His revelations and to make them grow, and to teach them the Scripture and Wisdom, though heretofore they were indeed in error manifest*} (62:2).
- And He said: {*Remember the grace of Allah upon you and that which He has revealed unto you of the Scripture and of wisdom, whereby He does exhort you*} (2:231).
- And He said: {*Allah reveals unto you the Scripture and wisdom, and teaches you that which you knew not. The grace of Allah toward you has been infinite*} (4:113).
- And He said: {*And bear in mind that which is recited in your houses of the revelations of Allah and wisdom. Lo! Allah is Subtle, Aware*} (33:34).

Al-Shāfiʿī said in commentary of these verses:

> Allah ﷻ mentioned the Book and that is the Qur'ān; He also mentioned wisdom. I have heard those whose opinion I trust among the people of knowledge of the Qur'ān say that "wisdom" means the Sunna of the Messenger of Allah ﷺ. This supports what Allah ﷻ said – and Allah knows best – because the Qur'ān is a Reminder and wisdom follows it, and Allah mentioned that He lavished favor on His creatures by teaching them the Book and wisdom. It is therefore impermissible – and Allah knows best – to say that wisdom here is anything other than the Sunna of the Messenger of Allah ﷺ. That is because it is coupled (*maqrūna*) with the Book, and Allah has made obedience to His Prophet a strict obligation, imposing upon people the absolute duty to follow his commands. Thus we cannot say of anything that it is a strict obligation (*farḍ*) except the book of Allah and the Sunna of His Messenger ﷺ. The reason, as we just said, is that Allah has coupled belief in His Messenger with belief in Him.[72]

Al-Shāfiʿī means to show that wisdom is the Sunna because in all these verses Allah ﷻ has joined it to the Book. This dictates differentiation (*mughāyara*), so "wisdom" cannot denote the Book. However, it cannot be anything other than either the Book or the Sunna, because Allah has lavished His favor upon us by teaching them to us. Favor cannot consist in other than what is right, true, and in conformity with what is with Him. Wisdom must therefore be obligatorily followed just like the Book, especially since Allah has coupled it with the Book. But He has not enjoined upon us such obligation throughout His Book except with regard to two things: following His Book and following the Sunna of His Prophet ﷺ. It follows that wisdom refers specifically to the Sunna.

[72] Al-Shāfiʿī, *al-Risāla* (p. 78).

c) Verses that indicate the obligatoriness of obeying the Prophet ﷺ in absolute terms in whatever he orders and whatever he prohibits

The third type of verses denoting the probativeness of the Sunna are the verses that indicate the obligatoriness of obeying the Prophet ﷺ in absolute terms in whatever he orders and prohibits, the fact that to obey him is to obey Allah, and the warning against contravening him or changing his Sunna.

- Allah ﷻ said: {*And obey Allah and the Messenger, that you may find mercy*} (3:132).
- And He said: {*Say: Obey Allah and the Messenger. But if they turn away, Lo! Allah loves not the disbelievers (in His guidance)*} (3:32).
- And He said: {*O you who believe! Obey Allah and His Messenger, and turn not away from him when you hear (him speak). Be not as those who say, We hear, and they hear not*} (8:20-21).
- And He said: {*And obey Allah and His Messenger, and dispute not one with another lest you falter and your strength depart from you; but be steadfast! Lo! Allah is with the steadfast*} (8:46).
- And He said: {*Obey Allah and obey the Messenger, and beware! But if you turn away, then know that the duty of Our Messenger is only plain conveyance (of the message)*} (5:92).
- And He said: {*O you who believe! Obey Allah and obey the Messenger, and render not your actions vain*} (47:33).
- And He said: {*Obey Allah and obey His Messenger; but if you turn away, then the duty of Our Messenger is only to convey (the message) plainly*} (64:12).

– And He said: {*O you who believe! Obey Allah, and obey the Messenger and those of you who are in authority; and if you have a dispute concerning any matter, refer it to Allah and the Messenger if you are (in truth) believers in Allah and the Last Day. That is better and more seemly in the end*} (4:59).

Al-Qāḍī ʿIyāḍ narrated from ʿAṭā' ibn Abī Rabāḥ, as did al-Ṭabarī, Ibn ʿAbd al-Barr, al-Bayhaqī and others from Mujāhid, Qatāda, and Maymūn ibn Mahrān: "Referring it to Allah ﷻ means to go back to His Book, while referring it to the Messenger ﷺ means to go back to him in his lifetime, and to his Sunna after his death."[73]

Al-Shāfiʿī said:

> Some of the people of knowledge said that {*those of you who are in authority*} refers to the commanders of the military detachments of the Messenger of Allah ﷺ, and Allah knows best. This is what was narrated to us, and it seems that this is what He said, and Allah knows best. For none of the Arabs that were around Makka were familiar with authority and they used to reject with contempt any notion of submitting to each other's authority. When they professed obedience to the Messenger of Allah ﷺ, they did not consider that such obedience could go to anyone other than him. Therefore, they were ordered to obey those in authority whom the Messenger of Allah had placed in authority, not with unconditional obedience, but with obedience respecting what stood for or against them. Then He said {*and if you have a dispute concerning any matter, refer it to Allah*} meaning if you differ about something. This is, if Allah wills,

[73] Al-Ṭabarī, *Tafsīr* (5:151, 25:78); al-Qurṭubī, *Tafsīr* (5:260-261); al-Lālikā'ī, *Iʿtiqād Ahl al-Sunna* (1:73); al-Naḥḥās, *Maʿānī al-Qur'ān* (2:123); al-Bayhaqī, *al-Iʿtiqād* (p. 227-228), *al-Madkhal* (p. 184); al-Bukhārī, *Khalq Afʿāl al-ʿIbād* (p. 61); Ibn ʿAbd al-Barr, *al-Tamhīd* (4:264), *Bayān Faḍl al-ʿIlm* (1:765-766, 2:910, 2:1177, 2:1189); Ibn al-Jawzī, *Zād al-Masīr* (2:117); al-Suyūṭī, *al-Durr al-Manthūr* (2:579).

> identical with what He said concerning those in authority except that He states {*and if you have a dispute*} meaning – Allah knows best – they and their leaders in authority whom they were ordered to obey. {*Refer it to Allah and the Messenger*} meaning – Allah knows best – refer it to what Allah and the Messenger said if you know of it. If you do not know of it, then ask the Messenger about it when you contact him or whoever is in touch with him. For that is the strict obligation about which there is no question because of His saying {*And it becomes not a believing man or a believing woman, when Allah and His Messenger have decided an affair (for them), that they should (after that) claim any say in their affair*} (33:36). Whoever is disputing something after the time of the Messenger of Allah ﷺ, has to refer the matter to the judgment of Allah ﷻ, then to His Messenger's judgment. If there is no extant judgment in them or in one of them textually on the matter under dispute, then they have to refer it to one of them analogically.[74]

The ḥadīth Master Ibn Ḥajar said:

> Al-Bukhārī alludes to his preference for the explanation of this verse to mean obedience to those in positions of leadership, as opposed to those who said that the verse was revealed in reference to the Ulema. This is also al-Ṭabarī's preference [....] Ibn ʿUyayna said: "I asked Zayd ibn Aslam about it at a time when no one in Madīna could explain the Qur'ān like him other than Muḥammad ibn Kaʿb. He said: 'Read what precedes it and you will know.' I read {*Lo! Allah commands you that you restore deposits to their owners, and, if you judge between mankind, that you judge justly. Lo! comely is this which Allah admonishes you. Lo! Allah is ever Hearer, Seer*} (4:58). Then he said: 'This verse refers to those who govern (*al-wulāt*).'"

[74] Al-Shāfiʿī, *al-Risāla* (p. 79-81).

The subtlety of repeating the verb for the Prophet ﷺ in {*Obey Allah, and obey the Messenger*} but not for {*and those of you who are in authority*} – although the one being obeyed in reality is Allah ﷻ – is the fact that the sources by which one determines legal responsibility are the Qur'ān and the Sunna. It is as if Allah ﷻ were saying: "Obey Allah in whatever He textually stipulates for you in the Qur'ān and obey the Messenger in whatever he elucidates from the Qur'ān for you and textually stipulates for you in the Sunna." Or: "Obey Allah in all He commands you in the revelation instituted for worship-through-recitation, and obey the Messenger in all he commands you in the revelation that is other than the Qur'ān."

One of the most remarkable answers was that given by one of the Successors to one of the Umayyad princes when the latter asked him: "Did not Allah ﷻ order you all to obey us when He said {*and those of you who are in authority*}?" whereupon the former replied: "Was not obedience denied you whensoever you contravened right, when He said {*and if you have a dispute concerning any matter, refer it to Allah and the Messenger if you are (in truth) believers in Allah and the Last Day*} (4:59)?"

Al-Ṭībī said: "He repeated the verb in {*and obey the Messenger*} as a sign that the Prophet ﷺ is obeyed independently, but he did not repeat it for {*and those of you who are in authority*} as a sign that some among them do not have to be obeyed. Then He expounded this by saying {*and if you have a dispute concerning any matter*}, as if saying: if they do not act according to right, then do not obey them, and refer whatever you differed about to the judgment of Allah and His Messenger."[75]

An example of a dispute with those in authority in which the matter was referred to the Prophet ﷺ is given in the following ḥadīth:

[75] Ibn Ḥajar, *Fatḥ al-Bārī* (1959 ed. 13:111).

> The Prophet ﷺ sent a military detachment under the command of one of the Companions after ordering those who were with him to obey him faithfully. In the course of the expedition the commander became angry with them. He lit a fire and ordered them to enter it. They refused, saying: "We have fled to the Messenger of Allah ﷺ to get away from the fire (*fararnā ilā Rasūlillāhi min al-nār*)!" When the Prophet ﷺ heard about the incident he said: "Had they entered it they would not have come out of it until the Day of Resurrection. Obedience is only in good matters!"[76]

Similarly the Prophet ﷺ said: "No obedience is due to any creature in disobedience of Allah!"[77] and "Whoever of your rulers and governors commands you to sin, neither hear nor obey him!"[78]

Ibn al-Qayyim said:

> Allah ﷻ ordered that whatever the believers are in dispute about is to be referred to Allah and His Messenger if they are, in truth, believers. He told them that that was better for them in this life and more seemly in the hereafter. This comprises several issues. First, it tells us that the people of belief may find themselves in dispute over certain rulings but this does not expel them from the fold of belief [...]. Secondly, The phrase {*and if you have a dispute concerning any matter*} (4:59) uses an indefinite object (matter) in the protasis of a conditional sentence to include generally all that the believers dispute over, whether great or small, manifest or hidden. Now if there were not, in the Book of Allah and His Messenger, the sufficient exposition of the ruling concerning what they were disputing

[76] Narrated from ʿAlī by al-Bukhārī and Muslim.
[77] Narrated from ʿAlī, Ibn Masʿūd, and ʿImrān by Aḥmad with four sound chains.
[78] Narrated with a fair chain from Abū Saʿīd al-Khudrī by Ibn Mājah and Aḥmad.

over, He would not have commanded that they refer back to them. For it is precluded that Allah ﷻ command them to refer to an arbiter at a time of dispute when that arbiter does not possess the means to settle the dispute. Thirdly, the scholars have reached Consensus that referring to Allah ﷻ means referring to His Book, while referring to the Messenger ﷺ means referring to him in person during his lifetime and to his Sunna after his death. Fourthly, Allah has made this reference one of the obligations and necessary conditions of belief. If this reference is denied, then belief is contradicted by virtue of the essential correlation that made one the obligation and necessary condition of the other. Then He told them that such a reference was a great good for them and that its consequence in the next world was the very best.[79]

Other explanations of the *Salaf*[80] for {*those who are in authority*} (4:59) are "the knowledgeable scholars of the Religion" (*al-ʿulamā'*),[81] "the people of Religion and knowledge,"[82] particularly "the Companions of Muḥammad who are the people of intelli-

[79] Ibn al-Qayyim, *Iʿlām al-Muwaqqiʿīn* (1:54).
[80] The *Salaf* are "The Predecessors," a name applied to the righteous Muslims of the first centuries. A "Salafī" is, properly speaking, a strict imitator of the *Salaf* such as the adherents of the Four Sunnī Schools but the *Salafiyya* today is a misnomer referring to an anti-traditional free-thinking *mutasallif* current spawned by the *Wahhābiyya*, both patching up views from modernism, the *Muʿtazila*, *Ẓāhiriyya*, and *Karrāmiyya*, and both claiming to represent *Ahl al-Sunna* in vociferous opposition to Ashʿarīs and Māturīdīs. The "Salafīs" also name themselves *Ahl al-Ḥadīth* (in Indo-Pakistan) and *Atharī* (in the Gulf). Their opponents name them *Ḥashwiyya*, *Mujassima*, *Khawārij*, and misguided deceivers.
[81] Narrated from Mujāhid and ʿAṭā' by Ibn Kathīr in his *Tafsīr* under this verse.
[82] Narrated from Ibn ʿAbbās by al-Ḥākim, Ibn al-Mundhir, al-Ṭabarī, Ibn Abī Ḥātim, and Ibn Kathīr in his *Tafsīr* under this verse; and from Jābir ibn ʿAbd Allah by Ibn Abī Shayba, ʿAbd ibn Ḥumayd, al-Ḥakīm al-Tirmidhī, al-Ṭabarī, Ibn al-Mundhir, al-Ḥākim, and Ibn Abī Ḥātim, both as related by al-Suyūṭī in *al-Durr al-Manthūr* for this verse.

gence, superlative understanding, and Religion"[83] specifically the Four Rightly-Guided Caliphs and Ibn Mas'ūd,[84] and more specifically Abū Bakr and 'Umar.[85]

- Allah ﷻ said: {*We sent no messenger save that he should be obeyed by the leave of Allah. And if, when they had wronged themselves, they had but come unto you and asked forgiveness of Allah and the Messenger had asked forgiveness for them, they would have found Allah Forgiving, Merciful*} (4:64).
- And He said: {*Whoso obeys Allah and the Messenger, they are with those unto whom Allah has shown favor, of the Prophets and the saints and the martyrs and the righteous. The best of company are they!*} (4:69).
- And He said: {*O you who believe! Guard your duty to Allah, and speak words straight to the point; He will adjust your works for you and will forgive you your sins. Whosoever obeys Allah and His Messenger, he verily has gained a signal victory*} (33:70-71).
- And He said: {*And whatsoever the Messenger gives you, take it. And whatsoever he forbids, abstain (from it)*} (59:7).
- And He said: {*Lo! those who swear allegiance unto you (Muḥammad), swear allegiance only unto Allah. The Hand of Allah is above their hands. So whosoever breaks his oath, breaks it only to his soul's hurt; while whosoever keeps his covenant with Allah, on him will He bestow immense reward*} (48:10).

[83] Narrated from Mujāhid by Ibn Abī Shayba, 'Abd ibn Ḥumayd, al-Ṭabarī, and Ibn al-Mundhir as related by al-Lacknawī in *Tuḥfat al-Akhyār* (p. 66); and from al-Daḥḥāk by Ibn Abī Ḥātim as related by al-Suyūṭī in *al-Durr al-Manthūr*.
[84] Narrated from al-Kalbī by 'Abd ibn Ḥumayd as related by al-Lacknawī in *Tuḥfat al-Akhyār* (p. 66) and al-Suyūṭī in *al-Durr al-Manthūr*.
[85] Narrated from 'Ikrima by 'Abd ibn Ḥumayd, al-Ṭabarī, Ibn Abī Ḥātim, and Ibn 'Asākir as related by al-Lacknawī in *Tuḥfat al-Akhyār* (p. 66) and al-Suyūṭī in *al-Durr al-Manthūr*.

- And He said: {*Whatever of good befalls you (O man) it is from Allah, and whatever of ill befalls you it is from yourself. We have sent you (O Muḥammad) as a Messenger unto mankind and Allah is sufficient as witness. Whosoever obeys the Messenger obeys Allah, and whosoever turns away: We have not sent you as a warder over them*} (4:79-80).

Concerning this verse al-Shāfiʿī said: "He has informed them that their allegiance to His Messenger was allegiance to Him, and that their obedience to him was obedience to Him."[86]

- And He said: {*These are the limits (imposed by) Allah. Whosoever obeys Allah and His Messenger, He will make him enter Gardens underneath which rivers flow, where such will dwell for ever. That will be the great success. And whosoever disobeys Allah and His Messenger and transgresses His limits, He will make him enter Fire, where such will dwell for ever; his will be a shameful doom*} (4:13-14).

- And He said: {*Make not the calling of the Messenger among you as your calling one of another. Allah knows those of you who steal away, hiding themselves. And let those who conspire to evade orders beware lest grief or painful punishment befall them*} (24:63).

- And He said: {*That is because they opposed Allah and His Messenger. Whosoever opposes Allah and His Messenger, (for him) lo! Allah is severe in punishment*} (8:13).

- And He said: {*Lo! Allah has cursed the disbelievers and has prepared for them a flaming fire, Wherein they will abide forever. They will find (then) no protecting friend nor helper. On the day when their faces are turned over in the fire, they say: Oh, would that we had obeyed Allah and had obeyed His Messenger!*} (33:64-66).

[86] Al-Shāfiʿī, *al-Risāla* (p. 82).

- And He said: {*Lo! those who disbelieve and turn from the way of Allah and oppose the Messenger after the guidance has been manifested unto them, they hurt Allah not a jot, and He will make their actions fruitless*} (47:32).

d) Verses that indicate the obligatoriness of following and imitating him ﷺ in whatsoever issues from him, as the necessary condition for being loved by Allah

- Allah ﷻ said: {*Say, (O Muḥammad, to mankind): If you love Allah, follow me; Allah will love you and forgive you your sins. Allah is Forgiving, Merciful*} (3:31).

  Some people came and said: "Messenger of Allah, verily we love Allah!" whereupon Allah revealed {*Say: If you love Allah...*}.[87] Al-Ḥasan said: "Thereafter, the mark of their love for Him was their adherence to the Sunna."[88]

- And He said: {*Verily in the Messenger of Allah you have a good example for him who looks unto Allah and the last Day, and remembers Allah much*} (33:21) Al-Qāḍī ʿIyāḍ quoted al-Ḥakīm al-Tirmidhī and other commentators as saying: "Following the exemplariness of the Messenger means taking him as one's leader, following his Sunna, and not contravening him whether in speech or in deed."[89]

- And He said: {*The Prophet is closer to the believers than their selves, and his wives are (as) their mothers*} (33:6).

- And He said: {*Say: If your fathers, and your sons, and your brethren, and your wives, and your tribe, and the wealth you have*

[87] Narrated from al-Ḥasan and Ibn al-Jurayj by al-Ṭabarī in his *Tafsīr* (3:232) and al-Qurṭubī in his (4:60).
[88] Narrated by al-Lālikāʾī in *Sharḥ Uṣūl Iʿtiqād Ahl al-Sunna* (1:70).
[89] In al-Qāḍī ʿIyāḍ, *al-Shifāʾ* (2:7).

acquired, and merchandise for which you fear that there will be no sale, and dwellings you desire are dearer to you than Allah and His Messenger and striving in His way: then wait till Allah brings His command to pass. Allah guides not wrong-doing folk} (9:24).

- And He said: {*And lo! you are of a tremendous nature. And you will see and they will see which of you is demented. Lo! your Lord is best aware of him who strays from his way, and He is best aware of those who walk aright*} (68:4-7).

- And He said: {*And ordain for us in this world that which is good, and in the Hereafter (that which is good), Lo! We have turned unto You. He said: I smite with My punishment whom I will, and My mercy embraces all things, therefore I shall ordain it for those who ward off (evil) and pay the poor due, and those who believe Our revelations; Those who follow the Messenger, the unlettered Prophet, whom they will find described in the Torah and the Gospel (which are) with them. He will enjoin on them that which is right and forbid them that which is wrong. He will make lawful for them all good things and prohibit for them only the foul; and he will relieve them of their burden and the fetters that they used to wear. Then those who believe in him, and honor him and help him, and follow the light which is sent down with him: they are the successful*} (7:156-157).

- And He said: {*And when you said unto him on whom Allah has conferred favor and you have conferred favor: Keep your wife to yourself, and fear Allah. And you did hide in your mind that which Allah was to bring to light, and you did fear mankind whereas Allah had a better right that you should fear Him. So when Zayd had performed the necessary formality (of divorce) from her, We gave her unto you in marriage, so that (henceforth) there may be no sin for believers in respect of wives of their adopted sons, when the latter have performed the necessary formality (of release) from them. The commandment of Allah must be fulfilled*} (33:37).

e) Verses indicating that Allah ﷻ has tasked the Prophet ﷺ with following and conveying whatever is revealed to him whether in recited (*matlū*) or non-recited form, forbidding him to neglect or alter or replace any part of it, and assuring him that He has protected him against people who would wish him to alter or cover up something of what was revealed to him

This type additionally includes verses that indicate that he fulfilled this command, conveyed the message fully and in the most perfect manner, and guided people to the straight path; that Allah ﷻ has completed and perfected the Religion for the Community by means of the Prophet's ﷺ conveyance of all that had been revealed to him; and that the Prophet ﷺ was {*of a tremendous nature and character*} (68:4), "nature" or "character" here meaning the source of all conscious and deliberate sayings and acts. If he is of the utmost greatness and excellence in the Divine presence, then everything that issues from him is of the same order. If the Prophet ﷺ were to announce a ruling or put it into practice when such a ruling contradicts the Divine Law, or if he were to command something forbidden or prohibit something permitted, he would not have fulfilled the order to convey, nor be guiding humanity to the straight path, but on the contrary he would be misguiding them and so would not have earned this praise on the part of Allah ﷻ. All this indicates the truthfulness and probativeness of the Sunna and the obligatoriness to adhere to it.

- Allah ﷻ said: {*O Prophet! Keep your duty to Allah and obey not the disbelievers and the hypocrites. Lo! Allah is Knower, Wise. And follow that which is revealed to you from your Lord. Lo! Allah is Aware of what you do*} (33:1-2).

- And He said: {*Follow that which is inspired in you from your Lord; there is no God save Him; and turn away from the idolaters*} (6:106).
- And He said: {*And now have We set you* (*O Muḥammad*) *on a clear road of* (*Our*) *commandment; so follow it, and follow not the whims of those who know not*} (45:18).
- And He said: {*And unto you have We revealed the Scripture with the truth, confirming whatever Scripture was before it, and as a watcher over it. So judge between them by that which Allah has revealed, and follow not their desires away from the truth which has come unto you. For each We have appointed a Divine law and a traced-out way. Had Allah willed He could have made you one community. But that He may try you by that which He has given you* (*He has made you as you are*)*. So vie one with another in good works. Unto Allah you will all return, and He will then inform you of that wherein you differ. So judge between them by that which Allah has revealed, and follow not their desires, but beware of them lest they seduce you from some part of that which Allah has revealed unto you. And if they turn away, then know that the will of Allah is to smite them for some sin of theirs. Lo! many of mankind are evil doers*} (5:48-49).
- And He said: {*O Messenger! Make known that which has been revealed unto you from your Lord, for if you do it not, you will not have conveyed His message. Allah will protect you from mankind. Lo! Allah guides not the disbelieving folk*} (5:67).
- And He said: {*And thus have We inspired in you* (*Muḥammad*) *a Spirit of Our command. You knew not what the Scripture was, nor the Faith. But We have made it a light whereby We guide whom We will of Our bondsmen. And lo! you verily do guide unto a right path, the path of Allah, unto Whom belongs whatsoever is in*

the heavens and whatsoever is in the earth. Do not all things reach Allah at last?} (42:52-53).

– And He said: {*But for the grace of Allah upon you (Muḥammad), and His mercy, a party of them had resolved to mislead you, but they will mislead only themselves and they will hurt you not at all. Allah revealed unto you the Scripture and wisdom, and taught you that which you knew not. The grace of Allah toward you has been infinite*} (4:113).

– And He said: {*But nay! I swear by all that you see and all that you see not, that it is indeed the speech of an illustrious Messenger. It is not poet's speech – little is it that you believe! Nor diviner's speech – little is it that you remember! It is a revelation from the Lord of the Worlds. And if he had invented false sayings concerning Us, We assuredly would have taken him by the right hand and then severed his life artery, and not one of you could have held Us off from him*} (69:38-47).

– And He said: {*Say: This is my Way: I call unto Allah with sure knowledge, I and whosoever follows me. Glory be to Allah! and I am not of the idolaters*} (12:108).

– And He said: {*He will enjoin on them that which is right and forbid them that which is wrong. He will make lawful for them all good things and prohibit for them only the foul; and he will relieve them of their burden and the fetters that they used to wear*} (7:157).

– And He said: {*And lo! you summon them indeed unto a right path*} (23:73).

– And He said: {*Yā Sīn. By the wise Qur'ān, Lo! you are of those sent on a straight path, a revelation of the Mighty, the Merciful*} (36:1-5).

- And He said: {*Therefore (O Muḥammad) put your trust in Allah, for you stand on the plain Truth*} (27:79).
- And He said: {*This day have I perfected your religion for you and completed My favor unto you, and have chosen for you as religion al-Islam*} (5:3).
- And He said: {*Nūn. By the pen and that which they write (therewith), you are not, for your Lord's favor unto you, a madman. And lo! yours verily will be a reward unfailing. And lo! you are of a tremendous nature*} (68:1-4).
- Allah ﷻ has also informed humanity that He was going to accept the Prophet's ﷺ testimony over his Community on the Day of Judgment when He said: {*Thus We have appointed you a middle nation, that you may be witnesses against mankind and that the Messenger may be a witness against you*} (2:143). Allah ﷻ does not accept testimony except if it comes from someone who is upright both outwardly and inwardly, and from whom nothing issues to violate that condition, whether in word or in deed and whether in the conveyance of the Message or otherwise. This is understood in the light of His complete awareness of all the Prophet's ﷺ states whether public or hidden.

We conclude this section by citing the saying of Allah ﷻ: {*We sent you not save as a mercy for the peoples*} (21:107) and {*O Prophet! Lo! We have sent you as a witness and a bringer of good tidings and a warner, and as a summoner unto Allah by His permission, and as a lamp that gives light*} (33:45-46). The content of these verses is obvious.

CHAPTER 4

Proofs from the Noble Sunna for the Sunna as Evidence

Someone may ask, how can the probativeness of the Sunna be inferred from the Sunna itself, and is this not a kind of logical circle that should be precluded?

First, the Qur'ān itself is not established as probative except through the Prophet's ﷺ own assertion that it is the word of Allah ﷻ, that is, on the basis of the mass-transmitted Sunna.

Second, whoever considers carefully the proofs given above under the heading of the Prophet's ﷺ exemption from error,[90] realizes that this objection is invalid. In that section we had said that the miracle of the Qur'ānic *iʿjāz* dictates that every Divinely-sanctioned discourse on his part is by Consensus truthful and in conformity with what comes from Allah ﷻ, therefore it is obligatory to accept and conform with it. This proof had lead us to establish as true a major corollary, namely, that revelation is divided into two kinds:

a) The Book, which is the evidentiary miracle used to worship by means of recitation.

b) Everything else, namely: the ḥadīth *qudsī* and the Prophetic ḥadīth, whose meaning was revealed but whose wording was chosen by the Prophet ﷺ.

We can now add a further specification that we can safely exclude from the second category those ḥadīths in which the Prophet ﷺ himself states that they are not part of the Divine disclosure but are his own opinion, meaning, not in his capacity as a prophet, but as an ordinary human being. Two of the best-known examples of this case are the ḥadīth of the pollination of

[90] See ch. "The Prophet's Immune State Dictates that Ḥadīth is Revelation" above.

the date palm trees[91] and the ḥadīth of al-Ḥubāb ibn al-Mundhir's tactical advice in the battle of Badr.[92] We are not concerned here with that type of ḥadīth, nor with the ḥadīths that describe the Prophet's ﷺ noble frame (*khalq*) and manners (*khuluq*), but with the ḥadīths that carry the force of timeless law – and therefore qualify as Divine ordinances conveyed by the Prophet ﷺ – outside the Book. Once one accepts that the Prophet ﷺ never lies in the conveyance of commands and prohibitions from his Lord, then one can no longer reject the law-probative force of the latter kind of ḥadīths provided they are established as authentic through the means elaborated to that effect.

Third and last, we may adduce the Prophet's ﷺ commands – whose probative nature is established by their inclusion in the definition of conveyance (*al-khabar al-balāghī*) – to establish the probativeness of his acts and tacit approvals and disapprovals. It can be seen from the above stipulations, that we only adduce as proof the kind of law-probative ḥadīth established independently from, and prior to, any other ḥadīth whose probativeness the law-probative ḥadīth may serve to establish. Therefore, there is no circular logic, *wal-ḥamdu lillāh*.

There are many types of proofs in the Sunna for the Sunna as evidence. These types can be reduced to three: ironclad conveyance from the one who never lies ﷺ, his orders and prohibitions, and his command to listen to his ḥadīth, memorize it, and convey it to others.

[91] Cf. n. 204.
[92] In Ibn Isḥāq, Ibn Sa'd and others cf. *Iṣāba*.

THE CONVEYANCE FROM THE ONE WHO NEVER LIES ﷺ THAT:

1. Allah ﷻ has revealed to him the Qur'ān and other than it;
2. Whatever legal rulings he has expounded and stipulated are His ﷻ own expositions and stipulations, not the Prophet's ﷺ;
3. It is impossible to understand the laws and ordinances of Islam from the Qur'ān alone, rather, it is necessary to have recourse to the Sunna;
4. Sunna-based practice is Qur'ān-based;
5. The Umma in its entirety and without exception has been ordered to accept his words, obey his commands and prohibitions, and follow his Sunna;
6. Whoever obeys him ﷺ and holds fast to his Sunna obeys Allah ﷻ and follows guidance, and as such, deserves Paradise and huge reward;
7. Whoever disobeys him ﷺ and rejects his sayings, preferring to follow his own opinion and whims, has disobeyed Allah, followed misguidance, and perished, such being deserving of hellfire and the curse of Allah – may Allah ﷻ protect us!;
8. Faith and belief remain incomplete until one follows all that he brought ﷺ;
9. Nothing but truth comes out of his blessed mouth ﷺ;
10. The best guidance of all is his guidance ﷺ;
11. Anything that he ﷺ did not himself bring but which people innovate after him according to their whims and caprice, or to serve their lusts, is an innovation in the Religion (*bid'a*) which is completely rejected.

All the above items presuppose that the Sunna is probative. Following are the narrations that pertain to each item, numbered accordingly.

1. Allah ﷻ has revealed to him ﷺ the Qur'ān and other than it

The Prophet ﷺ said: "Lo! Verily I was given the Qur'ān and something like it. Soon a man may say, leaning on his couch with his stomach full: 'Follow this Qur'ān, whatever you find in it to be [declared] permissible then declare it permissible, and whatever you find in it to be [declared] prohibited then declare it prohibited.' Verily whatever the Messenger of Allah has declared prohibited is just as what Allah ﷻ has declared prohibited. Lo! The meat of the domestic ass is prohibited to you. So is the meat of fanged beasts of prey. So is a find belonging to the beneficiary of a treaty unless its owner does not want it. If one or more people arrive among some people the latter must receive them hospitably; if they do not, they must give them the amount equivalent to their hospitality."[93]

Another narration of the above gives us a glimpse at the "circumstances of utterance" (*asbāb al-wurūd*) for this foundational ḥadīth:

> Al-ʿIrbāḍ ibn Sāriya said: "We alighted in Khaybar with the Prophet ﷺ and whoever of his Companions was with him. The leader of Khaybar was a rebellious, contemptible man. He came to the Prophet ﷺ and said, 'Muḥammad! Do you all have total licence to kill our donkeys, eat our crops, and beat our womenfolk?' The Prophet ﷺ became angry and said: 'Ibn ʿAwf, get on

[93] Narrated from al-Miqdām ibn Maʿdīkarb with sound chains by Abū Dāwūd and Aḥmad; also, in part, by al-Tirmidhī (*ḥasan gharīb*), Ibn Mājah, and al-Dārimī. Also narrated in part from Abū Nāfiʿ the Prophet's ﷺ *mawlā* by all but al-Dārimī as well as al-Shāfiʿī in *al-Umm* (7:15), al-Ṭaḥāwī in *Sharḥ Maʿānī al-Āthār* (4:209), Ibn Ḥazm in *al-Iḥkām* (6:310), etc. Al-Tirmidhī declared it *ḥasan ṣaḥīḥ*.

your horse and call out: Lo! Verily Paradise is forbidden except to a believer; then tell them to gather for the prayer.' They gathered and the Prophet ﷺ prayed with them. Afterwards he said: 'Does any of you think, leaning back on his couch, perhaps, that Allah prohibited nothing except what is in this Qur'ān? Truly, truly, I swear by Allah that I have exhorted and commanded and forbidden you certain matters in the amount of the Qur'ān or more! And I have said that fanged beasts of prey are not permissible for you to eat, nor domestic asses, and that Allah ﷻ did not make it permissible for you to enter the houses of the People of the Book except with their permission, nor beat their womenfolk, nor eat their crops if they give you what they are due to give.'"[94]

Muḥammad ibn Naṣr al-Marwazī (d. 294) said: "Allah revealed two types of revelation, naming one Qur'ān and the other *ḥikma*, differentiating between them, both being from Him, and the *ḥikma* is whatever the Messenger ﷺ instituted (*sanna*) that is not mentioned in the Book. Otherwise it would be as if He said 'Allah reveals unto you the Scripture and the Scripture' which is far-fetched. [...] None denies this except one who is dim-witted."[95]

The Prophet ﷺ stood speaking among the Companions and mentioned that *jihād* in the path of Allah, together with belief, is the best of all deeds. A man stood up and said: "Messenger of Allah, what do you say if I am killed in the way of Allah, does it expiate all my sins?" the Messenger of Allah ﷺ replied: "Yes, if you are killed in the way of Allah with patient endurance (*ṣābiran*), anticipating reward (*muḥtasiban*), and marching on not

[94] Narrated from al-ʿIrbāḍ ibn Sāriya by Abū Dāwūd, al-Bayhaqī in *al-Sunan al-Kubrā* (9:204 §18493) and Muḥammad ibn Naṣr al-Marwazī at the very end of his book *al-Sunna* (p. 111-112 §405 *isnād jayyid*), all with a fair chain according to al-Arnaʾūṭ and Maʿrūf's assessment of the narrators in their *Taḥrīr Taqrīb al-Tahdhīb*.

[95] In *al-Sunna* (p. 110 §401).

fleeing, except for any outstanding debt [of yours]. For Gibrīl ﷺ thus said to me."[96]

2. Whatever legal rulings he ﷺ has expounded and stipulated are the expositions and stipulations of Allah Himself, not his

When prices soared in Madīna it was said to the Prophet ﷺ: "Messenger of Allah, set the market prices for us." He replied: "Allah ﷻ will not ask me of any Sunna I innovated (*aḥdathtu*) among you without His commanding me to do so. But ask Allah for His favor."[97]

There are several other versions of the above narration, all indicating that the Prophet ﷺ does not proceed to ordain anything in daily practice except with Divine permission. Among them:

They said: "Messenger of Allah! set the market prices for us." He replied: "Allah is He Who sets the market prices (*al-Musaʿʿir*), the Straitener (*al-Qābiḍ*), the Expander (*al-Bāsiṭ*), and the Bestower of sustenance (*al-Rāziq*). Verily I hope to find my Lord without any of you complaining that I have wronged him either with regard to someone's death or with regard to property."[98]

The Prophet ﷺ also said, on the day of the campaign of Tabūk: "O people! Verily I do not command you anything except what Allah ﷻ has commanded you, and I do not prohibit you from anything except what Allah ﷻ has prohibited. Therefore be

[96] Narrated from Abū Qatāda by Muslim, Mālik, al-Tirmidhī (*ḥasan ṣaḥīḥ*), al-Nasāʾī, Aḥmad, and al-Dārimī; from Abū Hurayra by al-Nasāʾī and Aḥmad; and from Muḥammad ibn ʿAbd Allah ibn Jaḥsh by Aḥmad – all with a fair chains.

[97] Narrated from Talḥa ibn Nudayla by al-Bayhaqī in *al-Madkhal*. Ibn Ḥajar cited its different chains in *al-Iṣāba* (3:535).

[98] Narrated from Anas by al-Tirmidhī (*ḥasan ṣaḥīḥ*), Abū Dāwūd, Ibn Mājah, Aḥmad, al-Dārimī, and Abū Yaʿlā (5:245) all with sound chains as stated by Ibn Ḥajar in *Talkhīṣ al-Ḥabīr* (3:14), cf. Shaykh Ḥusayn Asad. Also narrated from Abū Saʿīd al-Khudrī by Aḥmad, and from Abū Hurayra by Aḥmad and Abū Dāwūd, both with fair chains as stated by Ibn Ḥajar. The latter mentioned two other chains for this ḥadīth, one from ʿAlī and one from Ibn ʿAbbās. This is an example of the narrations which Ibn al-Jawzī incorrectly included in his *Mawḍūʿāt*.

graceful in your requests from Him. By the One in Whose hand is Abū al-Qāsim's life, the sustenance of each one of you shall surely come to him just as his term of life shall surely come to pass. Therefore, if you find yourself in difficulty because of some need, ask for your sustenance through obedience to Allah ﷻ."[99]

3. It is impossible to understand the laws and ordinances of Islam from the Qur'ān alone, rather, it is necessary to have recourse to the Sunna

The Prophet ﷺ said: "Whoever speaks about the Qur'ān without knowledge, let him take from now his seat in the Fire."[100]

Another version states: "Whoever is asked about knowledge which he possesses but conceals it, shall be made to wear a bridle of fire on the Day of Resurrection."[101]

Another version states: "Whoever is asked about knowledge and conceals it shall come on the Day of Resurrection wearing a bridle of fire, and whoever says something about the Qur'ān without knowledge, shall come on the Day of Resurrection wearing a bridle of fire."[102]

[99] Narrated from al-Ḥasan ibn ʿAlī by al-Ṭabarānī in *al-Kabīr* (3:83) with a chain containing ʿAbd al-Raḥmān ibn ʿUthmān al-Ḥāṭibī whom Abū Ḥātim declared weak as stated by al-Haythamī (4:71-72), however, the contents of the ḥadīth itself are confirmed by other evidence and Abū Ḥātim's lone discreditation does not suffice, as he is known for his severity [al-Dhahabī in the *Siyar* (10:479) calls him "very prone to discreditation" (*jarrāḥ*)], and Allah knows best.

[100] Narrated from Ibn ʿAbbās by al-Tirmidhī (*ḥasan ṣaḥīḥ*), Aḥmad with two chains, al-Nasā'ī in *al-Sunan al-Kubrā* (5:30), Ibn Abī Shayba (6:136), al-Quḍāʿī in *Musnad al-Shihāb* (1:327), and al-Bayhaqī in *Shuʿab al-Īmān* (2:423).

[101] Narrated from Abū Hurayra by al-Tirmidhī (*ḥasan*) who said that Jābir and ʿAbd Allah ibn ʿAmr also narrate it, Abū Dāwūd, Ibn Mājah, and Aḥmad; and from Anas by Ibn Mājah.

[102] Narrated from Ibn ʿAbbās by Abū Yaʿlā (4:458) with a weak chain according to Shaykh Ḥusayn Asad, however, al-Haythamī (1:163) declared all its narrators trustworthy.

The Prophet ﷺ also said: "Allah never gave any learned person knowledge except He took from them a covenant they should not conceal it."[103]

Ibn ʿAbd al-Salām said: "The knowledge meant in the hadīth of the Prophet ﷺ 'Whoever is asked about knowledge which he possesses but conceals it shall be made to wear a bridle of fire on the Day of Resurrection' is whatever knowledge of sacred Law one is obliged to learn, not one of the crafts or trades one plies except what constitutes a communal obligation to learn, such as shooting and other martial skills. That is definitely knowledge, and Allah knows best."[104]

The Prophet ﷺ also said: "Beware of narrating something about me except what you know for sure, for whoever deliberately lies about me, let him take from now his seat in the Fire; and whoever says something about the Qur'ān on the basis of his own opinion, let him take from now his seat in the Fire."[105]

Another version has: "Whoever says something about the Qur'ān on the basis of his own opinion and happens to be correct, he is nevertheless wrong."[106] Meaning: in relation to the ruling on the conditions necessary for explaining the book of Allah.[107]

[103] Narrated from Abū Hurayra by al-ʿIrāqī wih his chain in *Faḍl al-ʿIlm* and in Ibn Ḥajar's *al-Qawl al-Musaddad* (p. 5). Cited by al-Suyūṭī in *al-Jāmiʿ al-Ṣaghīr* (§7767 *ṣaḥīḥ*).

[104] Ibn ʿAbd al-Salām, *Fatāwā Mawṣiliyya* (p. 49).

[105] Narrated from Ibn ʿAbbās by al-Tirmidhī (*ḥasan*), Aḥmad, al-Nasāʾī in *al-Sunan al-Kubrā* (5:31), al-Bayhaqī in *Shuʿab al-Īmān* (2:423). This ḥadith is mass-transmitted (*mutawātir*).

[106] Narrated with weak chains from Jundub ibn ʿAbd Allah by al-Tirmidhī (*gharīb*), Abū Dāwūd, al-Nasāʾī in *al-Sunan al-Kubrā* (5:31 §8026), Abū Yaʿlā (3:90) and in his *Mafārīd* (p. 42), al-Ṭabarānī in *al-Kabīr* (2:163), al-Bayhaqī in *Shuʿab al-Īmān* (2:423) and others. Al-Tirmidhī, Ibn Abī Ḥātim, al-Bayhaqī, Ibn ʿAdī, and others mentioned that the chain of this ḥadīth had been questioned by some of the Imāms of ḥadīth. However, its contents was heeded by the Companions and Successors as shown by the numerous narrations to that effect adduced by Ibn Kathīr at the beginning of his *Tafsīr* (1:6). Cf. al-Qurṭubī, *Tafsīr* (1:32).

[107] As stated in *ʿAwn al-Maʿbūd* in commentary of this ḥadīth.

The Prophet ﷺ also said: "What I most fear for my Community is three things: the scholar's lapse, the hypocrite who disputes about the Qur'ān, and [the riches of] the world that shall be opened up for you."[108]

Another version states: "In truth I fear two things for my *Umma*: the Qur'ān and milk (*al-laban*). As for [those who seek] milk [pastures], they cling to the countryside and run after pleasures, abandoning *ṣalāt*. As for the Qur'ān, the hypocrites learn it and then dispute with the Believers."[109]

Another version states: "What I most fear for my Community is the silver-tongued hypocrite."[110] Another version has: "the silver-tongued hypocrite that argues over the Qur'ān."[111]

4. Sunna-based practice is Qur'ān-based

The Prophet ﷺ said: "Faithful responsibility (*al-amāna*) alighted upon the roots of men's hearts. Then the Qur'ān alighted, whereupon they learned from the Qur'ān and they learned from the Sunna."[112]

[108] Narrated from Mu'ādh by al-Ṭabarānī in *al-Kabīr* (20:138) and Tammām al-Rāzī in *al-Fawā'id* (2:219). Something similar is narrated by al-Bayhaqī in *Shu'ab al-Īmān* (7:281) and *al-Madkhal* (p. 443) and Ibn al-A'rābī in *al-Zuhd* (p. 49) with a weak chain from Ibn 'Umar as stated by al-Haythamī (7:203).

[109] Narrated from 'Uqba ibn 'Āmir al-Juhanī by Aḥmad with two chains, Abū Ya'lā (3:285 §1746), al-Ṭabarānī in *al-Kabīr* (17:296), al-Bayhaqī in *Shu'ab al-Īmān* (3:104 §3009) cf. Ibn Kathīr, *Tafsīr* (3:129) and al-Haythamī (1:187 and 2:194).

[110] Narrated from 'Umar ibn al-Khaṭṭāb and 'Imrān ibn Ḥuṣayn by Aḥmad, Ibn Ḥibbān (1:282), al-Bazzār (1:434), al-Bayhaqī in *Shu'ab al-Īmān* (2:284), and al-Ṭabarānī in *al-Kabīr* (18:237) with a fair chain as stated by al-Maqdisī in *al-Mukhtāra* (1:344) and as indicated by al-Mundhirī in *al-Targhīb* (1997 ed. 1:75) and al-Haythamī (1:187). See also al-Dāraquṭnī, *'Ilal* (2:170 §196).

[111] Narrated without chain by Ibn 'Abd al-Barr in *Jāmi' Bayān al-'Ilm* (2:1200 §2360).

[112] Narrated as part of a longer ḥadīth from Ḥudhayfa by al-Bukhārī in two places, Muslim, al-Tirmidhī (*ḥasan ṣaḥīḥ*), Ibn Mājah, and Aḥmad.

5. The *Umma* in its entirety and without exception has been ordered to accept his ﷺ words, obey his commands and prohibitions, and follow his Sunna

The Prophet ﷺ said: "Whoever obeys me certainly obeys Allah. Whoever disobeys me certainly disobeys Allah. Whoever obeys my leader (*amīrī*), certainly obeys me. Whoever disobeys my leader, certainly disobeys me."[113]

Another version states: "Do you not know that whoever obeys me certainly obeys Allah, and part of obedience to Allah is obedience to me?" They said: "Yes! We bear witness to this." The Prophet ﷺ replied: "Then know that a part of obedience to me is that you obey your leaders (*umarā'*)." One version has: "Your imāms."[114]

6. Whoever obeys him ﷺ and holds fast to his Sunna obeys Allah ﷻ and follows guidance, and as such deserves Paradise and huge reward

The Prophet ﷺ said: "All of my Community shall enter Paradise except those who refuse." They said: "Messenger of Allah! Who could refuse?" He replied: "Whoever obeys me enters Paradise and whoever disobeys me has refused."[115]

He also said: "Verily this Qur'ān is difficult and felt as a burden to anyone who hates it, but it is made easy to anyone who follows it. Verily my sayings are difficult and felt as a burden to anyone who hates them, but they are made easy to anyone who follows them. Whoever hears my saying and preserves it, putting it into

[113] Narrated from Abū Hurayra by al-Bukhārī, Muslim, al-Nasā'ī, Aḥmad, and Ibn Mājah. The latter has the words "the imām" instead of "my *amīr*."

[114] Narrated from Ibn 'Umar by Aḥmad with a sound chain, Abū Ya'lā, and al-Ṭabarānī. Cf. Ibn Ḥajar in *Fatḥ al-Bārī* (1959 ed. 13:91): "This ḥadīth shows the obligatoriness of obeying those who govern, on condition that they do not command disobedience to Allah."

[115] Narrated from Abū Hurayra by al-Bukhārī and Aḥmad.

practice, shall come forth together with the Qur'ān on the Day of Resurrection. Whoever dismisses my sayings dismisses the Qur'ān, and whoever dismisses the Qur'ān has lost this world and the next."[116]

He also said: "Whoever eats wholesome food, puts a Sunna into practice, and spares people his wrongdoings, shall certainly enter Paradise." They said: "Messenger of Allah, today this is found in abundance among people." He replied: "It shall be found in the centuries after me."[117]

He also said: "Whoever gives life to one of my Sunnas which was eliminated after my time will receive the reward of all those who practice it without their reward being diminished. And whoever innovates an innovation of misguidance that pleases not Allah nor His Prophet[118] then upon his head rests the sin of whoever puts it into practice without their sins being diminished."[119] It was said that the meaning of "one of my Sunnas" here is one of the rulings of the Law which the Prophet ﷺ brought concerning the obligations of prayer, *zakāt*, etc.[120]

He also said: "Whoever gives life to my Sunna certainly loves me: and whoever loves me is with me in Paradise."[121]

[116] Narrated with a very weak chain from al-Ḥakam ibn ʿUmayr al-Thumālī by al-Khaṭīb in *al-Jāmiʿ li-Akhlāq al-Rāwī* (1983 ed. 2:189), al-Qurṭubī in his *Tafsīr* (18:17), Abū Nuʿaym, Abū al-Shaykh, and al-Daylamī cf. al-Jawzaqānī, *al-Abāṭīl* (1:13 §12).

[117] Narrated with weak chains from Abū Saʿīd al-Khudrī by al-Tirmidhī (*gharīb*), al-Ṭabarānī in *al-Awsaṭ*, al-Ḥākim (1990 ed. 4:117) who declared it *ṣaḥīḥ*, al-Bayhaqī in *Shuʿab al-Īmān*, (5:54), al-Lālikāʾī in *Sharḥ Uṣūl Iʿtiqād Ahl al-Sunna* (1:54), and others. All their chains contain Abū Bishr, who is unknown.

[118] *Man ibtadaʿa bidʿata ḍalālatin lā turḍillāha wa-rasūlah.*

[119] A sound ḥadīth narrated from ʿAmr ibn ʿAwf ibn Zayd al-Muzanī by al-Tirmidhī (*ḥasan*), Ibn Mājah, ʿAbd ibn Ḥumayd in his *Musnad* (p. 120), al-Baghawī in *Sharḥ al-Sunna* (1:233), al-Bayhaqī in *al-Iʿtiqād* (p. 231), and Ibn ʿAbd al-Barr in *al-Tamhīd* (24:328). The latter also narrates it from Jarīr ibn ʿAbd Allah.

[120] Al-Sindī in his commentary on Ibn Mājah's *Sunan*, *Muqaddima*.

[121] Narrated from Anas by al-Tirmidhī (*ḥasan gharīb*) as part of a longer ḥadīth, al-

He also said: "The keeper of my Sunna when my Community lapses into corruption will receive the reward of a hundred martyrs."[122]

He also said: "Islam began as a stranger and shall again be considered a stranger. Therefore, blessings and glad tidings to the strangers! Those who set aright what people have corrupted of my Sunna after me."[123]

7. Whoever disobeys him ﷺ and rejects his sayings, preferring to follow his own opinion and whims, has disobeyed Allah, followed misguidance, and perished, such being deserving of Hellfire and the curse of Allah – may Allah ﷻ protect us

Angels came to the Prophet ﷺ while he was sleeping.

One of them said: "He is sleeping."

Ṭabarānī in *al-Awsaṭ*, Muḥammad ibn Naṣr al-Marwazī in *Ta'ẓim Qadr al-Ṣalāt* (2:661), and al-Lālikā'ī in *Sharḥ Uṣūl al-I'tiqād* (1:53). Al-Munāwī declared al-Tirmidhī's chain very weak in *Fayḍ al-Qadīr* but said that the ḥadīth itself was fair (*ḥasan*) due to its numerous corroborating narrations.

[122] Narrated by al-Mundhirī in *al-Targhīb* (1:87=1997 ed. 1:41) and al-Ḥākim. Ibn 'Adī in *al-Kāmil* (2:327) indicated that the narration was fair (*ḥasan*). Al-Mundhirī said: "Al-Bayhaqī narrated it through al-Ḥasan ibn Qutayba, and al-Ṭabarānī from Ibn Hurayra with an unexceptionable chain, except that he said 'the reward of one martyr.'"

[123] Narrated from 'Amr ibn 'Awf ibn Zayd by al-Tirmidhī (*ḥasan ṣaḥīḥ*), al-Quḍā'ī in *Musnad al-Shihāb* (2:138), al-Ṭabarānī in *al-Kabīr* (17:16), Abū Nu'aym in *Ḥilyat al-Awliyā'* (1985 ed. 2:10), and al-Khaṭīb in *al-Jāmi' li-Akhlāq al-Rāwī* (1983 ed. 1:112). The ḥadīth is also narrated, without mention of the Sunna: from Abū Hurayra and Ibn 'Umar by Muslim; from Abū Hurayra, Anas, and Ibn Mas'ūd by Ibn Mājah; from Ibn Mas'ūd by al-Tirmidhī (*ḥasan ṣaḥīḥ gharīb*) who said that al-Bukhārī declared it *ḥasan*, and al-Dārimī; and from Ibn Mas'ūd and 'Abd al-Raḥmān ibn Sanna by Aḥmad with a chain he termed *munkar* as in Ibn Qudāma's *al-Muntakhab min al-'Ilal lil-Khallāl* (p. 57). Some versions have the continuation: "They asked: 'Who are the strangers?' The Prophet ﷺ replied: 'Those far away from their tribes (or: their families and countrymen).' One version in Muslim and Aḥmad states: "Islam shall coil back between the Two Mosques the way a snake coils back into its hole."

Another said: "Truly the eye sleeps while the heart is wide awake."

Then they said: "Truly there is a similitude for your friend here. Strike a similitude for him."

One of them said: "He is sleeping."

Another said: "Truly the eye sleeps while the heart is wide awake."

Then they said: "His similitude is that of a man who built a house then gave a banquet, sending a herald [to invite the people]. Whoever responded to the herald entered the house and partook of the banquet, and whoever did not respond to the herald neither entered the house nor ate of the banquet."

Then the angels said: "Interpret this parable for him so that he may understand it well."

Another said: "Truly the eye sleeps while the heart is wide awake."

Then they said: "The house stands for Paradise and the herald is Muḥammad ﷺ. Whoever obeys Muḥammad, obeys Allah; whoever disobeys Muḥammad, disobeys Allah. Muḥammad is the separator between the people (*farqun bayn al-nās*)."[124]

The Prophet ﷺ said: "Whoever marches against the rule(r) of Allah on earth (*sulṭān Allah fil-arḍ*) in order to abase it/him – then Allah shall certainly abase his neck on the Day of Resurrection, in addition to the punishment that lies in wait for him." Musaddad added: "The rule(r) of Allah on earth is the Qur'ān and Sunna."[125] Another version states: "Whoever denigrates the

[124] Narrated from Jābir ibn ʿAbd Allah by al-Bukhārī.

[125] Narrated from Ibn ʿAbbās by Ibn Abī ʿĀṣim in *al-Sunna* (p. 612-613 §1462= 2:627) and al-Ṭabarānī in *al-Kabīr* (11:214), both with weak chains as indicated by al-Haythamī (1:170) and Ibn ʿAdī (2:352). Also narrated from Ḥudhayfa by al-Azdī in *al-Jāmiʿ* (11:344) with the wording: "No people march against Allah's rule

rule(r) of Allah on earth (*sulṭān Allah fil-arḍ*), then may Allah denigrate him!"[126]

The Prophet ﷺ was reported to say: "Whoever hears of a ḥadīth of mine then belies it, has belied Allah, His Prophet, and the one who brought him that ḥadīth."[127]

The Prophet ﷺ also said: "I was ordered to fight people until they say 'There is no God but Allah' believing in me and in what I brought. Once they do, they have made their lives and properties untouchable by me except for the right due upon them, and their reckoning is with Allah."[128]

in order to abase it except Allah abases their necks before they die," without Musaddad's gloss.

[126] A fair ḥadīth due to its witness-narrations (*ḥasan li-ghayrih*), narrated from Abū Bakrah by al-Tirmidhī (*ḥasan gharīb*) with the wording: Ziyād ibn Kusayb al-'Adawī narrated: "I was with Abū Bakrah under Ibn 'Amir's pulpit while the latter was speaking, and he was wearing very fine clothes. Whereupon Abū Bilāl [Murādis ibn Udayya, one of the Khawārij] said: 'Look at our emir, he is wearing the garb of corrupt men!' Hearing this Abū Bakrah said: 'Be quiet! I heard the Messenger of Allah ﷺ say: 'Whoever denigrates Allah's ruler on earth, then Allah shall certainly denigrate him.'" Also narrated by Aḥmad, with some additions, through two chains and, as part of a longer ḥadīth, from Ibn 'Abbās by al-Khaṭīb in his *Tārīkh* (6:67) – he alluded to its weakness – and al-Ṭabarānī with a chain of sound narrators except for one unknown as stated by al-Haythamī (5:211-212). The prohibition against taking up arms against the Muslim ruler is mass-narrated.

[127] A "disclaimed" (*munkar*) ḥadīth according to al-Dhahabī in *Mīzān al-I'tidāl* (3:444 §7094) narrated from Jābir by al-Ṭabarānī in *al-Awsaṭ*, al-Khaṭīb in *al-Faqīh wal-Mutafaqqih* (1:90), Ibn 'Asākir (27:409-410), and Ibn 'Abd al-Barr in *Jāmi' Bayān al-'Ilm* (2:1183-1184 §2340), all with chains containing Maḥfūẓ ibn Miswar al-Fihrī who is unknown – as stated by al-Dhahabī and al-Haythamī – and Baqiyya ibn al-Walīd who used to conceal the weak links of his narrative chains so as to pass them off as strong ones.

[128] A mass-narrated (*mutawātir*) ḥadīth of the Prophet ﷺ narrated by al-Bukhārī, Muslim, and others from nineteen Companions as stated by al-Kattānī in *Naẓm al-Mutanāthir*.

8. Faith and belief remains incomplete until one follows all that he ﷺ brought

The Prophet ﷺ said: "None of you believes until his likes and dislikes are in conformity with what I have brought" (*ḥattā yakūna hawāhu taba'an limā ji'tu bih*).[129]

Al-Nawawī said this ḥadīth corresponds to the verse {*And it becomes not a believing man or a believing woman, when Allah and His Messenger have decided an affair (for them), that they should (after that) claim any say in their affair; and whosoever is rebellious to Allah and His Messenger, he verily goes astray in error manifest*} (33:36), adding: "One is obligated to evaluate his every deed in the light of the Qur'ān and the Sunna, contravening his likes and dislikes and following what the Prophet ﷺ brought."[130] Ibn Kathīr

[129] *Ṣaḥīḥ* through Abū Hurayra. Narrated from 'Abd Allah ibn 'Amr by al-Baghawī in *Sharḥ al-Sunna* (1:212-213 §104), Ibn Abī 'Āṣim in *al-Sunna* (p. 12 §15), al-Nasawī in *al-Arba'īn* (p. 52), al-Bayhaqī in *al-Madkhal* (p. 288 §209), al-Khaṭīb in *Tārīkh Baghdād* (4:369), the Shāfi'ī jurist Abū al-Fatḥ Nāṣir ibn Ibrāhīm al-Maqdisī in his book *al-Ḥujja 'alā Tārik al-Maḥajja*, and al-Harawī in *Dhamm al-Kalām* (2:254-256 §320), all with a weak or very weak chain because of Nu'aym ibn Ḥammād al-Marwazī who singled himself out with this ḥadīth: "Nu'aym is disclaimed in his narrations (*munkar al-ḥadīth*) despite his standing as an Imām," Ibn Ḥajar, *al-Amālī al-Ḥalabiyya* (p. 40) cf. Ibn Rajab in *Jāmi' al-'Ulūm wal-Ḥikam* (2:269-271=Risāla ed. p. 393-395), Khaldūn al-Aḥdab in *Zawā'id Tārīkh Baghdād* (4:168-172 §625), and 'Abd al-Qādir al-Arna'ūṭ in his edition of al-Nawawī's *Arba'īn* (p. 98 §41). However, Abū Nu'aym included it among the *ṣaḥīḥ* narrations in *al-Arba'īn 'alā Madhhab al-Mutaḥaqqiqīn min al-Ṣūfiyya* and narrated it through al-Ṭabarānī; al-Nawawī graded it *ḥasan ṣaḥīḥ*; and Ibn Ḥajar in *Fatḥ al-Bārī* (1959 ed. 13:289) said al-Ḥasan ibn Sufyān and others narrated it from Abū Hurayra "with a chain of trustworthy narrators." Ibn Rajab proceeds (2:271-275) to cite proofs from Qur'ān, ḥadīth, and the sayings of the scholars supporting the meaning of this ḥadīth. Among its proofs is the ḥadīth: "Say: O Allah! Inspire me with right guidance and protect me from the evil of my *nafs*." (*Allahumma alhimnī rushdī wa-qinī sharra nafsī.*). Narrated from 'Imrān ibn Ḥuṣayn by al-Tirmidhī (*ḥasan gharīb*), al-Bazzār (9:53), al-Bukhārī in *Khalq Af'āl al-'Ibād*, and others.

[130] Al-Nawawī, *Sharḥ Matn al-Arba'īn* (p. 134).

cited this ḥadīth[131] in elucidation of the same verse in addition to two more: {*But nay, by your Lord! they will not believe (in truth) until they make you judge of what is in dispute between them and find within themselves (fī anfusihim) no dislike of that which you decide, and submit with full submission*} (4:65) and {*And let those who conspire to evade orders beware lest grief or painful punishment befall them*} (24:63).

Anas ibn Mālik narrates: "The Prophet ﷺ said to me: 'Dearest son! If you are able to rise in the morning and retire at night without the least spite in your heart for anyone, then do so.' Then he said: 'Dearest son! That is part of my Sunna, and whoever gives life to my Sunna truly loves me: and whoever truly loves me shall be together with me in Paradise.'"[132]

The Prophet ﷺ also said: "Every servant of Allah goes through a phase of eagerness (*shirra*), and every eagerness wanes (*fatra*) – either to the Sunna, or to innovation. If one's eagerness wanes toward the Sunna he has succeeded. Otherwise, he has perished."[133]

[131] In his *Tafsīr* (3:491).

[132] Narrated by al-Tirmidhī (*ḥasan gharīb*) with a weak chain because of ʿAlī ibn Zayd, although al-Tirmidhī considers him "truthful" (*ṣadūq*) and – in full – by al-Ṭabarānī in *al-Ṣaghīr* (2:102) and Abū Yaʿlā (6:306-309) with weak chains because of Muḥammad ibn al-Ḥasan ibn Abī Yazīd as stated by al-Haythamī (1:272).

[133] Narrated from ʿAbd Allah ibn ʿAmr by Aḥmad with five chains, al-Ṭaḥāwī in *Sharḥ Mushkil al-Āthār* (2:88), Ibn Abī ʿĀṣim in *al-Sunna* (p. 27-28 §51), al-Bayhaqī in *Shuʿab al-Īmān* (3:399-400), Ibn Khuzayma (3:293-294 §2105), and his student Ibn Ḥibbān (1:187-188 §11), all with sound chains as stated by Shaykh Shuʿayb al-Arnaʾūṭ in the latter and al-Haythamī (3:193). Also narrated from Ibn ʿAbbās by al-Bazzār with a chain of sound narrators, and from Abū Hurayra by al-Ṭabarānī with a weak chain, both as indicated by al-Haythamī also (2:259). The collation of the various accounts in Aḥmad reveals the events in which the ḥadīth was uttered: ʿAbd Allah ibn ʿAmr married a Quraysh wo-man but did not cohabit with her, being engrossed in worship and fasting. News of this reached the Prophet ﷺ who said to him: "Fast three days of the months" but ʿAbd Allah kept saying that he could bear with more until the Prophet ﷺ told him to fast every other day. Then he told him to recite the Qurʾān (in prayer once a month), finally allowing him to recite it in whole every three days. This account is also narrated

In a closely-related context and meaning the Prophet ﷺ also said, when a certain woman who fasted days and prayed nights was mentioned to him: "I myself sleep and pray; I fast and break my fast. Whoever follows my example is part of me, and whoever desires other than my Sunna has nothing to do with me. Every deed stems from an eagerness and then it abates. If one's abatement is to innovation then he has gone astray. If one's abatement is to the Sunna then he has followed guidance."[134] A similar ḥadīth was uttered in response to the three Companions who had respectively vowed lifelong night vigil, lifelong chastity, and lifelong fasting.[135]

The Prophet ﷺ also said: "Truly Religion is nothing but[136] absolute good faith (*innamā al-dīn al-naṣīḥa*)! Truly Religion is nothing but absolute good faith! Truly Religion is nothing but absolute good faith!" They asked: "To whom, Messenger of Allah?" He replied: "To Allah; to His Book; and to His Messenger, the leaders of the Muslims and their multitude."[137]

by al-Bukhārī and Muslim. Cf. Ibn Ḥajar, *Fatḥ al-Bārī* (1959 ed. 4:218). ʿAbd Allah ibn ʿAmr's propensity for worship is one of the reasons why he reported less than Abū Hurayra, although the latter acknowledged that no one heard more than he from the Prophet ﷺ, except ʿAbd Allah ibn ʿAmr, because the latter could write, unlike Abū Hurayra; and Allah knows best.

[134] Narrated from an unnamed Companion by Aḥmad with a chain of sound narrators as stated by al-Haythamī (3:193).

[135] Narrated from Anas by al-Bukhārī, Muslim, al-Nasāʾī, Aḥmad with three chains; from ʿĀʾisha by Abū Dāwūd; and from Saʿd ibn Abī Waqqāṣ by al-Dārimī.

[136] In al-Nasāʾī's and Aḥmad's version from Tamīm al-Dārī.

[137] Narrated from Abū Hurayra by al-Tirmidhī (*ḥasan ṣaḥīḥ*) and Aḥmad, and from Tamīm al-Dārī by Abū Dāwūd. Also narrated – without the repetition – from Tamīm by Muslim and al-Nasāʾī, from Abū Hurayra by al-Nasāʾī and Aḥmad, from Ibn ʿUmar by al-Bazzār, and from Thawbān by al-Bukhārī in *al-Tārīkh al-Kabīr*. This ḥadīth is §7 of al-Nawawī's "*Forty*."

9. Nothing but truth comes out of his ﷺ blessed mouth

ʿAbd Allah ibn ʿAmr said: "I used to write down everything that I heard from the Messenger of Allah ﷺ, intending to memorize it. The Quraysh forbade me, saying: 'You write everything you hear from the Messenger of Allah ﷺ, but the Messenger of Allah is a human being that speaks sometimes in anger and sometimes in contentment!' Thereupon I stopped writing. I mentioned this to the Messenger of Allah ﷺ and he said: 'Write! By Him in Whose Hand is my soul! Nothing but truth ever comes out of this' and he indicated his mouth."[138]

10. The best guidance of all is his ﷺ guidance

The Prophet ﷺ delivered a sermon in which he said: "To proceed: The best of all discourse is the Book of Allah ﷻ and the best of all guidance is the guidance of Muḥammad. The worst of all matters are newfangled matters. Every newfangled matter is an innovation, and every innovation is misguidance."[139]

ʿUmar ؓ came to the Prophet ﷺ and said: "We hear from the Jews narrations that impress us, do you think we should write down some of them?" The Prophet ﷺ replied: "Are you all going to fall into the same chaos (*amutahawwikūn*) into which fell the Jews and Christians? I brought it [the Religion] to you pristine and pure. If Mūsā were alive, he would have no alternative but to follow me!"[140]

Another version states that ʿUmar ؓ passed by a man who was reciting a book, so he listened for a while and was pleased with what he heard. He asked the man: "Can you copy what is in that book?" He replied yes, whereupon ʿUmar bought a piece of

[138] Narrated by Abū Dāwūd, Aḥmad, and al-Dārimī with sound chains.
[139] Narrated from Jābir by Muslim.
[140] Narrated from Jābir by al-Bayhaqī in *Shuʿab al-Īmān* (1:200) and *mursal* from al-Ḥasan by al-Khaṭīb in *al-Jāmiʿ li-Akhlāq al-Rāwī* (1991 ed. 2:228 §1531=1983 ed. 2:161) with weak chains.

hide for himself and brought it to the man who copied on its front and back [in Arabic].¹⁴¹ Then ʿUmar brought it to the Prophet ﷺ and began to read it back to him. Immediately, the Prophet's ﷺ countenance changed. Whereupon one of the men of the Anṣār [ʿAbd Allah ibn Zayd]¹⁴² slapped down the book with his hand and said: "May your mother lose you, Ibn al-Khaṭṭāb! Can you not see the face of the Messenger of Allah since you began to read from that book?" The Prophet ﷺ then said: "I was not sent except as an opener and a sealer.¹⁴³ I was given the pithiest expressions with the vastest meanings and the openings of all discourse with true concision. Therefore let not those who are in chaos induce you into chaos."¹⁴⁴

Another version states that ʿUmar ؓ brought the Prophet ﷺ a book he had taken from one of the People of the Book. He read it to the Prophet ﷺ who became angry and said: "Are you all going to fall into chaos, Son of Khaṭṭāb? By Him in Whose Hand is my soul! Even if Mūsā ؏ were alive, he would have no alternative but to follow me."¹⁴⁵

---

¹⁴¹ As stated by Ibn Ḥajar in *Fatḥ al-Bārī* (1959 ed. 13:525).
¹⁴² *Ibid.*
¹⁴³ Cf. the ḥadīth of the Prophetic speeches during the Ascension (*Miʿrāj*): "Praise to Allah Who has sent me as a mercy to the worlds sent to all without exception..." until he said: "...Who has exalted my name, and made me the Opener and the Sealer!" Narrated from Abū Hurayra by al-Ṭabarī in his *Tafsīr* (15:8), Ibn Abī Ḥātim, al-Bazzār, Abū Yaʿlā, al-Bayhaqī in *Dalāʾil al-Nubuwwa*, Ibn Kathīr in his *Tafsīr* (3:19), and al-Suyūṭī in *al-Khaṣāʾiṣ al-Kubrā* with a chain of trustworthy narrators according to al-Haythamī (1:69-72).
¹⁴⁴ Narrated *mursal* from Abū Qilāba by ʿAbd al-Razzāq (6:112-113) but the bracketed segment is narrated from Abū Hurayra by al-Bukhārī, Muslim, al-Tirmidhī, and Aḥmad.
¹⁴⁵ Narrated from Jābir by Aḥmad, and Ibn Abī ʿĀṣim in *al-Sunna* (p. 27 §50) with weak chains because of Mujālid ibn Saʿīd as indicated by al-Haythamī (1:174) – notwithstanding Ḥamza al-Zayn's lax grading of a "fair chain" in the *Musnad* (12:85 §15094). Also narrated from Jābir by Ibn ʿAbd al-Barr in *Jāmiʿ Bayān al-ʿIlm* (2:805-806 §1497) with the addition: "Do not ask them about anything so that they will not tell you of something true which you might declare false, or

Another version states that ʿUmar came to the Prophet and said: "Messenger of Allah, I passed by a brother of mine from Banū Qurayẓa who wrote me some epitomes from the Torah, shall I not show them to you?" Hearing this the Prophet's face changed. ʿAbd Allah ibn Thābit said to ʿUmar: "Do you not see what is on the face of the Messenger of Allah?" ʿUmar said: "We are well-pleased with Allah for our Lord and Islam for our Religion and Muḥammad for our Messenger!" The Prophet's anger abated then he said: "By the One in Whose Hand is my soul! If Mūsā came to you one morning and you were to follow him and leave me, you would be going astray. You are my lot among the nations and I your lot among the Prophets."[146]

Another version states that ʿUmar came to the Prophet with a copy of the Torah in his hand and said: "Messenger of Allah! This is a copy of the Torah." The Prophet remained silent. As [ʿUmar] began to read the Prophet's face changed. Whereupon Abū Bakr said to ʿUmar: "May your mother and grandmother lose you! Can you not read the face of the Messenger of Allah?" ʿUmar looked up to the Prophet's face and said: "I seek refuge in Allah from the anger of Allah and the anger of His Prophet! We are well-pleased with Allah as our Lord and with Islam as our Religion and with Muḥammad as our Prophet!" Then the Prophet said: "By the One in Whose Hand is Muḥammad's soul! If Mūsā were to appear before you and you were to follow him and leave me, you would be going astray and leaving the straight path. And if he were alive and heard of my Prophethood, he would follow me."[147]

something false which you might declare true." Al-Dhahabī in the *Siyar* (al-Arna'ūṭ ed. 13:325) described the ḥadīth as *gharīb* while Albānī in his *Irwā' al-Ghalīl* (§1589) declares the narration fair on the basis of its witness-chains.
[146] Narrated from ʿAbd Allah ibn Thābit by Aḥmad, al-Ṭabarānī, ʿAbd al-Razzāq (6:113), and al-Bayhaqī in *Shuʿab al-Īmān* (3/4:307), all with weak chains because of Jābir ibn Yazīd ibn al-Ḥārith al-Juʿfī as indicated by al-Haythamī (1:173).
[147] Narrated from Jābir by al-Dārimī with a weak chain because of Mujālid.

Subsequently, in his caliphate, ʿUmar forbade the copying or keeping of Biblical material, as shown by his hitting with a stick a man who had copied down the book of the Prophet Daniel.[148]

The ḥadīth "I have left among you two matters..."

The Prophet ﷺ said: "I have left among you two matters by holding fast to which, you shall never be misguided: the Book of Allah and the Sunna of His Prophet."[149] Another version states instead: "The Book of Allah and my Sunna. And these two shall never part ways until they show up at the Pond."[150]

Zayd ibn Arqam narrated: "The Prophet ﷺ stood among us at a brook named Khumm between Makka and Madīna [three miles from al-Juḥfa]. He praised Allah ﷻ and glorified Him then said: 'To proceed: People! Truly I am now only waiting for a messenger [of death] sent by my Lord so that I may respond. Therefore I am leaving among you the two weighty matters: the Book of Allah – in it is the Guidance and the Light, therefore hold fast to the Book of Allah, and conform to it!' – and he encouraged people to do so, and urged them. Then he said: 'And the People of my House (*ahlu baytī*). I remind you by Allah ﷻ of the People of my House! I remind you by Allah ﷻ of the People of my House! I

[148] Cited by Ibn Ḥajar in *Fatḥ al-Bārī* (1959 ed. 13:525)

[149] Narrated from Ibn ʿAbbās by al-Bayhaqī in *al-Sunan al-Kubrā* (10:114 §20108) and – as part of a longer ḥadīth – by al-Ḥākim (1:93=1990 ed. 1:171) who declared it *ṣaḥīḥ* and – without chain – by Mālik and Ibn ʿAbd al-Barr in *al-Tamhīd* (24:331) who declared it *ṣaḥīḥ* as did Ibn Ḥazm in *al-Iḥkām*, al Suyūtī in *al-Jāmiʿ al-Ṣaghīr*, Aḥmad al-Ghumārī in his *Mudāwī*, and his brother ʿAbd Allah in *al-Kanz al-Thamīn* among others.

[150] Narrated from Abū Hurayra by al-Ḥākim (1:93=1990 ed. 1:172), al-Bayhaqī in *al-Sunan al-Kubrā* (10:114 §20109), al-Dāraquṭnī in his *Sunan* (4:245 §149), al-Lālikā'ī in *Sharḥ Uṣūl Iʿtiqād Ahl al-Sunna* (1:80), al-Khaṭīb, *al-Jāmiʿ li-Akhlāq al-Rāwī* (1983 ed. 1:111=1991 ed. 2:165-166 §89), Ibn ʿAbd al-Barr in *al-Tamhīd* (24:331), and Ibn Ḥazm who declared it *ṣaḥīḥ* in *al-Iḥkām* (6:243) while al-Suyūṭī declared it *ḥasan* in *al-Jāmiʿ al-Saghīr* (§3923).

remind you by Allah ﷻ of the People of my House!'" One version includes the wording, "I am only a human being."[151]

Another version adds: "Then he said: 'Truly Allah ﷻ is my Patron (*mawlāy*) and I am the patron of every believer.' Then he took ʿAlī by the hand and said: 'Anyone whose patron I am, this is his patron! O Allah, be the patron of whoever takes him as a patron, and be the enemy of whoever takes him as an enemy.'"[152]

Another version states that Jābir ibn ʿAbd Allah said: "I saw the Messenger of Allah ﷺ in his Pilgrimage on the Day of ʿArafa mounted on his camel al-Qaṣwā', addressing the people, and I heard him say: 'O people! I have left among you that which if you hold to it you shall never go astray: the Book of Allah and my mantle (*ʿitra*) – the People of my House.'"[153]

[151] Narrated from Zayd ibn Arqam by Muslim, Aḥmad with the addition of the words "I am only a human being," al-Dārimī, al-Ṭaḥāwī in *Mushkil al-Āthār* (9:89 §3464), Ibn Abī ʿĀṣim in *al-Sunna* (§1550), al-Ṭabarānī (§5028), and others.

[152] A sound ḥadīth narrated from Zayd ibn Arqam or Abū Sarīḥa from al-Tirmidhī (*ḥasan gharīb*) with a sound chain, from Saʿd ibn Abī Waqqāṣ by Ibn Mājah, from Ibn ʿAbbās by al-Ḥākim (3:134, *ṣaḥīḥ*), and from ʿAlī, al-Barā', Zayd ibn Arqam as already cited, and Burayda al-Aslamī by Aḥmad both in his *Musnad* and in *Faḍā'il al-Ṣaḥāba* (§947) through various chains both fair and sound as well as al-Ṭabarānī in *al-Kabīr*, Ibn Abī ʿĀṣim (§1354), Ibn Abī Shayba (12:57), Ibn Ḥibbān with two chains, one sound by Muslim's criterion, one fair (15:374-376 §6930-6931), al-Ḥākim (2:130 *ṣaḥīḥ* as per al-Bukhārī and Muslim's criteria; 3:109-110, 3:371), al-Bazzār (§2535) and Abū Yaʿlā, and – from ʿAlī with two fair chains and one weak chain – al-Ṭaḥāwī in *Sharḥ Mushkil al-Āthār* (2:307f.=5:13-15 §1760-1762). Al-Ṭaḥāwī also narrated it with a sound chain from Jābir ibn ʿAbd Allah from ʿAlī (5:16 §1763) and three weak chains from Saʿd ibn Abī Waqqāṣ (5:20-22 §1766-1768), cf. al-Nasā'ī in *Khaṣā'iṣ ʿAlī* (94-96). Al-Nawawī in his *Fatāwā* (p. 262) and al-Dhahabī in the *Siyar* (1/2:621) declared the ḥadīth sound while al-Suyūṭī declared it *mutawātir* and al-Kattānī confirmed him in *Naẓm al-Mutanāthir* (p. 194) where he names twenty-five narrators of this ḥadīth among the Companions. The ḥadīth master Ibn ʿUqda gathered all its chains in a large monograph. Al-Zaylaʿī's questioning of its authenticity in *Naṣb al-Rāya* (1:189) is meaningless, and Allah knows best.

[153] Narrated by al-Tirmidhī (*ḥasan gharīb*) with a weak chain because of Zayd ibn al-Ḥasan al-Qurashī.

Other versions state: "I am leaving among you that which if you hold to it, you shall never go astray, one of them greater than the other: the Book of Allah – a rope extended down from heaven to earth – and my mantle (*ʿitra*), the People of my House. These two shall never part ways until they come to me at the Pond. Look well to how you act with them after me."[154]

It is established that when the verse of mutual invocation of curses (*mubāhala*) was revealed (3:61), the Prophet ﷺ summoned ʿAlī, Fāṭima, al-Ḥasan, and al-Ḥusayn, and said: "O Allah, my Lord! These are my Family" (*Allahumma hā'ulā'i ahlī*).[155] He repeated this act when the verse of the cleansing of the People of the House was revealed (33:33).[156]

Allah ﷻ said in Sūrat al-Aḥzāb (33:28-34):

28. {*O Prophet! Say unto* **thy wives**: *If you* [F] *desire the world's life and its adornment, come! I will content you* [F] *and will release you* [F] *with a fair release*;}

29. {*But if you* [F] *desire Allah and His Messenger and the abode of the Hereafter, then lo! Allah has prepared for the good among you* [F] *an immense reward.*}

[154] Narrated from Zayd ibn Arqam by al-Tirmidhī (*ḥasan gharīb*) and al-Ḥākim (3:148), the latter with a sound chain, but without the last sentence and the words "my mantle"; from Abū Saʿīd al-Khudrī by al-Tirmidhī (*ḥasan gharīb*) and Aḥmad with weak chains because of ʿAtiyya ibn Saʿd al-ʿAwfī; and from Zayd ibn Thābit by Aḥmad and al-Ṭabarānī in *al-Kabīr* (5:153) with chains containing al-Qāsim ibn Ḥassān who is passable (*maqbūl*) and not trustworthy, contrary to al-Haythamī's claim in *Majmaʿ al-Zawā'id* (1:170). The latter version states: "I am leaving among you two successors (*khalīfatayn*)..." Also narrated from Zayd ibn Arqam by al-Nasā'ī in *al-Sunan al-Kubrā* (5:45, 5:130) with the wording: "I am leaving among you the two weighty matters..."

[155] Narrated from Saʿd ibn Abī Waqqāṣ by Muslim and al-Tirmidhī (*ḥasan ṣaḥīḥ gharīb*).

[156] Narrated from Umm Salama by Aḥmad with six chains, al-Tirmidhī with several chains (*ḥasan ṣaḥīḥ*), al-Ḥākim, al-Ṭabarānī, and others.

30. {*O you* **wives of the Prophet!** *Whosoever of you* [F] *commits manifest lewdness, the punishment for her will be doubled, and that is easy for Allah,*}

31. {*And whosoever of you* [F] *is submissive unto Allah and His Messenger and does right, We shall give her reward twice over, and We have prepared for her a rich provision.*}

32. {*O you* **wives of the prophet!** *You are not* [F] *like any other women. If you* [F] *keep your duty (to Allah), then be not* [F] *soft of speech, lest he in whose heart is a disease aspire (to you), but utter customary speech.*}

33. {*And stay in your* [F] *houses. Bedeck not yourselves* [F] *with the bedecking of the Time of ignorance. Be regular* [F] *in prayer, and pay* [F] *the poor due, and obey* [F] *Allah and His Messenger. The wish of Allah is but to remove uncleanness far from you* [M/F], *O* **Folk of the Household**, *and cleanse you* [M/F] *with a thorough cleansing.*}

34. {*And bear in mind that which is recited in your* [F] *houses of the revelations of Allah and wisdom. Lo! Allah is Subtle, Aware.*}

The Ulema of Qur'ānic commentary agree one and all that the meaning of *ahl al-bayt* in these verses, similar to its recurrence in the address of the angels to the family of Ibrāhīm in Sūrat Hūd (11:73), includes both the wives of the Prophet ﷺ and his grandchildren together with ʿAlī ؓ:

- Al-Rāzī said: "Allah ﷻ quit using the feminine pronoun in his address and turned to the masculine by saying {*liyudhhiba ʿankum al-rijsa*} = '*to remove uncleanness far from you* [masculine plural],' so as to include both the women of his ﷺ house and the men [beginning with the Prophet ﷺ]. Explanations have differed concerning the '*Ahl al-Bayt*' but the most appropriate and correct is to say they are his children and wives; al-Ḥasan and al-Ḥusayn being among them and ʿAlī being among them... due to his cohabitation with the daughter of the Prophet ﷺ and his close companionship with the Prophet ﷺ."[157]

- Al-Baghawī said: "In this verse [Hūd 73] there is a proof that wives are part of Ahl al-Bayt. ... He means by *Ahl al-Bayt* [in 33:33] the wives of the Prophet ﷺ because they are in his house. This is the narration of Saʿīd ibn Jubayr from Ibn ʿAbbās."[158]

- Al-Bayḍāwī said: "The *Shīʿa's* claim that verse 33:33 is specific to Fāṭima, ʿAlī, and their two sons – Allah be well-pleased with them – [...] and their adducing it as proof of their immunity from sin (*ʿiṣma*) and of the probative character of their Consensus, is weak, because restricting the meaning to them is not consistent with what precedes the verse and what follows it. The thread of speech means that they are part of the *Ahl al-Bayt*, not that others are not part of it also."[159]

- Al-Khāzin said: "They [*Ahl al-Bayt*] are the wives of the Prophet ﷺ because they are in his house." Then he mentions the other two explanations, namely, that they are the *ʿItra* or that they are the families of ʿAlī, ʿAqīl, Jaʿfar, and al-ʿAbbās.[160]

- Al-Nasafī said: "There is in it [verse 33:33] a proof that his wives are part of the Folk of his Household (*min ahli baytihi*). He said '*from you* [M] (*ʿankum*)' because what is meant are both the men and women of his family (*āl*) as indicated by {(*wa-yuṭahhirakum taṭhīran*) '*and cleanse you* [M/F] *with a thorough cleansing*' *from the filth of sins*}."[161]

[157] *Al-Tafsīr al-Kabīr* (6:615).
[158] *Maʿālim al-Tanzīl* (2:393, 3:428).
[159] *Anwār al-Tanzīl* (4:374).
[160] *Lubāb al-Taʾwīl fī Maʿānī al-Tanzīl* (3:490).
[161] *Madārik al-Tanzīl wa-Ḥaqāʾiq al-Taʾwīl* (3:490).

- Al-Ṭabarī [after citing reports explaining *Ahl al-Bayt* to mean the *ʿItra*] and al-Wāḥidī said: "From ʿIkrima [concerning 33:33]: 'It is not as they claim, but the verse was revealed concerning the wives of the Prophet ﷺ.'"[162]

- Al-Zamakhsharī said: "In this [33:33] there is an explicit proof that the wives of the Prophet ﷺ are among the People of his House (*min Ahli Baytihi*)."[163]

- Al-Shawkānī and al-Mubārakfūrī said: "Ibn ʿAbbās, ʿIkrima, ʿAṭāʾ, al-Kalbī, Muqātil, and Saʿīd ibn Jubayr said the wives of the Prophet ﷺ are specifically meant [in 33:33], and by "house" are meant the houses of his wives as mentioned before in the verses. While Abū Saʿīd al-Khudrī, Mujāhid, and Qatāda – it is also related from al-Kalbī – said that those meant are specifically ʿAlī, Fāṭima, al-Ḥasan, and al-Ḥusayn. They adduced the fact that the pronouns are in the masculine, but this was refuted by the fact that the noun *Ahl* is masculine and therefore necessitates a masculine gender as in the verse [Hūd 73] [...]. A third group stands midway between the two and includes both [the wives and the *ʿItra*] [...] A number of the verifying authorities consider this the most correct explanation, among them al-Qurṭubī, Ibn Kathīr, and others."[164]

- Al-Jalālayn: "*Ahl al-Bayt* [in 33:33] *i.e.* the wives of the Prophet ﷺ."

- Al-Ṣāwī said in *Ḥāshiyat al-Jalālayn*: "It was said the verse [33:33] is comprehensive (*ʿāmma*) to mean the People of his House in the sense of his dwelling and these are his wives, and the People of his House in the sense of his lineage and these are his offspring."

[162] *Jāmiʿ al-Bayān* (22:7) and *Asbāb al-Nuzūl* (p. 299 §734).
[163] *Al-Kashshāf* (2:212).
[164] *Fatḥ al-Qadīr* (4:278-280) and *Tuḥfat al-Aḥwadhī* (9:48-49).

- Al-Suyūṭī said [after citing the narrations of the *ʿItra*] that Ibn Saʿd narrated from ʿUrwa that he said: "*Ahl al-Bayt* [in 33:33] means the wives of the Prophet ﷺ and it was revealed in the house of ʿĀ'isha."[165]

- Ibn al-Jawzī said: "Then He showed their superiority over all women when He said: {*You* [feminine] *are not like anyone* [masculine] *of the women*} (33:32). Al-Zajjāj [the philologian] said that He did not say, '*like any other woman*' in the feminine, because the masculine form denotes a general exclusion of both male and female [human beings], one and all."[166]

- Ibn Juzayy said: "The *Ahl al-Bayt* of the Prophet ﷺ are his wives, his offspring, and his near relatives such as al-ʿAbbās, ʿAlī, and all for whom receiving *ṣadaqa* is unlawful."[167]

- Al-Bukhārī in his *Ṣaḥīḥ* narrated from Anas that the Prophet ﷺ visited ʿĀ'isha and, upon entering her house, said: "*As-Salāmu ʿalaykum Ahl al-Bayt! wa-raḥmatullah.*" Whereupon she responded: "*Wa-ʿalayka as-Salām wa-raḥmatullāh*, how did you find your wives (*ahl*)? May Allah bless you." Then he went around to see all of his wives and said to them exactly what he had said to ʿĀ'isha.

- Al-Wāḥidī said: "*Ahl al-Bayt* [in 33:33] meaning, the wives of the Prophet ﷺ and the men [and women] of the People of his House."[168]

- Al-Thaʿālibī said: "This verse [11:73] shows that the wife of a man is part of the people of his house (*min ahli baytihi*) [...]

[165] *Al-Durr al-Manthūr* (6:603).
[166] *Zād al-Masīr* (6:378).
[167] *Tafsīr Ibn Juzayy* (p. 561).
[168] *Al-Wajīz* (2:865).

and '*the House*' in Sūrat al-Aḥzab [33:33] refers to the dwelling quarters [*i.e.* of the wives]."[169]

- Ibn Kathīr and al-Wāḥidī said: "From Ibn 'Abbās: 'This verse [33:33] was revealed concerning the wives of the Prophet ﷺ.' "[170]

- Ibn Jamā'a and al-Suyūṭī said: "*Ahl al-Bayt* in verse 33 are the Prophet ﷺ and his wives. It was also said they are 'Alī, Fāṭima, al-Ḥasan, and al-Ḥusayn, and it was also said they are those for whom *ṣadaqa* is unlawful *[i.e. Āl 'Aqīl, Āl 'Alī, Āl Ja'far*, and *Āl al-'Abbās*]."[171]

- Al-Zarkashī said: "The phrasing of the Qur'ān [in Surat al-Aḥzāb] shows that the wives are meant, that the verses were revealed concerning them, and that it is impossible to exclude them from the meaning of the verse. However, since others were to be included with them it was said with the masculine gender: {*Allah desires to remove uncleanness far from you* [masculine plural], *O Folk of the Household*}. It is then known that this desire comprises all the Folk of the Household – both male and female – as opposed to His saying {*O wives of the Prophet*} and it shows that 'Alī and Fāṭima are more [specifically] deserving of this description ['*Ahl al-Bayt*'] than the wives."[172]

- Al-Jaṣṣāṣ said: "It [11:73] shows that the wives of the Prophet ﷺ are of the People of his House (*min Ahli Baytihi*) because the angels name Ibrahim's wife as being of the People of his House, and so has Allah Most High said when addressing the wives of the Prophet ﷺ when He said: {*Allah desires to remove uncleanness far from you, O Folk of the Household*} (33:33). His wives are

[169] *Al-Jawāhir al-Ḥisān* (2:212).
[170] *Tafsīr Ibn Kathīr* (3:532) and *Asbāb al-Nuzūl* (p. 299 §733).
[171] *Ghurar al-Tibyān* (p. 421 §1201) and *Mufhamāt al-Aqrān*.
[172] *Al-Burhān fi 'Ulum al-Qur'ān* (2:197).

part of those meant because the beginning of the address concerns them."[173]

- Abū al-Su'ūd said: "This [33:33], as you see, is an explicit verse and a radiant proof that the wives of the Prophet ﷺ are among the People of his House (*min Ahli Baytihi*), ruling once and for all the invalidity of the opinion of the Shī'īs who narrow it to mean only Fāṭima, 'Alī, and their two sons – Allah be well-pleased with them. As for what they claim as their proof [ḥadīth of the Mantle], it only shows that they [the Four] are part of *Ahl al-Bayt*, not that others are excluded."[174]

The term *ahlu baytī* in the ḥadīth was further defined among the pious *Salaf* as follows:

> Ḥusayn ibn Ṣabra said to Zayd: "Who are the People of his House, O Zayd? Are not his wives among the People of his House?" Zayd replied: "His ﷺ wives are among the People of his House, but the People of his House are [primarily] those for whom *ṣadaqa* is unlawful after him ﷺ." Ḥusayn said: "And who are they?" He replied: "The family of 'Alī, the family of 'Aqil, the family of Ja'far [all sons of Abū Ṭālib], and the family of 'Abbās [ibn 'Abd al-Muṭṭalib]." Ḥusayn said: "Is *ṣadaqa* unlawful for all of these?" Zayd replied yes.[175]

Lexically, the term *'itra* – literally "mantle" – was defined as "A man's relatives such as his children, grandchildren, and paternal cousins"[176] while in the context of the ḥadīths it was explained to mean "Those of the Prophet's Family who follow his Religion and cling to his commands."[177] What emerges from these meanings

[173] *Aḥkām al-Qur'ān* (4:378-379).
[174] *Irshād al-'Aql al-Salīm* (7:103).
[175] Narrated by Aḥmad with a sound chain.
[176] *Mu'jam Maqāyīs al-Lugha* (4:217).
[177] Al-Ṭaḥāwī, *Sharḥ Mushkil al-Āthār* (9:88).

together with the two wordings of the ḥadīth "I have left among you two matters" is firm evidence that there is an inseparable connection, until the Last Day, between the Qur'ān, the Sunna, and the Family of the Prophet ﷺ.

One of the meanings of the Family version is the Prophet's ﷺ specific recommendation of ʿAlī ibn Abī Ṭālib ؓ to the Muslims as explicited by the following two narrations:

> At the tree of Khumm the Prophet ﷺ took ʿAlī by the hand and said: "People! Do you not bear witness that Allah ﷻ is your Lord?" They said yes. He said: "Do you not bear witness that Allah is nearer and His Prophet is nearer to you all (*awlā bikum*) than your own selves [cf. Qur'ān 33:6], and that Allah ﷻ and His Prophet are your two protecting friends (*mawlayākum*) [cf. Qur'ān 3:150, 8:40, 22:78, 66:2]?" They said yes. He said: "Anyone whose patron (*mawlā*) I am, this is his patron!" Or he said – Ibn Marzūq, one of the narrators, was unsure – "ʿAlī is his patron.[178] Truly I have left among you that which if you hold to it, you shall never go astray: the book of Allah – which is His rope in your very hands – and the people of my House."[179]

> On his way back from his Farewell Pilgrimage when the Prophet ﷺ alighted at the brook of Khumm (*Ghadīr Khumm*), he ordered a stop under the large trees then he said: "I seem to be called back [by my Lord], therefore I am responding [to Him]. Truly I have left among you the two weighty matters, one of them greater than the other: the Book of Allah and my mantle (*ʿitra*), the People of my House. Look well to how you treat

[178] See n. 152.

[179] Narrated from ʿAlī by al-Ṭaḥāwī with a fair chain as stated by al-Arna'ūṭ in his edition of *Sharḥ Mushkil al-Āthār* (5:13 §1760), while Ibn Ḥajar declared the chain sound (*ṣaḥīḥ*) in *al-Maṭālib al-ʿĀliya* (§3972).

them after me! For these two shall never part ways until they show up at the Pond." Then he said: "Truly Allah ﷻ is my Patron, and I am the patron of every believer!" Then he took 'Alī ؓ by the hand and said: "Anyone whose patron (*mawlā*) I am, this is his patron! O Allah! Be the Patron of whoever takes him as a patron, and be the enemy of whoever takes him as an enemy." The Companion Abū al-Ṭufayl said to Zayd ibn Arqam: "You heard this from the Messenger of Allah?" He replied: "There was no one under those large trees except he saw it with his two eyes and heard it with his two ears."[180]

11. **Anything that he ﷺ did not himself bring but which people innovate after him according to their whims and caprice, or to serve their lusts, is an innovation in the Religion (*bid'a*) which is completely rejected**

A mass-transmitted ḥadīth states that the Prophet ﷺ said:

"There shall dawn upon my Community exactly what dawned upon the Israelites, as near [in resemblance] as a sandal-span. If the Israelites had a man openly commit incest with his mother then there shall also be someone who does this in my Community. Truly the Israelites divided into seventy-two sects and my Community shall divide into seventy-three – all of them in the Hellfire except one group." They asked: "Who are they,

[180] A sound ḥadīth narrated from Zayd ibn Arqam by al-Ṭaḥāwī in *Mushkil al-Āthār* (5:18 §1765) as stated by Shaykh Shu'ayb al-Arna'ūṭ, also by al-Nasā'ī in his *Khaṣā'iṣ 'Alī* (§79) and *Faḍā'il al-Ṣaḥāba* (§45), al-Ḥākim (3:109) who declared it sound, and al-Ṭabarānī (§4969). The stand-alone ḥadīth "I am leaving among you the two weighty matters: the Book of Allah and the People of my House" is also narrated from Zayd ibn Arqam with a sound chain – as stated by al-Arna'ūṭ – by Aḥmad, al-Ṭaḥāwī in *Mushkil al-Āthar* (9:88 §3463), and al-Ṭabarānī (§5040); from Abū Sa'īd al-Khudrī by Aḥmad with a weak chain because of 'Aṭiyya ibn Sa'd al-'Awfī; and from 'Alī by al-Bazzār with a weak chain as indicated by al-Haythamī (9:163).

> Messenger of Allah?" He replied: "[Those that follow] that which I and my Companions follow."[181]

Another version states that the Prophet ﷺ said:

> "Truly the People of the Book divided into seventy-two sects and this Community shall divide into seventy-three sects, all of them in the Fire except one – the Congregation (*al-jamāʿa*). There shall come out of my Community people in whom unspeakable lusts run amok, the way rabies runs through its victim. There shall not be one nook or cranny except they enter it."[182] ʿAmr ibn ʿUthmān – Abū Dāwūd's Shaykh – said: "Rabies does not leave one artery or joint in its victim except it enters it."

Close to this is the ḥadīth that states:

> "A trial (*fitna*) is coming which shall not leave one house of the Arabs intact except it shall enter it."[183] Another version is that of

[181] Narrated from ʿAbd Allah ibn ʿAmr by al-Tirmidhī (*ḥasan gharīb*), Muḥammad ibn Naṣr al-Marwazī in *al-Sunna* (p. 23), Ibn ʿAsākir, Abū Nuʿaym in *Maʿrifat al-Ṣaḥāba*, al-Ṭabarānī in *al-Saghīr*, and al-Ḥākim (1:129=1990 ed. 1:218), with chains containing ʿAbd al-Raḥmān ibn Zyād al-Ifrīqī, who was declared weak by some but fair in his narrations by others, and from Anas by al-Ṭabarānī in *al-Awsaṭ*. Al-Lālikā'ī declared this ḥadīth sound (*ṣaḥīḥ*) in his *Sharḥ Uṣūl Iʿtiqād Ahl al-Sunna* (1:100) and it was included – with its variant versions – by al-Kattānī in his *Naẓm al-Mutanāthir* (p. 45-47) and Ibn al-Athīr in *Jāmiʿ al-Uṣūl* (10:408). The second half of the ḥadīth beginning with the words "Truly the Israelites divided..." is often quoted as a stand-alone narration and is the subject of a monograph by al-Ṣanʿānī. For the ḥadīth: "You must follow my Sunna and the Sunna of the Rightly-Guided Successors" see note 32 above and the second volume of our *Sunna Notes* entitled *The Excellent Innovation.*

[182] Narrated from Abū Hurayra by Ibn Mājah and, as part of a longer ḥadīth, from Muʿāwiya by Abū Dāwūd and Aḥmad all with good chains as stated by al-ʿIrāqī in *al-Mughnī* while al-Ḥākim (1:128=1990 ed. 1:218) said "a sound chain", and in part from Anas by Abū Yaʿlā (7:32-36 §3938 and §3944 *isnād ḍaʿīf*).

[183] Narrated from ʿAwf ibn Mālik by al-Bukhārī. Some saw in this ḥadīth a reference to television.

> Ḍirār ibn ʿAmr whereby the Prophet ﷺ said concerning the saying of Allah ﷻ {*He is able to bewilder you with dissension*} (6:65): "Four dissensions shall appear: in the first, the taking of lives will be made licit; in the second, the taking of lives and property will be made licit; in the third, the taking of lives, property, and sexual liberty will be made licit; the fourth dissension will be an overwhelming, blind darkness which shall cover all like a tidal wave until not one house of the Arabs remains except it enters it."[184]

Another version states that the Prophet ﷺ said:

> "You shall adopt the practices of the People of the Book [that went] before you as closely as a sandal-span, not missing a step of the way, nor shall their way be any different from yours." A man among the people said: "Messenger of Allah, will they even worship the golden calf of the Israelites?" The Prophet ﷺ replied: "Yes, and the golden calf of my Community is So-and-So" (*wa-ʿijlu ummatī fulān*).[185]

Another word the Prophet ﷺ used for the Congregation is "the largest mass" (*al-sawād al-aʿẓam*), as in the following narrations:

> "My Community shall never concur on error. Therefore, when you see disagreement, you must stay with the largest mass."[186] Another version states: "Allah shall not make my [or: this]

[184] Cited by al-Suyūṭī in *al-Durr al-Manthūr* (6:65) from Nuʿaym ibn Ḥammād's *Kitāb al-Fitan*. Also narrated from ʿAwf ibn Mālik al-Ashjaʿī, ʿUmayr ibn Hānī', and – *mawqūf* –from Abū Hurayra by Nuʿaym ibn Ḥammād in *al-Fitan* (1:50, 1:57, 1:238). "Nuʿaym is disclaimed in his narrations (*munkar al-ḥadīth*) despite his standing as an Imām." Ibn Ḥajar, *al-Amālī al-Ḥalabiyya* (p. 40).

[185] Narrated from Ḥudhayfa by al-Ṭabarānī in *Musnad al-Shāmiyyīn* (2:100).

[186] Narrated from Anas by Ibn Mājah, ʿAbd ibn Ḥumayd in his *Musnad* (p. 367 §1220), and al-Lālikā'ī in his *Sharḥ Uṣūl al-Iʿtiqād* (1:105 §153), all with very weak chains cf. al-Būṣīrī in the *Miṣbāḥ* (4:169) but the ḥadīth is declared sound by al-Ṣuyūṭī in *al-Jāmiʿ al-Ṣaghīr* due to the multiplicity of its chains.

Community ever concur on error. The Hand of Allah is with the *Jamāʿa*."[187] Another version continues: "Whoever dissents from them departs to Hell."[188]

"The Hand of Allah is with the *Jamāʿa*."[189] Al-Ṭabarī defined the *Jamāʿa* as "the largest mass."[190] Another version continues: "Follow the largest mass, for verily whoever dissents from them departs to Hell."[191]

"The Israelites divided into seventy-one sects, seventy of which are in the Fire; the Christians into seventy-two sects, seventy-one of which are in the Fire; and this Community shall separate into seventy-three sects, all of them in the Fire except one which will enter Paradise." We said: "Describe it for us." He said: "The *Sawād al-Aʿẓam*."[192]

Abū Umāma is also related to say, "You must stick with the largest mass." When asked to define it, he said, "This verse in Sūrat al-Nūr: {*Say: Obey Allah and obey the Messenger. But if you turn away, then it is for him to do only that wherewith he has been*

[187] Narrated from Ibn ʿAbbās by al-Bayhaqī in *al-Asmā' wal-Ṣifāt* (al-Ḥāshidī ed. 2:136 §702 *isnād ṣaḥīḥ*).
[188] Narrated from Ibn ʿUmar by al-Tirmidhī (*gharīb*) with a weak chain.
[189] Narrated from Ibn ʿAbbās by al-Tirmidhī (*gharīb*) with a chain of trustworthy narrators.
[190] Cf. *Fatḥ al-Bārī*, ḥadīth of Ḥudhayfa: "People used to ask the Messenger of Allah ﷺ about the good, but I wished to ask him about the evil..." and al-Mubārakfūrī, *Tuḥfat al-Aḥwadhī*, ḥadīth "The Hand of Allah is with the *Jamāʿa*."
[191] Narrated from Ibn ʿAbbās by al-Ḥākim and al-Ṭabarī, and from Ibn ʿUmar by Abū Nuʿaym in the *Ḥilya* (3:37), al-Ḥākim with three chains (1:115-116=1990 ed. 1:199-201), al-Lālikā'ī in his *Sharḥ Uṣūl* (1:106), al-Dānī in *al-Sunan al-Wārida fil-Fitan* (3:748), al-Ḥakīm al-Tirmidhī in *Nawādir al-Uṣūl* (Aṣl 88), and al-Daylamī in *Musnad al-Firdaws* (5:258). Shaykh ʿAbd al-Fattāḥ Abū Ghudda denounced al-Albānī's misdocumentation of this ḥadīth cf. our *Sunna Notes II* (p. 53-54 n. 103).
[192] Narrated from Abū Umāma by al-Ṭabarānī in *al-Kabīr* and *Awsaṭ* with trustworthy narrators cf. al-Haythamī (7:258-259), Ibn Abī Shayba (7:554), Ibn Abī ʿĀṣim in *al-Sunna* (1:34), Abū Naṣr al-Marwazī in *al-Sunna* (p. 22 §55), and al-Bayhaqī in *al-Sunan* (8:188).

charged, and for you to do only that wherewith you have been charged. If you obey him, you will go aright. But the Messenger has no other charge than to convey (the message), plainly} (24:54)."[193]

The *Sawād al-Aʿẓam* means "a massive gathering of human beings" as ascertained by the narration that during his Ascension the Prophet ﷺ passed by Prophets followed by their nations and he passed by Prophets followed by their groups and he passed by Prophets followed by no one until he saw a tremendous throng (*sawād ʿaẓīm*) and said: "Who are these?" The answer came: "These are Mūsā and his nation, but raise your head and look up," whereupon the Prophet ﷺ said: "[I saw] a tremendous throng (*sawād ʿaẓīm*) that had blocked up the entire firmament from this side and that!" And it was said: "These are your Nation ."[194]

The *Sawād al-Aʿẓam* is therefore as Ibn Masʿūd said in his authentic narration: "That which the Muslims deem good, Allah deems good."[195]

A Companion-narration or *mawqūf* report from Ḥudhayfa al-Yamānī states: "The first thing you will lose from your Religion is humility (*khushūʿ*) and the last, prayer (*ṣalāt*). You shall undo the bonds of Islam one by one. Women shall pray in their menses. You shall tread the path of those that came before you as closely as the arrow-feather and the sandal-span, not missing a step of the way, nor shall their way be any different from yours. In the end two out of many [wayward] sects shall remain. The first shall say: 'What are these five prayers? Surely those that came before us went astray. Allah ﷻ only said: {*Establish worship at the two ends of the day and in some watches of the night*} (11:114). Do not pray except three prayers!' The other sect shall say: 'The faith of the believers in Allah is just like the faith of the angels. There is

[193] Narrated by Aḥmad, al-Bazzār, and al-Ṭabarānī with trustworthy narrators cf. al-Haythamī.
[194] Narrated from Ibn ʿAbbās by al-Tirmidhī (*ḥasan ṣaḥīḥ*).
[195] Aḥmad relates it from the words of Ibn Masʿūd (*mawqūf*) with a sound chain.

not, among us, a single apostate nor dissimulator!' It shall be right that Allah raise them together with the Antichrist."[196]

Although the chain of this narration is not raised up to the Prophet ﷺ, nevertheless its status is that of a Prophetic ḥadīth as it pertains to unseen matters which are not subject to the Companion's opinion and which he can only have said upon hearing them from the Prophet ﷺ.

The Prophet ﷺ said: "My similitude and that of the message Allah sent me with is that of a man who came to his people and said: 'O my people! I have seen the [enemy] army with my own two eyes, and I am warning you of the plain truth, so save yourselves!' Then a group of his people obeyed him and fled when night came, proceeding stealthily until they were safe, while another group disbelieved him and stayed where they were until morning. At that time the army came upon them, destroying and trampling them. This is the similitude of those who obey me and follow what I have brought [*i.e.*, the Qur'ān and the Sunna], and the example of those who disobey me and disbelieve the truth I have brought."[197]

The Prophet ﷺ is also related to say: "There are six types whom I have cursed and whom Allah has cursed as well as every Prophet that ever was:

- He who adds something to the Book of Allah;

- He who denies the Divine foreordained Decree (*qadar*);

- He who imposes himself upon others [in some versions: upon my *Umma*] through tyranny, elevating thereby those whom Allah abased, and abasing those whom He elevated;

[196] Narrated by al-Ḥākim (4:469=1990 ed. 4:516) who declared its chain *ṣaḥīḥ*.
[197] Narrated from Abū Mūsā al-Ash'arī by al-Bukhārī and Muslim, but al-Bukhārī omits the last sentence.

- He who treats as licit what Allah has made forbidden;
- He who treats as licit those of my Family (*ʿitra*) whom Allah has made forbidden;
- He who abandons my Sunna for an innovation."[198]

The Prophet ﷺ is also related to say: "Knowledge (*al-ʿilm*) consists in three matters and whatever else is superfluous: [1] a verse of Qur'ān unabrogated and unambiguous (*āyā muḥkama*); [2] a Sunna firmly established (*qā'ima*); or [3] a just inheritance law (*farīḍa*)."[199]

[198]Narrated from ʿĀ'isha by al-Tirmidhī, al-Ṭaḥāwī in *Sharḥ Mushkil al-Āthār* (9:84-86 §3460-3462=4:366-367), Ibn Ḥibbān (13:60 §5749), al-Ṭabarānī in *al-Kabīr* (3:126 §2883) and *al-Awsaṭ* (2:186 §1667), Ibn Abī ʿĀṣim in *al-Sunna* (§44, §337), "with a sound chain" per al-Suyūṭī in *al-Jāmiʿ al-Saghīr* (§4660) and al-Daylamī as stated by al-Munāwī, "a weak chain" per al-Arna'ūṭ in his edition of Ibn Ḥibbān, al-Ḥākim – also from Ibn ʿUmar – (1:36, 2:525, 4:90), and al-Bayhaqī chainless in *Shuʿab al-Īmān* (3:443 §4010), a ḥadīth *ḥasan* according to the editor of al-Harawī's *Dhamm al-Kalām* (5:10). Also narrated with seven items from ʿAmr ibn Shaghawī by al-Ṭabarānī in *al-Kabīr* (17:43) with a fair chain according to al-Suyūṭī in *al-Jāmiʿ al-Saghīr* (§4648) – confirmed by al-Munāwī but contradicted by al-Haythamī (1:176). See also al-Haythamī, *Mawārid al-Ẓam'ān* (p. 42) and al-Suyūṭī, *Miftāḥ al-Janna* (p. 31 §39-40). Al-Dhahabī in his notes on the *Mustadrak* once declares its chain sound (1:36) and once calls it "a wholly disclaimed narration" (*ḥadīth munkar bi-marra* 4:90) while in *al-Kabā'ir* (p. 166) he supposedly declares its chain sound. Al-Tirmidhī declared as "more correct" the same ḥadīth narrated through a *mursal* chain from Zayn al-ʿĀbidīn ʿAlī ibn al-Ḥusayn ibn ʿAlī, from the Prophet ﷺ, as does Abū Zurʿa cf. *Mīzān* (ʿAbd al-Raḥmān ibn Abī al-Mawālī), Ibn Abī Ḥātim's *ʿIlal al-Ḥadīth* (2:91), al-Dāraquṭnī's *Afrād*, al-Khaṭīb's *Muttafaq*, al-Suyūṭī's *Iḥyā' al-Mayt bi-Faḍā'il Ahl al-Bayt* (§58), and *Kanz* (§33024, 44032).

[199]Narrated from ʿAbd Allah ibn ʿAmr by Abū Dāwūd, Ibn Mājah, al-Ḥākim (4:332=1990 ed. 4:369), al-Dāraquṭnī in his *Sunan* (4:67-68 §2), and al-Bayhaqī in his (6:208 §11942), all with weak chains because of ʿAbd al-Raḥmān ibn Rāfiʿ al-Tanūkhī and ʿAbd al-Raḥmān ibn Zyād ibn Anʿum. However, the narration is deemed acceptable by Abū Dāwūd, Ibn Kathīr in his *Tafsīr* (1:458), al-Qurṭubī in his (5:56), al-ʿAẓīm Ābādī in his commentary on al-Dāraquṭnī, and Ibn Qudāma in *al-Mughnī* (6:162).

Something similar is related *mawqūf* from Ibn ʿUmar.[200] Imām Mālik ؓ said: "A ruling is one of two kinds (*al-ḥukmu ḥukmān*): a ruling brought by the book of Allah, and a ruling stipulated by the Sunna." He also said: "And the opinion of a *mujtahid* for it may be that he shall be granted success." He also mentioned the pretender and disparaged him.[201]

The Prophet ﷺ also said: "Whosoever innovates in this matter of ours [*i.e.*, the Religion] what does not belong to it, it is null and void."[202]

---

[200] Cf. Ibn Ḥazm in *al-Iḥkām* (8:509-510), and al-Dhahabī in the *Siyar* (Arna'ūṭ ed. 15:61) and *Tadhkirat al-Ḥuffāẓ* (3:807). Ibn Ḥajar in *Tahdhīb al-Tahdhīb* (6:159) related that Sufyān al-Thawrī said that none of the people of knowledge considered this narration raised up to the Prophet ﷺ.

[201] Narrated from Ibn Wahb by Ibn ʿAbd al-Barr in *al-Tamhīd* (4:266).

[202] Narrated from ʿĀʾisha by al-Bukhārī, Muslim, Abū Dāwūd, Ibn Mājah, and Aḥmad.

HIS ﷺ ORDER TO HOLD FAST TO HIS SUNNA AND HIS PROHIBITION TO FOLLOW OR PRACTICE ONLY WHAT IS FOUND IN THE QUR'ĀN IN ABANDONMENT OF THE SUNNA AND IN PURSUIT OF LUSTS AND INDEPENDENT OPINION.

As the proofs previously adduced show, the Prophet ﷺ does not command other than what Allah made required, and he does not prohibit other than what Allah forbade. Al-ʿIrbāḍ ibn Sāriya said:

> The Messenger of Allah ﷺ prayed among us that day then turned to face us and admonished us intensely so that the eyes wept and the hearts trembled. A man said: "Messenger of Allah! This resembles the admonishment of one who bids farewell, therefore what solemn promise do you require of us?" He replied: "I exhort you to beware of Allah ﷻ. I exhort you to hear and obey even if your leader is a black Ethiopian. Lo! Whoever of you lives shall live to see great divisions. You must follow my Sunna and the Sunna of the rightly-guided, upright caliphs after me. Hold on to it firmly, bite upon it with your very jaws! Beware of newfangled matters. Every newfangled matter is an innovation, and every innovation is misguidance."[203]

The Prophet ﷺ heard voices coming from the date palm groves and he enquired about them. They said: 'They are pollinating the trees." He said: "If they did not [pollinate them] it would be fine." So they did not pollinate them that year, and the dates grew undersized. When they mentioned this to the Prophet ﷺ he said: "If it is something that pertains to your world then it is up to you, and if it is something that pertains to your Religion then it is up to me."[204]

[203] See n. 32 above and Ibn Rajab's commentary on this foundational ḥadīth in the second volume of our *Sunna Notes, The Excellent Innovation*.

[204] Narrated from Anas, Thābit, and ʿĀ'isha with sound chains by Ibn Mājah, Aḥmad, Ibn Ḥibbān (1:201 §22), and Abū Yaʿlā (6:198, 6:237). Also narrated by

Another version states that the Prophet ﷺ replied: "I am only a human being. If I tell you something that pertains to your Religion then follow it, but if I tell you something that pertains to your mundane matters, then I am only a human being."[205]

Another time, the Prophet ﷺ inadvertently omitted something in prayer. Asked if the prayer had changed, he said: "I am only a human being and I forget just as you forget. If I forget something, remind me [of it]."[206]

The Prophet ﷺ said: "People! Allah ﷻ has made pilgrimage obligatory upon you, so accomplish the pilgrimage." A man asked: "Every year, Messenger of Allah?" The Prophet ﷺ kept silent. The man asked again, and then asked a third time. Whereupon the Prophet ﷺ said: "If I said yes it would become obligatory and you would not be able to fulfill it." Then he said: "Leave me alone as long as I leave you alone. Those before you perished for no other reason than asking too many questions and then differing with their Prophets. If I order you to do something, do it to the extent that you can, and if I forbid you something, then leave it!"[207]

The Prophet ﷺ did something by following the easier dispensation (*rukhṣa*), whereupon some people disdained to avail themselves of it. When news of this reached him he praised Allah ﷻ

Muslim with the wording: "You know best about your mundane matters." Also narrated from the words: "If it is something..." by al-Dāraquṭnī in his *Sunan* (1:382), Also narrated with sound chains as part of a long ḥadīth that arose in a different circumstance by Aḥmad and Ibn Khuzayma (1:214 §410). The position of our *Shuyūkh* and theirs is that the Prophet's ﷺ advice was to be understood in the long term and that two or more years were needed for the expected results.

[205] Narrated from Rafiʿ ibn Khadīj by al-Ṭabarānī in *al-Kabīr* (4:280) and Ibn Ḥibbān (1:202 §23) with a fair chain as stated by Shaykh Shuʿayb al-Arnaʾūṭ.

[206] Narrated from Ibn Masʿūd by al-Bukhārī, Muslim, al-Nasāʾī, Abū Dāwūd, Ibn Mājah, and Aḥmad.

[207] Narrated from Abū Hurayra by Muslim, al-Nasāʾī, and Aḥmad. Also narrated from the words "Leave me alone" to the end by al-Bukhārī, al-Tirmidhī (*ḥasan ṣaḥīḥ*), Ibn Mājah, and Aḥmad.

and glorified Him then said: "What is the matter with certain people who disdain to avail themselves of something which I practice? By Allah! I am the most knowledgeable of Allah ﷻ among them, and the most intense of them in fear of Him."[208]

Ibn Ḥajar said:

> Ibn al-Tīn related from al-Dāwūdī that the latter said: "Disdaining to take up whatever dispensation the Prophet ﷺ used is among the greatest sins because one sees himself as more Godwary than the Messenger of Allah ﷺ." There is no doubt that one who believes this is a heretic. However, those that did it in the ḥadīth gave as their reason, that the Prophet's ﷺ past and future sins had been forgiven and so his case was different from theirs. Hence – according to their reasoning – those whose sins have not been forgiven are in need of following the stricter and harder way in order to be saved. So the Prophet ﷺ informed them that even if Allah ﷻ had forgiven him, he was still the most Godwary and most intense of all of them in fear of Him. Therefore, whatever he does – whether in the way of dispensation or strictness – he does with the most Godwariness and intense fear of Allah. The immense favor of being forgiven in no way impelled him to leave earnest effort in his deeds. On the contrary, he showed gratitude.[209]

[208] Narrated from 'Ā'isha by al-Bukhārī, Muslim, and Aḥmad.
[209] Ibn Ḥajar, *Fatḥ al-Bārī* (1959 ed. 13:279).

HIS ﷺ COMMAND TO LISTEN TO HIS HADITH, MEMORIZE IT, AND CONVEY IT TO WHOEVER DID NOT HEAR IT, BOTH HIS CONTEMPORARIES AND POSTERITY, PROMISING THEM IMMENSE REWARD FOR IT.

This command of the Prophet ﷺ to memorize and convey his ḥadīth necessitates the probative nature of the Sunna. Al-Shāfiʿī ؓ said:

> The fact that the Messenger of Allah ﷺ made it desirable for each individual to listen to his sayings, memorize them, and convey them, indicates that he did not command that there be conveyed from him other than what constitutes a proof against him to whom it is conveyed. For nothing is conveyed from him ﷺ except [the stipulations of] what is lawful so that it be followed, what is illicit so that it be avoided, legal punishment, trade and transactions of goods, as well as faithful advice concerning the Religion and the present life.[210]

Similar evidence is provided by the Prophet's ﷺ prohibition of lying about him and that of concealing any knowledge that came from him, which would be tantamount to changing the ruling of Allah ﷻ, failing to inform people of it, and putting into practice other than that which Allah ﷻ revealed. If the ḥadīth were not probative as we said, there would have been no difference between lying and otherwise, or between concealment of what the Prophet ﷺ brought and lying about him. Nor would the latter two offences incur such heavy punishment as Hellfire.[211]

Abū Dharr ؓ said: "The Prophet ﷺ ordered us not to be overcome in commanding the good, forbidding the wrong, and teaching people the *sunan*."[212] Al-Bayhaqī narrated it then added:

[210] Al-Shāfiʿī, *al-Risāla* (p. 402-403).
[211] See chapter 'Proofs from the Noble Sunna for the Sunna as Evidence', section 7.
[212] Narrated by al-Dārimī and al-Bayhaqī in *al-Madkhal* (p. 258), *Shuʿab al-Īmān*

> If following the Messenger of Allah ﷺ in what he made a Sunna is obligatory and knowing it is an enduring obligation, it is also true that following his Sunna is impossible until we know it, and knowing it is impossible until we accept truthful reports from him. Accepting such reports is therefore a precondition for followership. Hence, we were commanded to teach them [the Sunan] and to invite people to them.[213]

The Prophet ﷺ said in his Farewell Pilgrimage: "Lo! Let every witness among you tell the one who is absent. Perhaps the one who is conveyed to shall understand better than the one who heard in the first place."[214] Al-Bayhaqī said: "If it were not for the definite proof adduced by the Sunna, the Prophet ﷺ would not have said in his address, after teaching whoever saw him the matter of their Religion: 'Let every witness tell the absent one, etc.'"[215]

Similar to the above ḥadīth is the mass-transmitted report that the Prophet ﷺ said:

> Allah brighten the face of him among His servants who hears my words, remembers [or preserves] them, guards them, and transmits them! Many a transmitter of knowledge does not himself understand it, and many may transmit knowledge to others who are more versed in it than they. The heart of a Muslim shall never harbor vindictive feelings towards three

(6:18), and *al-I'tiqād* (p. 232) with a chain of sound narrators except for one unknown narrator as stated by al-Haythamī (5:216).

[213] Al-Bayhaqī, *al-I'tiqād* (p. 232).

[214] Narrated from Abū Bakrah by Ibn Mājah and Ibn 'Abd al-Barr in *Jāmi' Bayān al-'Ilm* (1:182-184 §192-194) with three chains, two of them sound; also, as part of a longer narration, by al-Bukhārī, Muslim, Aḥmad, and al-Dārimī. Also narrated from 'Ubāda ibn al-Sāmiṭ by al-Ṭabarānī in *al-Kabīr* with a chain of sound narrators as stated by al-Haythamī (1:139). The second sentence is narrated without the first from 'Abd Allah ibn 'Amr by Ibn 'Abd al-Barr in *Jāmi' Bayān al-'Ilm* (1:190 §200) with a very weak chain because of 'Abd al-'Azīz ibn 'Ubayd Allah.

[215] Al-Bayhaqī as cited by 'Abd al-Khāliq in *Ḥujjiyyat al-Sunna* (p. 320).

> things: sincerity in deeds done for the sake of Allah; faithfulness to Muslims; and conformity to the community of believers. For truly their supplication encompasses the rest of the people.[216]

The Prophet ﷺ also said: "Whoever lies about me willfully, let him take now his seat in the Fire!"[217] We related another version of this mass-narrated ḥadīth.[218] A third version states: "Truly if one lies about me it is not like lying about anyone else. Whoever lies about me willfully, let him take now his seat in the Fire!"[219]

The Prophet ﷺ also said: "Whoever innovates something new (*aḥdatha ḥādithan*) or abets someone who does (*aw āwā muḥdithan*), upon him is the curse of Allah, the angels, and that of all the people! There shall be accepted from him neither barter (*ṣarf*) nor balance (*'adal*)."[220] Another version states: "When innovations appear in my Community, the person of knowledge has to show his knowledge. If he does not do so, then upon him be the curse of Allah, that of the angels, and that of all the people! There shall be accepted from him neither barter nor balance."[221]

[216] A mass-transmitted (*mutawātir*) ḥadīth beginning with the words *naḍḍar Allahu imra'an* (May Allah brighten the face = grant prosperity and felicity) and narrated from nineteen Companions. See its documentation in volume 1 of our *Sunna Notes* entitled *Ḥadīth History and Principles.*

[217] A mass-narrated (*mutawātir*) ḥadīth from many Companions in al-Bukhārī and Muslim. One version narrated from Ibn 'Abbās by Aḥmad with three chains, al-Tirmidhī (*ḥasan*), and – with a sound chain – Ibn Abī Shayba begins with the words: "Avoid relating my words except what you know for sure."

[218] See above, n. 105.

[219] Narrated from al-Mughīra ibn Shu'ba by al-Bukhārī, Muslim, and Aḥmad. In al-Bukhārī's version al-Mughīra continues and says: "I heard the Prophet ﷺ say: 'Whoever is wailed over [at burial] shall be punished to the extent of the [people's] wailing over him.'"

[220] Part of a longer ḥadīth narrated from 'Alī by al-Bukhārī, Abū Dāwūd, Aḥmad, and others.

[221] Narrated from Jābir ibn Zayd by al-Rabī' al-Azdī in his *Musnad* (p. 365).

Another versions states: "When innovations appear and my Companions are insulted, the person of knowledge has to show his knowledge. If he does not do so, then upon him be the curse of Allah, that of the angels, and that of all people!"[222] Al-Walīd ibn Muslim, Abū Bakr ibn ʿAyyāsh, and ʿAbbād ibn al-ʿAwwām said in explanation of "his knowledge": "It means the Sunna."[223]

Al-Suyūṭī said:

> From the beginning of Prophethood until the death of the last of the Companions there are 120 years. The century of the Successors starts at the year 100 and extends to the year 170. Then that of the Successors' Successors from then to about 220. At that time innovations appeared en masse, the Muʿtazila let their tongues loose, the philosophers raised their heads, the people of knowledge were put on trial for not saying that the

[222] Narrated from Jābir by al-Dānī in *al-Sunan al-Wārida fīl-Fitan* (3:632) and from Muʿādh ibn Jabal by al-Khallāl in *al-Sunna* (3:495).

[223] *Ibid.* Cf. the narration : "When my Companions are mentioned, hold back [*i.e.* from criticism of them]; when the stars are mentioned [*i.e.* astrology], hold back; and when the Divine Foreordained Decree (*al-qadar*) is mentioned, hold back." Narrated by al-Ṭabarānī in *al-Muʿjam al-Kabīr* (2:93-96, 10:198, 10:244) from Ibn Masʿūd and Thawbān; Ibn ʿAdī in *al-Kāmil fīl-Duʿafa'* (6:2172) from ʿUmar, Ibn Masʿūd, and Thawbān; al-Jurjānī in *Tārīkh Jurjān* (p. 294, 358) from Ibn ʿUmar; Abū al-Shaykh in *Ṭabaqāt al-Muḥaddithīn fī Aṣbahān* (4:134); Ibn Ḥajar in *al-Iṣāba* (4:159) from ʿAbd Allah ibn ʿAbd al-Ghafir the *mawlā* of the Prophet ﷺ; and Ibn Abī Usāma in his *Musnad* (2:748), Ibn ʿAbd al-Barr in *al-Tamhīd* (6:68), Abū Nuʿaym in *al-Ḥilya* (4:108), al-Muḥibb al-Ṭabarī in *al-Riyāḍ al-Naḍira* (1:194), and Ibn Ḥajar in *al-Maṭālib al-ʿĀliya* (3:79 §2932) from Ibn Masʿūd. Al-ʿIrāqī in *al-Mughnī ʿan Ḥaml al-Asfār* [Book of knowledge] said: "Al-Ṭabarānī narrated it from Ibn Masʿūd with a fair (*ḥasan*) chain." Al-Haythamī (7:202, 223 §11395-6, 11515) said: "From Thawbān: al-Ṭabarānī narrated it with a chain containing Yazīd ibn Rabīʿa who is weak; from ʿAbd Allah ibn Masʿūd: al-Ṭabarānī narrated it and its chain contains Mus-hir ibn ʿAbd al-Mālik (in *al-Taqrīb*: *layyin al-ḥadīth*), whom Ibn Ḥibbān and others declared trustworthy but there is disagreement about him, while the rest of the narrators are the men of sound ḥadīth." Al-Suyūṭī also graded it *ḥasan* in *al-Jāmiʿ al-Saghīr* (§615) while al-Ghumārī declares it weak in *al-Mudāwī* (1:364-365 §304/615).

Qur'ān was created, and the state of affairs changed radically. This has not changed until now, and witnesses to the truth of his saying ﷺ: "After that, lying will spread"[224] [in the narration of al-Bukhārī and Muslim from ʿAbd Allah ibn Masʿūd: "The best of people are my century, then those that follow them, then those that follow the latter. After that, lying will spread"].

[224] Al-Suyūṭī in al-Mubārakfūrī, *Tuḥfat al-Aḥwadhī* (6:482) and al-ʿAẓīm Ābādī, *ʿAwn al-Maʿbūd* (12:267). Cf. Ibn Ḥajar, *Fatḥ al-Bārī* (1959 ed. 6:7).

CHAPTER 5

It is Unfeasible to Act Solely on the Basis of the Qur'ān

It is impossible for any human being upon whom Divine revelation did not descend with Divine support to understand the *Sharīʿa*, its details, and its rulings autonomously, from the Qur'ān alone. It is therefore inevitable that one must look into the Sunna which was revealed together with the Qur'ān and the Sunna which the Prophet ﷺ inferred from striving to understand the Qur'ān, in which inference he received Divine confirmation.

One must therefore turn to the Sunna in order to understand Allah Almighty's meaning and infer the details of rulings from the Qur'ān, because the Sunna is the only path to achieve that objective. If the Sunna were not probative then this would not be the case. Nor would it be correct for any of those who exert scholarly striving to look into the Sunna and avail himself of it toward that end. As a result no one would have un-derstood what exactly they are held responsible for, the rulings would have been disregarded, the legal liabilities (*al-takālīf*) would have been cancelled and in vain, all of which is absurd and impossible on the part of Allah ﷻ.

What makes it clear that it is impossible for a *mujtahid* to rely solely on the Qur'ān to extract what we mentioned, is that because the Qur'ān has reached such a level of miraculous inimitability (*iʿjāz*) and the farthest limit of eloquence and economy, it contains many secondary meanings, treasure troves and secrets, many of which are known only to Him Whose Speech this is, and to him ﷺ upon whom their exposition was descended and revealed.

Al-Bukhārī narrated in this respect that when the Prophet ﷺ was asked about the status of donkeys (*i.e.* in comparison with horses in merit, especially in *jihād*), he replied: "Nothing was revealed to me concerning them except this all-encompassing, peerless verse: {*And whoso does good an atom's weight will see it then, and whoso does ill an atom's weight will see it then*} (99:7-8)."[225] Consider how the Prophet ﷺ took the ruling concerning donkeys from that verse, and is anyone else able to do this?[226]

Furthermore, the Qur'ān contains stipulations that are unexplained (*mujmala*) and others that are of indefinite meaning (*mushkala*). It is therefore necessary, in order to put them into practice, to have an explanation that expounds, clarifies, interprets, and explains them. It is further necessary that such an exposition come from Allah ﷻ because it is He that has thrust responsibility upon His servants and therefore He knows what is being meant before anyone else. And this explanation is the Sunna that revelation brought or upon which Allah ﷻ confirmed His Prophet ﷺ if it originated in elucidatory striving on his part. Hence, Allah ﷻ said {*And We have revealed unto you the Remembrance that you may explain to mankind that which has been revealed for them*} (16:44).

[225] Narrated from Abū Hurayra by al-Bukhārī, Muslim, Mālik, al-Nasā'ī, and Aḥmad.

[226] The commentators said that this means that whatever end to which the donkeys are used determines their legal status as instruments of good or evil. Ibn Ḥajar said in commentary upon this ḥadīth: "It provides a firm affirmation for basing practice on the external senses of the general statement (*al-ʿamal bi-ẓawāhir al-ʿumūm*) and the binding nature of the latter until the proof of specificity (*dalīl al-takhṣīṣ*) is pointed out. There is also in the ḥadīth an indication of the difference between a specific ruling explicitly stipulated (*al-ḥukm al-khāṣṣ al-manṣūṣ*) and a general ruling in external terms (*al-ʿāmm al-ẓāhir*), the latter being inferior to the former as an evidentiary proof."

Following are some examples for the unfeasibility of acting solely on the basis of the Qur'ān.

- Allah ﷻ said: {*Establish prayer* (*ṣalāt*) *and pay the poor-due* (*zakāt*)} (2:43, 2:83, 2:110, 4:77, 24:56, 73:20). From this it is understood that both prayer and the poor-due are obligatory. However, what is the exact description of this obligatory prayer? What is its modality? What is its timing? What is its quantity and number? Upon whom is it obligatory? How many times is it obligatory in one's lifetime?

  And what is the exact description of this poor-due? Upon whom is it obligatory? Concerning what kind of property is it obligatory? What is its amount? And what is the condition of its obligation?

- Allah ﷻ also said: {*So* (*give*) *glory to Allah when you enter the night and when you enter the morning*} (30:17). We understand from this the obligatoriness of giving glory and its time in general terms. However: what is meant by such glorification? Is it the same as prayer in His saying {*Establish prayer*}? Or is it something else, such as saying *subḥān Allah*?

- Allah ﷻ also said: {*Recite, then, of the Quran that which is easy for you*} (73:20). We understand from this the obligation of reciting whatever is easy for us of the Qur'ān. However, what is meant by such recitation? Is it the same as prayer? Or is it mere recitation of the Qur'ān? If it means prayer, is one *rak'a* sufficient? And if one *rak'a* is sufficient, what are the actions which such a *rak'a* consists in?

- Allah ﷻ also said: {*O you who believe! Bow down and prostrate yourselves*} (22:77). We understand from this the obligation of bowing down and prostrating. However, what is their exact modality and what is precisely meant by such bowing and prostrating? Are they the same as prayer or something else? If what is meant by them is prayer, then are the number of bows and the number of prostrations in it equal? Or is one superior to the other?

– Allah ﷻ also said: {*Lo! Allah and His angels make ṣalāt upon the Prophet. O you who believe! Make ṣalāt upon him and salute him with a worthy salutation*} (33:56).[227] Is what is meant by this *ṣalāt* the very same as the prayer which Allah ﷻ made obligatory upon us when He said {*Establish prayer*}? Or is it something different? And what does it consist of when it proceeds from Allah and His angels as opposed to when it proceeds from us?

– Allah ﷻ also said: {*They who hoard up gold and silver and spend it not in the way of Allah, unto them give tidings* (*O Muḥammad*) *of a painful doom*} (9:34). We understand from this the prohibition of hoarding up gold and silver and not spending it. However, what is meant by "spending" here as opposed to hoarding up?[228] Does it consist in spending the entire amount of one's property as the Companions understood it when the verse was revealed? Or does it mean spending part of one's property? And what is the precise amount of that part?

– Allah ﷻ also said: {*Perform to completion the pilgrimage* (*al-ḥajj*) *and the visit* (*al-ʿumra*) *for Allah*} (2:196). We understand from

[227] "Allah ﷻ willed that the Community benefit by serving him ﷺ just as he himself owns an immense favor for them which consists in his intercession. Consequently Allah ﷻ commanded them to invoke blessings upon him, then He rewarded them amply for it. For the Prophet ﷺ said: 'Whoever invokes blessings upon me once, Allah blesses him ten times.' [Narrated from Abū Hurayra by Muslim, al-Tirmidhī (*ḥasan ṣaḥīḥ*), al-Nasā'ī, Abū Dāwūd, Aḥmad, and al-Dārimī.]" Al-Qushayrī, *Laṭā'if* (5:170).

[228] The Sunna reveals that what is meant by the "spending" stipulated here is the *zakāt*.

this the obligation of performing to completion *ḥajj* and *ʿumra*. However, what is meant by *ḥajj* and *ʿumra*? Does it consist of the totality of what the Arabs used to do in the Time of Ignorance or of something else and what would that be? And how many times are they obligatory in one's lifetime?

- Allah ﷻ also said: {*Those who believe and obscure not their belief by wrong-doing, theirs is safety and they are rightly-guided*} (6:82). What is meant here by "wrong-doing", the preclusion of which Allah made a precondition for the obtainment of safety and right guidance? Does it mean the totality of the various types of wrong-doing as the Companions understood it, or only a specific type, and what would the latter be?[229]
- Allah ﷻ also said: {*As for the thief, both male and female, cut off their hands/arms. It is the reward of their own deeds, an exemplary punishment from Allah. Allah is Mighty, Wise*} (5:38). We understand by this the obligation of severing the hand/arm (*yad*) of each of them. However, what is the nature of the theft that makes such cutting off obligatory? Is it what is meant lexically by theft in all its varieties or something else? And if the latter, then what exactly? And what are its conditions? What is the amount of property the stealing of which makes cutting off the hand or arm obligatory? And what is the modality of this cutting off? Is the limb cut off from the shoulder-joint? From the wrist? From the elbow? Is the cutting off repeated upon recidivism?

There are many such examples in the Glorious Qur'ān. Try to empty your mind from all that the Sunna explicitly provided in the way of explanation pertaining to the above verses as well as what the jurists mentioned on the basis of the Sunna through

[229] The Sunna reveals that what is meant by "wrong-doing" here is *shirk*.

analogy (*qiyās*) and other methods of elucidating the Sunna. Then see if anyone is able to answer a single question among those we have mentioned above, and other questions of the same type. And supposing one is able to answer some of the questions about these necessary issues, can he answer them all? And if no one can do that, can we then fulfill those responsibilities thrust upon us? And is it rationally conceivable that Allah Sublime and Exalted should task us with responsibilities which He has concealed from us, and made us blind as to what He meant by them? Would it not be the height of absurdity and nonsense to claim that such as this issued from Allah ﷻ?

All of the above shows that Allah ﷻ did not task us with these responsibilities which He listed in broad terms in His Book – in the full knowledge that our minds fall short of understanding His meaning – except that He first put in place an elucidator and patent explainer in charge of clarifying all these matters. This is the Messenger of Allah ﷺ. And He did this by means of His revelation and His support.

The following excerpt from Ibn Ḥazm on the principles of the Law illustrates what we just said:

> Where in the Qur'ān does it state that:
>
> - *Ẓuhr* prayer is four rakʿas?
> - *Maghrib* is three rakʿas?
> - *Rukūʿ* is done in such-and-such a way?
> - *Sujūd* is done in such-and-such a way?
> - Qur'ānic recitation in the prayer is done in such-and-such a way?
> - *Salām* is given at the conclusion of prayer, in such-and-such a way?

- What one must avoid when fasting?
- The modality of *zakāt* for gold and silver, sheep, camels, and cattle?
- The determination of the *zakāt*able capitals and amount of their *zakāt*?
- The rituals of *ḥajj* from the time one stands in ʿArafa?
- The modality of prayer at ʿArafa and Muzdalifa?
- The modality of stoning at the three *jimār* in Minā?
- The description of the pilgrim's sanctified state (*iḥrām*)?
- What must be avoided in *iḥrām*?
- The amputation of the thief's limb?
- The definition of the breast-feeding that creates non-marriageable kinship?[230]
- What prepared foods are prohibited to eat?
- The description and definition of butchering and sacrificial slaughters?
- The modalities of penal rulings (*aḥkām al-ḥudūd*)?
- The description of the enactment of divorce?
- The rulings that pertain to selling?
- The exposition of usurious transactions (*al-ribā*)?
- The modalities of juristic verdicts and appeals?
- Those of solemn oaths, water-dams (*al-aḥbās*), life tenancy resulting in ownership of the tenant's heirs (*al-ʿumrā*), collection of legal alms (*al-ṣadaqāt*), and all the other topics of the Law?

[230] An excellent summation of this topic from the two perspectives of the legal rulings of the Four Schools and their evidences is Dr. Saʿd al-Mirṣafī's *Aḥādīth al-Riḍāʿ Ḥujjiyyatuhā wa-Fiqhuhā* ("The Ḥadīths of Breastfeeding: Their Probativeness and Jurisprudence") (Kuwait and Beirut: al-Manār and al-Rayyān, 1994).

> We find in the Qur'ān only comprehensive clauses (*jumal*). If we were left with them, we would not know how to apply them. In all this, the reference is none other than what is transmitted from the Prophet ﷺ. It is the same with scholarly Consensus (*al-ijmāʿ*) for the latter formed over but a few matters which we all gathered in a single book.[231] [...] Therefore, it is indispensable to refer back to the ḥadīth. And if someone were to say: "We do not take except what we find in the Qur'ān," that person would be an apostate by Consensus of the Community, and would not thereby be obligated to pray more than one *rakʿa* between the going down of the sun and the dark of night, and another one at dawn [cf. 17:78]. For this is the least that has been called *ṣalāt*, and there is no limit (*ḥadd*) set for the most in that chapter. One who follows such a position is an idolatrous disbeliever (*kāfir mushrik*) whose life and property are licit. The only ones to go that path are some of the extremist Rāfiḍīs upon whose apostasy Consensus has formed in the Community. And success is from Allah ﷻ. Now, should someone follow only what the entire Community has agreed upon and nothing else, leaving all that they differed about with regard to what the texts mention: such a person is a transgressor (*fāsiq*) by Consensus of the Community. These two preliminaries make it obligatory to accept what is transmitted.[232]

We have already cited several ḥadīths in illustration of the principles in this chapter.[233] Here are some of the countless Companion-reports and reports of the *Salaf* to that effect.

[231] *Marātib al-Ijmāʿ*, which Ibn Taymiyya critiqued in his *Naqd Marātib al-Ijmāʿ*.
[232] Ibn Ḥazm, *al-Iḥkām fī Uṣūl al-Aḥkām* (2:79-80).
[233] In the chapters entitled 'Proofs from the Noble Qur'ān for the Sunna as Evidence' and ' Proofs from the Noble Sunna for the Sunna as Evidence' above.

- Abū Bakr said: "What heaven will shade me, what earth will carry me, if I say about the Book of Allah something of which I have no knowledge?"[234]

- ʿUmar said: "I only fear for you two matters: A man that interprets the Qur'ān in a way other than the interpretation in which it is meant, and a man who vies with his brother in acquiring property."[235]

- He also said: "I do not fear for this Community a believer whose faith holds him in check nor a dissolute man whose corruption is evident. However, I fear for it a man who read the Qur'ān until he slickened his tongue with it, then he misconstrues it."[236]

- He also said: "Beware of those who put forward opinions (*aṣḥāb al-ra'ī*) for they are the enemies of the Sunna. They have despaired of memorizing the Prophet's ﷺ narrations and have resorted to forwarding opinions. As a result they went astray and also misguided others."[237] Also narrated from him: "Hold in

[234] Narrated from ʿĀmir al-Shaʿbī by al-Khaṭīb in *al-Jāmiʿ li-Akhlāq al-Rāwī* (2:285 §1643), and Ibn Ḥazm in *al-Muḥallā* (1:61) where he declares it *ṣaḥīḥ* and – in a slightly different wording – from Ibn Abī Mulayka and ʿĀ'isha by Ibn Qayyim al-Jawziyya in *Iʿlām al-Muwaqqiʿīn* (1:53-54, 1:82, 2:184) who declared it sound (*ṣaḥīḥ*). Also narrated with a broken (*munqaṭiʿ*) chain from Ibrāhīm al-Taymī by al-Qāsim ibn Sallām as cited in Ibn Kathīr's *Tafsīr* (4:473). After al-Shāfiʿī narrated a ḥadīth to a man the latter said: "Do you also say the same?" whereupon al-Shāfiʿī jumped, his color changed, and he said: "Woe to you! What earth would carry me, what heaven would shade me if I narrated from the Messenger of Allah ﷺ something but did not adhere to it? Yes, I adhere to it heart and soul! Yes, I adhere to it heart and soul!" Narrated by al-Ḥākim as cited by Ibn al-Qayyim in *Iʿlām al-Muwaqqiʿīn* (2:286).

[235] Narrated with a missing *Tābiʿī* link from ʿAmr ibn Dīnār by Ibn ʿAbd al-Barr in *Jāmiʿ Bayān al-ʿIlm* (2:1202 §2364).

[236] Narrated from ʿAbd al-ʿAzīz ibn Abī Ḥāzim by Ibn ʿAbd al-Barr in *Jāmiʿ Bayān al-ʿIlm* (2:1204 §2368) with a weak chain as stated by al-Zuhayrī.

[237] Narrated from ʿAmr ibn Ḥurayth and others by al-Dāraquṭnī in his *Sunan*

the highest suspicion any personal opinion as against [proofs provided by] the Religion (*ittahimū al-ra'ī 'alā al-dīn*)."[238] The same words are related from Sahl ibn Ḥunayf[239] while 'Alī said: "If the Religion went according to personal opinion, then wiping the bottom of the *khuff* would have been more appropriate than wiping its top."[240]

– 'Umar also said: "Certain people shall appear who will dispute with you concerning the Qur'ān: reply to them with the *Sunan*. For the possessors of the *Sunan* are the most knowledgeable about the book of Allah."[241] 'Alī said the same thing to Ibn 'Abbās when he sent him to debate the Khawārij: "Do not argue with them by means of the Qur'ān for it bears many interpretations (*innahu dhū wujūh*), but argue with them by means of the Sunna."[242] Another version states that Ibn 'Abbās said: "Commander of the believers, I know the Qur'ān better than them for it is in our homes that it was revealed," whereupon 'Alī replied: "You said the truth, but the Qur'ān is laconic in its phrasing (*jammāl*) and bears many interpretations. You will say [it means one thing] and they will say [it means another].

(4:146), al-Bayhaqī in *al-Madkhal* (p. 190), Ibn Ḥazm in *al-Iḥkām* (6:213), Ibn 'Abd al-Barr in *Jāmi' Bayān al-'Ilm* (2:1041-1042 §2001-2005) and al-Lālikā'ī in *Sharḥ Uṣūl I'tiqād Ahl al-Sunna* (1:123). Also attributed to al-Zuhrī, cf. Ibn 'Abd al-Barr *Jāmi'* (2:1052 §2032). See the definition of praiseworthy *ra'ī* by Ibn Ḥajar in *Fatḥ al-Bārī* (1959 ed. 13:189 and 13:287-288) and Ibn al-Qayyim in *I'lām al-Muwaqqi'īn* (1:83) as well as al-Kawtharī's *Fiqh Ahl al-'Iraq* and the introduction to al-Tahānawī's *I'lā' al-Sunan*.

[238] Narrated by al-Ṭabarānī in *al-Kabīr* with a chain declared strong by al-Haythamī (1:179), al-Lālikā'ī in *I'tiqād Ahl al-Sunna* (1:126), al-Bazzār cf. *Fatḥ* (5:346), and al-Bayhaqī in *al-Madkhal* cf. *Fatḥ* (13:289) and *Fayḍ al-Qadīr* (5:295).

[239] In al-Bukhārī and Muslim.

[240] Narrated by Abū Dawūd and al-Dārimī with a chain of trustworthy narrators.

[241] Narrated by al-Dārimī, al-Khaṭīb in *Tārīkh Baghdād* (14:286), and al-Lālikā'ī in *Sharḥ Uṣūl I'tiqād Ahl al-Sunna* (1:123 [also from 'Alī]).

[242] Narrated from 'Ikrima by Ibn Sa'd according to al-Suyūṭī in *al-Durr al-Manthūr* in his commentary on the verse {*show us the straight path*} (1:6).

Rather, argue with them by means of the *Sunan*, for they will not be able to find an escape from them."[243]

- Ibn Masʿūd said: "You must hold fast to knowledge [*i.e.*, Sunna] before it is taken away. This taking away consists in the departure of those who possess it. None of you knows when he shall sorely need one of them, or needs what he has. Verily you shall encounter a people who claim that they are calling you unto the book of Allah when in fact they have tossed it behind their backs. So hold fast to knowledge, beware of innovating (*al-tabaddu*ʿ), beware of excessive contention (*al-tanaṭṭu*ʿ), and beware of deep involvement (*al-ta*ʿ*ammuq*). Hold fast to the ancient (*al-*ʿ*atīq*)."[244]

- Muʿāwiya said: "Truly the most delusive misguidance (*aghrā al-ḍalāla*) is for a man to read the Qur'ān without understanding it, then he teaches it to boys, slaves, women, and slave-girls who then take to arguing with the people of knowledge over it."[245]

- ʿImrān ibn Ḥuṣayn said: "The Qur'ān was revealed and the Messenger of Allah ﷺ instituted the *Sunan*." Then he said: "Follow us [Companions] or, by Allah! if you do not, you shall go astray."[246]

[243] *Ibid.*
[244] Narrated with a *mursal* chain of sound narrators from Abū Qilāba – who did not meet Ibn Masʿūd as stated by al-Haythamī (1:126) – by al-Dārimī, al-Azdī in his *Jāmi*ʿ (11:252), Ibn Waḍḍāḥ in *al-Bida*ʿ (§25), Muḥammad ibn Naṣr al-Marwazī in *al-Sunna* (p. 29-30), al-Lālikā'ī in *Sharḥ Uṣūl I*ʿ*tiqād Ahl al-Sunna* (1:87 §108), al-Ṭabarānī in *al-Kabīr* (9:170), and Ibn ʿAbd al-Barr in *Jāmi*ʿ *Bayān al-*ʿ*Ilm* (2:1202 §2363), the latter with a weak chain according to al-Zuhayrī. Al-Dārimī's chain is strengthened by al-Bayhaqī's uninterrupted chain to Ibn Masʿūd from the trustworthy *Tābi*ʿ*ī* ʿĀ'idh Allah ibn ʿAbd Allah in *al-Madkhal* (p. 272).
[245] Narrated by Ibn ʿAbd al-Barr in *Jāmi*ʿ *Bayān al-*ʿ*Ilm* (2:1203 §2365) with a chain containing an unknown narrator.
[246] Narrated by Aḥmad with a weak chain because of ʿAlī ibn Zayd – although al-Tirmidhī considers him "truthful" (*ṣadūq*). Al-Zayn declared its chain fair (*ḥasan*)

- While ʿImrān ibn Ḥuṣayn was relating ḥadīths from the Prophet ﷺ, a man said to him: "O Abū Nujayd! Talk to us from the Qur'ān." Whereupon ʿImrān said to him: "You and your friends all read the Qur'ān: can you tell me about the *ṣalāt*, what it contains specifically and what its features are? Can you tell me of what consists the *zakāt* for gold? Camels? Cows? the different types of goods? No. But I witnessed it, and you were not there." Then he said: "The Messenger of Allah ﷺ imposed upon us such-and-such in the *zakāt* etc." The man said: "You have given me new life, may Allah ﷻ give you new life also!" Al-Ḥasan said: "This man did not die before he had become one of the authoritative jurists of the Muslims."[247]

- Another version states: The people were rehearsing the narrations of ḥadīth whereupon a man stood and said: "Enough of that, bring us something from the book of Allah!" ʿImrān ibn Ḥuṣayn became angry and said: "You are an idiot! Allah ﷻ mentioned *zakāt* in His Book; where then, is it mentioned that it consists in five parts out of every two hundred? Allah ﷻ mentioned *ṣalāt* in His Book; where then is it mentioned that *ẓuhr* consists of four *rakʿas*?" Then he mentioned all the other prayers. He continued: "Allah mentioned circumambulation in His Book; but where did He say that *ṭawāf* consists in seven circumambulations? And where did He say that coursing between Safa and Marwa is sevenfold? We rule according to what is in there [*i.e.* the Qur'ān], but the Sunna explains it."[248]

in the *Musnad* (15:96 §19883) on the grounds that al-Haythamī at one time declared ʿAlī ibn Zayd weak and another time fair in his narrations.

[247] Narrated from al-Ḥasan al-Baṣrī by Ibn Ḥibbān cf. Ibn Ḥajar in *Lisān al-Mīzān* (1:3) and by al-Ḥākim (1:109-110) with a sound chain. Cf. al-Suyūṭī, *Miftāḥ al-Janna* (p. 73 §131, p. 23-25 §23).

[248] Narrated by Abū Nadra by Ibn al-Mubārak in *al-Zuhd* (p. 23).

- A third version states: A man questioned the Companion ʿImrān ibn Ḥuṣayn. When the latter answered him, the man said: "Talk to us from the book of Allah and do not talk to us from other than it." ʿImrān said: "Idiot! Can you find it in the book of Allah that *ẓuhr* is four *rakʿas* in which one does not recite loud?" He went on to enumerate prayer, *zakāt*, and other than that, then said: "Do you find all these explained in the book of Allah? Rather, the book of Allah has ruled all this, and the Sunna explains it."[249]

- Similarly one of ʿImrān's students, Muṭarrif ibn ʿAbd Allah ibn al-Shikhkhīr replied: "By Allah! We never seek a substitute for the Qur'ān but only him who is more knowledgeable of the Qur'ān than we,"[250] meaning the Messenger of Allah ﷺ.

- A man asked ʿAbd Allah ibn ʿUmar: "Abū ʿAbd al-Raḥmān, we find the prayer of fear (*ṣalāt al-khawf*) and the prayer of residence (*ṣalāt al-ḥadar*) in the Qur'ān, but we do not find the prayer of travel (*ṣalāt al-safar*)." Ibn ʿUmar replied: "Cousin! Allah ﷻ sent forth Muḥammad ﷺ and we knew nothing. We only do whatever we saw him ﷺ do."[251]

- Similarly Jābir ibn ʿAbd Allah said: "The Messenger of Allah ﷺ was among us while the Qur'ān was being revealed to him and he knew its explanation. Whatever he ﷺ put into practice, we put into practice."[252]

[249] Narrated from Abū Nadra by Ibn al-Mubārak in his *Musnad* (p. 143), al-Ājurrī in *al-Sharīʿa* (p. 51), and Ibn ʿAbd al-Barr in *Jāmiʿ Bayān al-ʿIlm* (2:1192 §2348), where it is declared authentic by al-Zuhayrī.
[250] Narrated by Ibn ʿAbd al-Barr in his *Jāmiʿ* (2:1193 §2349) with a sound chain per al-Zuhayrī.
[251] A sound narration from Ibn Shihāb by Mālik, al-Nasāʾī, Ibn Mājah, and Aḥmad.
[252] Narrated from Muḥammad al-Bāqir as part of a long ḥadīth by Muslim, Abū Dāwūd, and Aḥmad.

– ʿAbd Allah ibn ʿUmar met Jābir ibn Zayd in *ṭawāf* and told him: "Abū al-Shaʿthā'! You are one of the *fuqahā'* of Baṣra. Therefore, do not give any response except with the communication of the Qur'ān (*bi-qur'ānin nāṭiqin*) or a Sunna with precedent (*sunnatin māḍiya*). If you do otherwise, you have perished and caused others to perish."[253]

– Ḥudhayfa ibn al-Yamān said: "Only three types of persons give *fatwās* to people: A man who is either an Imām or a governor, and a man who can tell the abrogating verses of the Qur'ān from the abrogated." They asked: "Who is such a man?" He said: "ʿUmar ibn al-Khaṭṭāb. Other than those three types, there are only overreaching fools."[254]

– Imām al-Shāfiʿī said: "Most of what is abrogated in the book of Allah is known only through the indications of the *Sunan* of the Messenger of Allah ﷺ."[255]

– The *Tābiʿī* Saʿīd ibn Jubayr, was narrating a ḥadīth of the Prophet ﷺ when a man said: "There is something contrary to this in the Book of Allah." Saʿīd replied: "Do not, when I narrate to you from the Messenger of Allah ﷺ, claim a contradiction with the Book of Allah. For the Messenger of Allah ﷺ was more knowledgeable of the Book of Allah than you."[256]

– Another *Tābiʿī*, Ḥassān ibn ʿAṭiyya, said: "Revelation would descend upon the Messenger of Allah ﷺ and Gibrīl ﷺ would also tell him the Sunna that expounded it."[257]

[253] Narrated from Jābir ibn Zayd by al-Dārimī.
[254] Narrated from Muḥammad ibn Sīrīn by al-Dārimī with a chain of sound narrators.
[255] Al-Shāfiʿī, *al-Risāla* (p. 222).
[256] Narrated from Yaʿlā ibn Ḥākim by al-Dārimī with a chain of sound narrators.
[257] Narrated from al-Awzāʿī by al-Dārimī, Abū Dāwūd in *al-Marāsīl* (p. 361 §18490), Muḥammad ibn Naṣr al-Marwazī in *al-Sunna* (p. 28), al-Lālikā'ī in *Sharḥ*

- Another *Tābi'ī*, Maymūn ibn Mahrān, said: "Truly this Qur'ān has been torn to tatters (*akhlaqa*) in many breasts. Therefore, learn the ḥadīths that are beside it [*i.e.*, to defend it]. Truly there are some who seek this knowledge as a commodity for worldly gain, while others learn it for self-display, and others for fame. But the best of them are those who learn it in order to obey Allah by means of it."[258] Ibn 'Abd al-Barr said: "By the words 'this Qur'ān has been torn to tatters' he means – and Allah knows best – that its interpretation has been torn to tatters except [the interpretation] conveyed in the narrations of the practicing *Salaf*. So its interpretation is limited to whatever sound ḥadīths are narrated from them and excludes what people come up with in their minds or dispute about in their opinions, in the fashion of those who follow their lusts."[259]

- The *Tābi'ī* Abū Wa'il Shaqīq ibn Salama said: "Do not sit with those who say: 'Suppose' (*ara'ayt*)." Similarly the *Tābi'ī* al-Sha'bī said: "There is no expression I hate more than 'Suppose'" and "Those that came before you perished because of 'Suppose'."[260]

- The *Tābi'ī* Ayyūb al-Sikhtiyānī said: "If you tell someone of Sunna and he then says: 'Never mind this, tell us from the Qur'ān': Know that that person is gone astray (*ḍāll*)."[261]

Uṣūl I'tiqād Ahl al-Sunna (1:83), and Ibn 'Abd al-Barr in his *Jāmi'* (2:1193 §2350) and it is a sound narration according to Ibn Ḥajar in *Fatḥ al-Bārī* (13:291) and al-Zuhayrī.

[258] Narrated by Abū Nu'aym in the *Ḥilya* (1985 ed. 4:84) and Ibn 'Abd al-Barr in *Jāmi' Bayān al-'Ilm* (2:1203 §2366) with a fair chain according to al-Zuhayrī.

[259] Ibn 'Abd al-Barr, *Jāmi' Bayān al-'Ilm* (2:1203).

[260] Narrated respectively from al-Zabarqān al-Sarrāj, Ibn Abī Khālid, and Dāwūd ibn Abī Hind by Ibn 'Abd al-Barr in *Jāmi' Bayān al-'Ilm* (2:1076-1077 §2094, §2095, and §2097) with one fair chain and two sound ones according to al-Zuhayrī.

[261] Narrated from Makhlad ibn al-Ḥusayn by al-Ḥākim in *Ma'rifat 'Ulūm al-Ḥadīth* (p. 65) and from al-Awzā'ī by al-Khaṭīb in *al-Kifāya* (Madīna ed. p. 15).

- Al-Shaʿbī said: "Those before you perished only when their paths multiplied and they diverged from the main road, leaving the transmitted reports (*al-āthār*) behind. They went astray and also misguided others."[262]

- ʿAbd Allah ibn al-Mubārak said: "Let your reliance be upon transmitted reports, and use, for personal opinion, only whatever the ḥadīth expounds to you."[263]

- One of Ḥassān ibn ʿAṭiyya's students, Imām al-Awzāʿī, similarly said: "The Book stands more in need of the Sunna than the Sunna stands in need of the Book."[264] Ibn ʿAbd al-Barr explains: "He means that the Sunna presupposes the Book and expounds its purport, and this is the meaning of the saying of the Ulema: 'The Book left room (*mawḍiʿan*) for the Sunna, and the Sunna left room for [qualified] opinion (*ra'ī*).'"[265]

- Another *Tābiʿī*, Yaḥyā ibn Abī Kathīr, said: "The Sunna adjudicates on (*qāḍiya ʿalā*) the Qur'ān, but not the Qur'ān on the Sunna." Aḥmad ibn Ḥanbal said: "I do not go so far as to say that the Sunna adjudicates on the Qur'ān, but the Sunna expounds the Book and explains it."[266]

[262] Narrated from al-Ḥasan ibn Wāṣil by Ibn ʿAbd al-Barr in *Jāmiʿ Bayān al-ʿIlm* (2:1050 §2026).

[263] Narrated from ʿAbdān ibn ʿUthmān by Ibn ʿAbd al-Barr in *Jāmiʿ Bayān al-ʿIlm* (2:1050 §2023, 2:1070 §2073) with a sound chain according to al-Zuhayrī.

[264] Narrated by Ibn ʿAbd al-Barr in his *Jāmiʿ* (2:1193 §2350) and it is sound according to al-Zuhayrī. Ibn ʿAbd al-Barr also cites it (2:1194 §2352) as narrated by al-Awzāʿī from Makḥūl.

[265] Ibn ʿAbd al-Barr, *Jāmiʿ Bayān al-ʿIlm* (2:1194).

[266] Narrated respectively from al-Awzāʿī and al-Faḍl ibn Zyad by Ibn ʿAbd al-Barr in *Jāmiʿ Bayān al-ʿIlm* (2:1194 §2353-2354).

- 'Abd al-Raḥmān ibn Mahdī said: "A man stands more in need of the Sunna than he stands in need of food and drink."[267]

- Imām Aḥmad further said: "The Sunna in our definition consists in the reports transmitted from the Messenger of Allah ﷺ, and the Sunna is the commentary (*tafsīr*) of the Qur'ān and contains its directives (*dalā'il*)."[268]

- Imām Aḥmad further said: "Allah revealed His Book to His Prophet ﷺ and made the latter the indicator (*al-dāll*) of both its outward meaning (*ẓāhiruhu*) and its hidden meaning (*bāṭinuhu*); its specific meaning (*khāṣṣuhu*) and its general meaning (*'āmmuhu*); its abrogating verses (*nāsikhuhu*) and its abrogated ones (*mansūkhuhu*); and all that the Book purports. So the Messenger of Allah ﷺ is the expounder (*al-mu'abbir*) of the Book of Allah, indicating its meanings. His Companions witnessed him in this act, the very same men whom Allah ﷻ was content to choose as his Companions and elect for him. They transmitted all this from him. Therefore, they were, of all people, the most knowledgeable of the Messenger of Allah ﷺ and of what Allah ﷻ meant by His Book, by witnessing him and watching firsthand that which the Book addressed. They were the expounders of all this after the Messenger of Allah ﷺ.

  "Thus did Jābir say: 'The Messenger of Allah ﷺ was among us while the Qur'ān was being revealed to him and he knew its explanation. Whatever he put into practice, we put into practice.'"[269]

[267] Narrated from 'Alī ibn al-Madīnī by al-Khaṭīb in *Tārīkh Baghdād* (2:187) and *al-Kifāya* (Madīna ed. p. 15).
[268] Narrated from 'Abdūs ibn Mālik al-'Aṭṭār by al-Lālikā'ī in *Sharḥ Uṣūl* (1:156). In Ibn al-Qayyim, *I'lām al-Muwaqqi'īn* (1973 ed. 2:290-291).
[269] For Jābir's ḥadīth see above, n. 252.

Here ends the text adapted from the book of our teachers' teacher, Shaykh ʿAbd al-Ghanī ʿAbd al-Khāliq al-Miṣrī, titled *Ḥujjiyyat al-Sunna*, abridged, revised, and annotated in English over a period of eight years, as faithfully as possible to this noble subject, by the sinful servant dependent on his Lord, Gibrīl Fouād Ḥaddād. Forgiveness is from the Lord and lenience from the reader for any mistake committed. May Allah send blessings and greetings upon our Master the Messenger of Allah, his Family, and all his Companions! And praise belongs to Allah the Lord of the worlds.

Ibn Ḥajar's Commentary on the Ḥadīth of *Islām*, *Īmān*, *Iḥsān*

The following chapter is a complete translation of Ibn Ḥajar's commentary on the Ḥadīth of *Islām, Īmān, Iḥsān* from *Fatḥ al-Bārī* (1959 ed.), Book of *Īmān*, ḥadīth §50. I was privileged with access to my Teacher – may Allāh bless and keep him – Mawlana al-Shaykh Muḥammad Nāẓim's original volumes of Muḥammad al-Zuhrī al-Ghamrāwī's 1896 and 1905 "Yunīniyya" editions and Aḥmad ʿAlī al-Sihāranfūrī al-Isḥāqī al-Ḥanafī's 1856 edition. The latter contains the exact same narration that Ibn Ḥajar refers to – as ascertained externally by their respective *isnād*s and, internally, by his commentary. Its *isnād* is al-Firabrī's narration through the ḥadīth Master Shaykh al-Islām ʿAbd al-Awwal ibn ʿĪsā, Abū al-Waqt al-Ṣūfī al-Sijzī al-Harawī (d. 553), taken from Ibrāhīm ibn Aḥmad al-Tanūkhī by Ibn Ḥajar who passed it on to Zakariyyā al-Anṣārī until it reached al-Sihāranfūrī through Shāh Walī Allāh al-Dihlawī and Imām ʿAbd al-Ḥayy al-Lacknawī (d. 1202). Abū al-Waqt's narration is referred to with the siglum ط in the Yunīniyya edition. Present-day editions of *Fatḥ al-Bārī* – including that used here – comprise a text of al-Bukhārī's *Ṣaḥīḥ* different from that which Ibn Ḥajar actually refers to in this ḥadīth, as shown by our remarks below (notes a-b and Section 6, par. **when a man came to him** p. 170). The Imām and ḥadīth Master Sharaf al-Dīn Abū al-Ḥusayn ʿAlī ibn Shaykh al-Islām Muḥammad ibn Aḥmad al-Hāshimī al-Yunīnī al-Baʿlabakkī al-Ḥanbalī (621-701) is famed for his meticulous transmission of al-Bukhārī's *Ṣaḥīḥ*. Al-Dhahabī accompanied him and narrated from him in Baʿlabakk and Damascus, as he related in the *Siyar* (Fikr ed. 17:120 §6086).

The Ḥadīth of *Islām, Īmān, Iḥsān* from Bukhārī's and Muslim's *Ṣaḥīḥs* with Ibn Ḥajar's Commentary from *Fatḥ al-Bārī*

The Prophet ﷺ said: "*Islām* is an outward proclamation while *Īmān* is in the heart."[270]

"*Īmān* is one of the characteristics of *islām*. Every *īmān* is *islām* but not vice-versa."

– Ibn al-Bāqillānī [271]

"Belief weakens in two ways, one bad, one good. The bad way is the weakening of certitude and the increase of doubt; the good way is the thinning of the veil, as belief can only be from behind a veil. So, the more one rises toward the station of excellence (*al-iḥsān*), which is the station of "being present and beholding" (*maqām ḥaḍrat al-shuhūd*), the more the veil of belief weakens and thins, and one's vision grows stronger."

– Al-Shaʿrānī [272]

[270] Narrated from Anas by Aḥmad, al-Bazzār, Abū Yaʿlā, and Ibn Abī Shayba with a chain of trustworthy narrators per al-Haythamī.
[271] In his *Tamhīd al-Awā'il* (p. 390).
[272] In *al-ʿUhūd al-Muḥammadiyya*, commentary on the ḥadīth: "Change the wrong with your heart, and that is the weakest belief." The Prophet ﷺ said: "Whoever of you sees wrongdoing, let him change it with his hand; if he cannot, then with his tongue; if he cannot, then with his heart, and that is the weakest belief." Narrated from Abū Saʿīd al-Khudrī by Muslim. Al-Shaʿrānī related from Shaykh Ibrāhīm al-Matbūlī: "The changing of wrongs with the tongue is specific to the Ulema, that with the hand is specific to the governors, and that with the heart is specific to the Friends of Allāh."

1. Al-Bukhārī's Chapter-Title and First Narration: Book of *Īmān*[273]

CHAPTER OF GIBRĪL'S QUESTION TO THE PROPHET ﷺ ON ĪMĀN, ISLĀM, IHSĀN, AND KNOWLEDGE OF THE FINAL HOUR, AND THE PROPHET'S ﷺ EXPOSITION TO HIM. THEN HE SAID: "GIBRĪL عليه السلام CAME TO TEACH YOU YOUR RELIGION," THEREBY MAKING THIS – ALL OF IT – THE RELIGION. HOW THE PROPHET ﷺ EXPOUNDED (*BAYYANA*) ĪMĀN TO ʿABD AL-QAYS'S DELEGATION, AND ALLĀH ALMIGHTY'S SAYING: {AND WHOSO SEEKS AS RELIGION OTHER THAN THE SURRENDER (TO ALLĀH) IT WILL NOT BE ACCEPTED FROM HIM, [AND HE WILL BE A LOSER IN THE HEREAFTER]} (3:85).

Musaddad narrated to us: Ismāʿīl ibn Ibrāhīm narrated to us: Abū Ḥayyān al-Taymī told us: From Abū Zurʿa: From Abū Hurayra who said:

> The Messenger of Allāh ﷺ was in full sight of the people one day when Gibrīl[274] came to him and said: "What is belief (*mā al-īmān*)?" The Prophet ﷺ replied: "Belief is that you believe in Allāh, His angels, His Books,[275] His encounter, His Messengers, and that you believe in the resurrection." He said: "What is submission (*mā al-islām*)?" The Prophet ﷺ replied: "Submission is that you worship Allāh without associating anything with Him, accomplish the prayer, remit the obligatory purification-tax, and fast Ramaḍān." He said: "What is excellence (*mā al-iḥsān*)?" The Prophet ﷺ replied: "That you worship Allāh as if you were seeing Him; for if you do not see Him, He certainly sees you."

---

[273] Book of *Īmān*, *Bāb* 37 (*Fatḥ al-Bārī* 1959 ed. 1:114).

[274] Sahāranfūrī has: "when a man came to him." The Yunīniyya has "Gibrīl," but indicates in the margins that "a man" is found in most narrations including Abū al-Waqt's. Both are sound transmissions as indicated by al-Yunīnī in his own marginalia. Ibn Ḥajar's commentary has: "'and a man came to him,' meaning an angel."

[275] "His Books" is missing from Sahāranfūrī and the Yunīniyya. Only one narration mentions it according to the latter.

He said: "When is the Final Hour?" The Prophet replied ﷺ: "The one who is questioned about is no more informed at all than the questioner, but I shall tell you of its preconditions (*ashrāṭihā*): when the slave girl gives birth to her master and when the destitute camelherds (*ruʿātu al-ibili al-buhmu*)/the herders of jet-black camels (*ruʿātu al-ibili al-buhami*) compete in building tall structures. [It is] among five things none knows but Allāh."[276] Then the Prophet ﷺ recited: {*Lo! Allāh! With Him is knowledge of the Hour*} (31:34), [to the end of] the verse. Then he [Gibrīl] turned around and left. Then the Prophet ﷺ said: "Bring him back!" But they could not see anything. He said: "This was Gibrīl. He came teaching the people their Religion."

Abū ʿAbd Allāh [al-Bukhārī] said: "He made this – all of it – part of belief (*jaʿala dhālika kulluhu min al-īmān*)."

2. Al-Bukhārī's Second Narration: Book of *Tafsīr*[277]

Isḥāq narrated to me: From Jarīr: From Abū Ḥayyān: From Abū Zurʿa: From Abū Hurayra ؓ:

That the Messenger of Allāh ﷺ was in full sight of the people one day when suddenly a man came to him on foot and said: "Messenger of Allāh! What is belief?" The Prophet ﷺ replied: "Belief is that you believe in Allāh, His angels, His Books, His Messengers, His encounter, and that you believe in the next resurrection." He said: "Messenger of Allāh! What is submission?" The Prophet ﷺ replied: "Submission is that you worship Allāh without associating anything with Him, accomplish the prescribed prayer, remit the obligatory purification-tax, and fast Ramaḍān." The man said: "Messenger of Allāh!

---

[276] This phrase forms an independent ḥadīth which al-ʿIrāqī discussed in *Ṭarḥ al-Tathrīb* (8:253-255).
[277] Book of *Tafsīr*, ḥadīth §4777 (*Fatḥ al-Bārī* 1959 ed. 8:514).

What is excellence?" The Prophet ﷺ replied: "Excellence is that you worship Allāh as if you were seeing Him; for if you do not see Him, He certainly sees you." The man said: "Messenger of Allāh! When is the Final Hour?" The Prophet ﷺ replied: "The one who is questioned about it is no more informed at all than the questioner. I shall tell you about its preconditions (*ashrātihā*): when a woman gives birth to her mistress – that is one of its preconditions. And when the barefoot and naked are the top leaders of the people – that is one of its preconditions. [It is] among five things none knows but Allāh." Then the Prophet ﷺ recited: {*Lo! Allāh! With Him is knowledge of the Hour. He sends down the rain and knows that which is in the wombs*} (31:34), [to the end of] the verse. The man went away. Then the Prophet ﷺ said: "Bring [him] back to me!" But they could not see anything. He said: "This was Gibrīl. He came to teach the people their Religion."

3. Muslim's First Set of Narrations[278]

a. Abū Khaythama Zuhayr ibn Ḥarb narrated to me: Wakīʿ narrated to us: From Kahmas: From ʿAbd Allāh ibn Burayda: From Yaḥyā ibn Yaʿmar;

b. Also, ʿUbayd Allāh ibn Muʿādh al-ʿAnbārī narrated to us – and this is his version: My father narrated to us: Kahmas narrated to us: From Abū Burayda: From Yaḥyā ibn Yaʿmar who said:

The first one to speak about *al-qadar* [in heresy] in al-Baṣra was Maʿbad al-Juhanī.[279] I went on the major or minor pilgrimage together with Ḥumayd ibn ʿAbd al-Raḥmān al-Ḥimyarī. We said: Would that we met one of the Companions of the Messenger of Allāh ﷺ, so that we could ask him about what those

[278] Muslim, *Ṣaḥīḥ*, Book of *Īmān*, ḥadīth §8 [ʿAbd al-Bāqī ed. 1:36-38].
[279] Maʿbad al-Juhanī (d. 80) was "the first who spoke about *qadar* in al-Baṣra." Narrated from Yaḥyā ibn Yaʿmar by Muslim, al-Tirmidhī, and Abū Dāwūd.

people say concerning foreordained destiny (*al-qadar*). We were happy to meet ʿAbd Allāh ibn ʿUmar ibn al-Khaṭṭāb ﷺ as he was entering the mosque. We went by his side, I and my friend, one on his right, one on his left. I assumed that my friend would entrust me to speak, so I said: "Abū ʿAbd al-Raḥmān! Some people have appeared before us who recite the Qur'ān and pursue obscure and difficult questions." He [Yaḥyā ibn Yaʿmar] then spoke about them and said that they claimed there was no such thing as foreordained destiny, and that everything was spontaneous and unplanned.

Ibn ʿUmar said: "If you meet those people, tell them that I am clear of them and they are clear of me. By the One by Whom ʿAbd Allāh ibn ʿUmar now swears! If anyone of them had the weight of Mount Uhud in gold and spent it [for the sake of Allāh], Allāh would not accept it until he believes in fore-ordained destiny." Then he said:

My father ʿUmar ibn al-Khaṭṭāb narrated to me: "As we sat with the Messenger of Allāh ﷺ one day, all of a sudden a man came up to us. He wore exceedingly white clothes. His hair was jet-black. There was no sign of travel on his person. None of us knew him. He went to sit near the Prophet ﷺ, leaning his knees against his and placing his hands on his thighs. He said: 'O Muḥammad! tell me about submission (*islām*).' The Messenger of Allāh ﷺ said: 'Submission is that you bear witness that there is no God but Allāh and that Muḥammad is the Messenger of Allāh; accomplish the prayer; remit the purification-tax; fast during Ramadan; and make the pilgrimage to the House if you are able to go there.' The man said: 'You have spoken the truth!' We wondered at him: how could he be asking the Prophet ﷺ and confirming him at the same time? Then he said: 'Tell me about belief (*īmān*).' The Prophet said ﷺ: 'Belief is that you believe in Allāh, His angels, His books, His Messengers, and the Last Day; and to believe in foreordained destiny, for better or worse.' The man said: 'You have spoken the truth! Now tell me about excellence (*iḥsān*).' The Prophet replied ﷺ: 'Excellence is that you worship Allāh as if you were seeing Him; for if you do not see Him, He certainly sees you.' The man said: 'Now tell me about the Final Hour.' The Prophet replied ﷺ: 'The one who is questioned about it is no more informed at all than the questioner.' He said: 'Then tell me about its portent (*amāratihā*).' He replied: 'The slave girl shall give birth to her mistress and you shall see the barefoot, naked, indigent (*al-ʿāla*) shepherds compete in building tall structures.' Then he left and a long time passed. Later the Prophet ﷺ said to me: 'O ʿUmar, do you know who the questioner was?' I said: 'Allāh and His Messenger know best.' He said: 'That questioner was none other than Gibrīl. He came to you to teach you your Religion.'"

c. Muḥammad ibn ʿUbayd al-Ghubarī, Abū Kāmil al-Jahdarī, and Aḥmad ibn ʿAbda narrated to me and said: Ḥammād ibn Zayd narrated to us: From Maṭar al-Warrāq: From ʿAbd Allāh ibn Burayda: From Yaḥyā ibn Yaʿmar who said: "When Maʿbad began saying what he said in the matter of foreordained destiny we condemned it, so I went on pilgrimage with Ḥumayd ibn ʿAbd al-Raḥmān al-Ḥimyarī." Then they related the rest of the narration in the same sense as that of Kahmas and the same chain of transmission, with some words added and some subtracted here and there.

d. Muḥammad ibn Ḥātim narrated to me: Yaḥyā ibn Saʿīd al-Qaṭṭān narrated to us: ʿUthmān ibn Ghiyāth narrated to us: ʿAbd Allāh ibn Burayda narrated to us: From Yaḥyā ibn Yaʿmar and Ḥumayd ibn ʿAbd al-Raḥmān who both said: "We met ʿAbd Allāh ibn ʿUmar and mentioned foreordained destiny and what they were saying about it." The rest of the ḥadīth was recounted in similar fashion to their narration from ʿUmar ☸ from the Prophet ﷺ, with something added and something missing.

e. Ḥajjāj ibn al-Shāʿir narrated to me: Yūnus ibn Muḥammad narrated to us: al-Muʿtamir [ibn Sulaymān ibn Ṭarkhān] narrated to us: From his father: From Yaḥyā ibn Yaʿmar: From Ibn ʿUmar: From ʿUmar: From the Prophet ﷺ, a similar version.

4. Muslim's Second Set of Narrations[280]

a. Abū Bakr ibn Abī Shayba and Zuhayr ibn Ḥarb narrated to us: Both from [Ismāʿīl ibn Ibrāhīm ibn Miqsam al-Asadī al-Baṣrī] Ibn ʿUlayya: Zuhayr [ibn Ḥarb, Abū Khaythama] said: Ismāʿīl ibn Ibrāhīm narrated to us: From Abū Ḥayyān: From Abū Zurʿa ibn ʿAmr ibn Jarīr: From Abū Hurayra who said:

> The Messenger of Allāh ﷺ was in full sight of the people one day when a man came to him and said: "Messenger of Allāh! What is belief?" The Prophet ﷺ replied: "That you believe in Allāh, His angels, His Books, His encounter, His Messengers, and that you believe in the next resurrection." He said: "Messenger of Allāh! What is submission?" The Prophet ﷺ replied: "Submission is that you worship Allāh without associating anything with Him, accomplish the prescribed prayer, remit the obligatory purification-tax, and fast Ramaḍān." The man said: "Messenger of Allāh! What is excellence?" The Prophet ﷺ replied: "That you worship Allāh as if you were seeing Him; for even if you do not see Him, He certainly sees you." The man said: "Messenger of Allāh! When is the Final Hour?" The Prophet replied ﷺ: "The one who is questioned about it is no more informed at all than the questioner. However, I shall tell you about its preconditions (*ashrāṭihā*). When the slave girl

[280] Muslim, *Ṣaḥīḥ*, Book of *Īmān*, ḥadīth §9 [ʿAbd al-Bāqī ed. 1:39].

> gives birth to her master – that is one of its preconditions. And when the naked and barefoot are the top leaders of the people – that is one of its preconditions. And when the shepherds compete in building tall structures – that is one of its preconditions. [It is] among five things none knows but Allāh." Then he recited: {*Lo! Allāh! With Him is knowledge of the Hour. He sends down the rain and knows that which is in the wombs. No soul knows what it will earn tomorrow, and no soul knows in what land it will die. Lo! Allāh is Knower, Aware*} (31:34). Then the man turned around and left. Then the Prophet ﷺ said: "Bring that man back to me!" They went to bring him back but saw nothing. The Messenger of Allāh ﷺ said: "This was Gibrīl. He came to teach the people their Religion."

b. Muḥammad ibn ʿAbd Allāh ibn Numayr narrated to us: Muḥammad ibn Bishr narrated to us: Abū Ḥayyān al-Taymī narrated to us the same ḥadīth with this chain, except that his version has: "If the slave girl gives birth to her husband, meaning the concubines."[281]

5. Muslim's Third Narration[282]

Zuhayr ibn Ḥarb narrated to me: Jarīr narrated to us: From ʿUmāra – this is Ibn al-Qaʿqāʿ – from Abū Zurʿa: From Abū Hurayra who said:

> The Messenger of Allāh ﷺ said: "Ask me questions!" (*salūnī*) but the people were too intimidated to ask. Then a man came and sat by his knees and said: "Messenger of Allāh! What is submission?" The Prophet ﷺ replied: "When you associate nothing

[281] Due to the accession of the sons of slave-girls to the throne and their subsequent purchase of concubines among whom, unbeknown to them, are their own mothers.

[282] Muslim, *Ṣaḥīḥ*, Book of *Īmān*, ḥadīth §10 [ʿAbd al-Bāqī ed. 1:40].

with Allāh, accomplish the prayer, remit the obligatory purification-tax, and fast Ramaḍān." The man said: "You have spoken the truth! Messenger of Allāh! What is belief?" The Prophet ﷺ replied: "That you believe in Allāh, His angels, His Books, His encounter, His Messengers, and that you believe in the resurrection, and that you believe in foreordained destiny completely." He said: "You have spoken the truth! Messenger of Allāh! What is excellence?" The Prophet ﷺ replied: "That you fear Allāh as if you were seeing Him; for if you see Him not, He certainly sees you." The man said: "You have spoken the truth! Messenger of Allāh! When shall the Final Hour rise?" The Prophet replied ﷺ: "The one who is questioned about it is no more informed at all than the questioner. However, I shall tell you about its preconditions (*ashrāṭihā*). When a woman gives birth to her master – that is one of its preconditions. And when you see that the barefoot and naked, the deaf and dumb are the kings of the earth – that is one of its preconditions. And when you see the cattleherds compete in building tall structures – that is one of its preconditions. [It is] among five things of the Unseen that none knows but Allāh." Then he recited: {*Lo! Allāh! With Him is knowledge of the Hour. He sends down the rain and knows that which is in the wombs. No soul knows what it will earn tomorrow, and no soul knows in what land it will die. Lo! Allāh is Knower, Aware*} (31:34). The man rose and left. Then the Prophet ﷺ said: "Bring that man back!" They looked for him but did not find him. The Messenger of Allāh ﷺ said: "This was Gibrīl. He wanted you to learn despite your not asking."

6. Ibn Ḥajar's Commentary on al-Bukhārī's Chapter-Title and First Narration as well as the Variants[283]

Chapter of Gibrīl's question on *īmān*, *islām*, etc. We have seen that al-Bukhārī considers *īmān* and *islām* expressions of a single meaning.[284] Since Gibrīl's question about *īmān* and *islām* and the answer he received appeared, of necessity, to differentiate between them – the former signifying truthfulness in specific matters, the latter, the display of specific matters – he [al-Bukhārī] attempted to cancel out the distinction by interpreting it figuratively (*bil-ta'wīl*), according to his preconception.

and the [**Prophet's** ﷺ] **declaration** [**to Gibrīl**] That is: "together with the declaration that conviction (*al-iʿtiqād*), together with deeds, makes up Religion."

and how he expounded [***īmān*** **to ʿAbd al-Qays's delegation**] That is: "together with what he expounded to the delegation to the effect that *īmān* is *islām* itself," since he explained *īmān* in the narration to the delegation in the same terms in which he explained *islām* here.[285]

[283] *Fatḥ al-Bārī* (1959 ed. 1:115-125 §50).

[284] Cf. *Fatḥ al-Bārī*, beginning of the book of *Īmān* (1959 ed. 1:45-55) and chapter previous to this (1:111). Al-Zaʿfarānī reported that al-Shāfiʿī in his commentary on the ḥadīth "Free her, for she is a believer," said: "Islām is *īmān*." In al-Bayhaqī, *Manāqib al-Shāfiʿī* (1:395). On the contextual difference of the two terms, Ibn Khafīf said in his *ʿAqīda* (§70 and §77): "Belief *(al-īmān)* is different from submission *(al-islām)*.... Every believer *(mu'min)* is a Muslim, but not every Muslim is a believer." Ibn al-Bāqillānī said in *Tamhīd al-Awā'il* (p. 390): "*Īmān* is one of the characteristics *(khiṣāl)* of *islām*. Every *īmān* is *islām* but not vice-versa." See also Ibn ʿAbd al-Salām's short treatise, *Maʿnā al-Īmān wal-Islām*, *Ṭabaqāt al-Ḥanābila* (1:25, 2:14, 2:302) and Shaykh Muḥyī al-Dīn Ibn ʿArabī's epistle *al-Mu'min wal-Muslim wal-Muḥsin*.

[285] The Prophet ﷺ imposed upon the delegation of the tribe of ʿAbd al-Qays belief in Allāh alone and said: "Do you know what belief in Allāh Alone is?" They replied: "Allāh and His Messenger know best." He said: "The testimony that there is no god but Allāh, and that Muḥammad is the Messenger of Allāh; the accomplish-

and the Saying of Allāh That is: "together with the verse's indication that *islām* itself is the Religion, and the indication of Abū Sufyān's relation that *īmān* is the Religion.[286] All this requires that *islām* and *īmān* be one and the same." This is the gist of al-Bukhārī's words.

[The Difference Between *Islām* and *Īmān*]

Abū ʿAwāna al-Isfarāyīnī reports in his *Ṣaḥīḥ* from al-Shāfiʿī's companion, al-Muzanī, the categorical opinion that they are the expressions of a single meaning, and that he heard it from al-Shāfiʿī; Abū ʿAwāna also reports from Imām Aḥmad the catego-

ment of prayer; the remittance of the purification-tax; the fasting of Ramaḍan; and that you give one fifth of the spoils." Narrated from Ibn ʿAbbās as part of a longer ḥadīth by al-Bukhārī in the book of *Īmān* (§53, *Fatḥ al-Bārī* 1959 ed.) and Muslim.

[286] There are two relations of Abū Sufyān to that effect, both narrated by al-Bukhārī at the end of the first book of his *Ṣaḥīḥ* (Book of the Beginning of Revelation):

(1) "Heraclius summoned the Roman authorities to his villa *(daskara)* in Ḥims, ordered the gates locked, then looked at them and said: 'O Romans! Do you want to reap success, do what is right, and ensure that your empire will endure? Follow this Prophet.' At this, they fled like wild asses and made for the gates, but found them locked. When Heraclius saw their loathing of what he had proposed to them he despaired of their belief *(īmān)*. 'Bring them back to me,' he ordered; then he addressed them again: 'I said this just now only in order to test the strength of your attachment to your religion *(dīn)*, of which I am satisfied.' At this they prostrated to him and they were happy again. That was the last we heard of Heraclius." Narrated as part of a longer ḥadīth by al-Bukhārī and Muslim.

(2) Heraclius asked me [Abū Sufyān] about the Prophet's ﷺ followers: "Are their numbers increasing or decreasing?" I said they are increasing. He said: "Does any of them recant out of discontent with his religion after entering it?" I said no [...] Then Heraclius said to the translator: "Say to him [Abū Sufyān]: "I asked you whether their numbers were increasing or decreasing and you said the former; and indeed such is the case with belief *(īmān)* until it is complete. I asked you if any of them reneged out of discontent with their religion *(dīn)* after entering it and you said no; and indeed such is belief *(īmān)* when its elation *(bashāsha)* pervades the heart." Narrated both as part of a longer ḥadīth by al-Bukhārī and Muslim, and as an independent ḥadīth by al-Bukhārī.

rical opinion that they are two different meanings.[287] Each position has mutually contradictory proofs. Al-Khaṭṭābī said: "Two great Imāms have compiled texts on this question with much evidence supporting each position, and they hold opposite opinions.[288] The truth is that there is a general understanding and a

[287] Al-Shāfi'ī, Aḥmad, and the Ash'arī School – contrary to Abū Ḥanīfa and Mālik – prefer that one add *inshā' Allāh* to the affirmation "I am a believer." "If a man is asked: 'Are you a *mu'min*?' Let him say: 'I am a *mu'min*, if Allāh wills.' Or let him say: 'I hope that I am a *mu'min*.' Or: 'I believe in Allāh, His angels, His Books, and His Messengers.'" Narrated as a saying of Imām Aḥmad from al-Iṣṭakhrī by Ibn Abī Ya'lā in *Ṭabaqāt al-Ḥanābila* (1:25). Abū Bakr al-Marwazī said: "Abū 'Abd Allāh [Aḥmad ibn Ḥanbal] was asked: 'Should we say that we are *mu'minūn*?' He replied: 'No, but we should say that we are *muslimūn*.'" Ibid. (2:14). Abū Muḥammad Rizq Allāh al-Tamīmī: "He [Aḥmad] used to say: '*Īmān* is definitely other than *islām*.'" Ibid. (2:302). Al-Qushayrī in *al-Risāla* (p. 35) narrates that Abū al-'Abbās al-Sayyārī said: "His bestowal is of two kinds: Generosity *(karāma)* and entrapment *(istidrāj)*. Whatever He causes to abide in you is Generosity. Whatever He removes from you is entrapment. Therefore say: 'I am a Believer if Allāh wills' *(anā mu'minun in shā' Allāh)*." This is the Shāfi'ī, Ash'arī, and Ḥanbalī position. As for Ḥanafīs and Mālikīs they allow it. Sīdī Muṣṭafā Baṣīr said to this author: "One may say he is a real believer on the evidence of the verse {*Those are they who are in truth believers*} (8:4) for possessing five traits: their hearts tremble at the mention of Allāh; His signs increase them in faith; they rely on Him; they pray; and they spend of what Allāh has granted them. And Mālik used to say – Allāh have mercy on him: 'I am a believer, and praise belongs to Allāh.'" Cf. al-Qāḍī 'Iyāḍ, *Tartīb al-Madārik* (2:42). See also al-Haytamī's commentary on the ḥadīth of Islām and *Īmān* in his *Al-Tabyīn fī Sharḥ al-Arba'īn* (Cairo: 'Īsā al-Ḥalabī, n.d.). Ibn al-Subkī mentioned as one of the proofs of the Ash'arī position the ḥadīth of the Prophet ﷺ that "A man assuredly does the deeds of the people of Paradise as far as the people can see but he is in fact one of the people of Hellfire; and another man assuredly does the deeds of the people of Hellfire as far as the people can see but he is in fact one of the people of Paradise." Narrated from Sahl ibn Sa'd al-Sā'idī by al-Bukhārī and Muslim. Ibn al-Subkī said in *Ṭabaqāt al-Shāfi'iyya al-Kubrā* (4:39): "The addition *as far as the people can see* there is of huge import, immense benefit [as a proof] for Ash'arīs, and greatly useful for *Ahl al-Sunna wal-Jamā'a* in relation to the question of 'I am a *mu'min* if Allāh wills.' Let whoever can understand what its signals, understand." See, on the other hand, the ḥadīth of Ḥāritha cf. our *Sunna Notes I* (p. 150), "This morning I am a real believer."

[288] See also Ibn Rajab's discussion in the beginning of his *Jāmi' al-'Ulūm wal-*

particular understanding for each of the two. Every *mu'min* is a Muslim, but not every Muslim is a *mu'min*." This is the gist of what he said. It presupposes that *islām* is not applied, as a word, to belief and performance together, as opposed to *īmān*, which supposedly applies to both of them. This is refuted by the saying of Allāh: {*And I have chosen for you as religion Islām*} (5:3) for *Islām* entails both performance and belief, since an unbelieving performer does not have an acceptable religion.[289] This is the argument used by al-Muzanī and Abū Muḥammad al-Baghawī.

Al-Baghawī said concerning the ḥadīth of Gibrīl: "The Prophet ﷺ used *islām* here as a word for visible performance of deeds, and *īmān* as a word for the hidden aspect of belief. This is not because performance is not part of *īmān*, nor because confirmation (*al-taṣdīq*) is not part of *islām*, but only as the itemization of a unified whole whose heading is the Religion (*al-dīn*). This is why the Prophet ﷺ said: 'He came to teach you your religion,' and Allāh ﷻ said: {*And I have chosen for you as religion Islām), (And whoso seeks as religion other than the Surrender (to Allāh) it will not be accepted from him*} (3:85). For religion does not deserve Divine pleasure and acceptance except if confirmation is part of it." This is the end of al-Baghawī's words.

[The Complementariness of *Islām* and *Īmān*]

What emerges from the sum of the proof-texts is that *islām* and *īmān* each have a proper legal sense (*ḥaqīqa shar'iyya*) as well as

Ḥikam; al-Ṭabbā''s edition of Ibn 'Abd al-Salām's *Ma'nā al-Īmān wal-Islām*; and Shaykh Muḥyī al-Dīn Ibn 'Arabī's epistle *al-Mu'min wal-Muslim wal-Muḥsin.*

[289] Al-Khaṭṭābī is correct in that he is paraphrasing the Qur'ān, {*Say: You believe not, but rather say 'We submit' for īmān has not yet penetrated your hearts*} (49:14) and is confirmed by the ḥadīth of the Prophet ﷺ from Anas in Aḥmad, "*Islām* is proclaimed while *īmān* is in the heart" cited by Ibn Kathīr in his *Tafsīr* in explanation of the verse {*but Allāh has endeared the faith* (*al-īmān*) *to you and has beautified it in your heart*} (49:7) nor is it necessarily true that al-Khaṭṭābī's statement presupposes what Ibn Ḥajar said.

a proper lexical sense (*ḥaqīqa lughawiyya*). However, each term presupposes the other to complete its own meaning (*kullun minhumā mustalzimun lil-ākhar bi-maʿnā al-takmīl*). For just as the performer of an action is not a perfect *muslim* unless he believes, so is the believer not a perfect *mu'min* unless he performs. Whenever the word *īmān* is used in the place of *islām* or vice-versa, and whenever one is used in the sense of both, it is a metaphorical usage (*ʿalā sabīl al-majāz*). The actual sense becomes clear through the context. If they occur together in the course of a question, they are construed in the literal sense; if they do not occur together or if it is not in the course of a question, then they may be construed either literally or metaphorically depending on whatever is mentioned along with them.

Al-Ismāʿīlī said that the above explanation was that of *Ahl al-Sunna wal-Jamāʿa*: "They said that the meaning of *īmān* and *islām* differs only when they are mentioned together. If one is mentioned alone, the other enters into its definition." Likewise, what Muḥammad ibn Naṣr related – and Ibn ʿAbd al-Barr followed him – saying that the majority equated between the two regardless of what is mentioned in the ḥadīth of ʿAbd al-Qays, and what al-Lālikā'ī and Ibn al-Simʿānī said to the effect that *Ahl al-Sunna wal-Jamāʿa* differentiated between the two on the basis of the content of the ḥadīth of Gibrīl. Allāh is the Grantor of all success.

and knowledge of the Hour This [specifying of the word "knowledge"] is al-Bukhārī's explanation of the meaning of Gibrīl's words in the question: "When is the Hour?" That is: "When is the Final Hour going to be known?" and, of course, what is implicit is: "When is the timing of the Final Hour going to be known?

and the announcement of the Prophet ﷺ. The words are in the genitive form [in Arabic] because they are in conjunction with "knowledge" which is itself in the genitive as it is in construct [with "Chapter"]. If it is asked that since the Prophet ﷺ did not announce the timing of the Final Hour, how could al-Bukhārī speak of the Prophet's ﷺ announcement to that effect? The answer is that the meaning of "declaration" here is "what addresses most of what the question is raising." Al-Bukhārī therefore used the word in an absolute sense, as the status that applies to most of a thing is the same as that which applies to all of it. Or else al-Bukhārī represented the status of the Final Hour as being exclusively in Allāh's knowledge, a declaration of the Prophet ﷺ in itself.

Ismāʿīl ibn Ibrāhīm narrated to us: This is al-Baṣrī, known as Ibn ʿUlayya, who said:

Abū Ḥayyān al-Tamīmī told us: Al-Bukhārī also cites him in the commentary of Sūrat Luqmān, as per the ḥadīth of Jarīr ibn ʿAbd al-Ḥamīd from the same Abū Ḥayyān. Muslim related the ḥadīth through another chain, also from Jarīr but through ʿUmāra ibn al-Qaʿqāʿ, while Abū Dāwūd and al-Nasāʾī also narrated it as per Jarīr's ḥadīth from Abū Farwa [ʿUrwa ibn al-Ḥārith al-Ḥamdānī], all three groups (al-Bukhārī, Muslim, Abū Dāwūd and al-Nasāʾī):

from Abū Zurʿa [ibn ʿAmr ibn Jarīr al-Bajalī], from Abū Hurayra ؓ: Abū Farwa adds "and from Abū Dharr also," and conveys all of his narration from both of them [Abū Hurayra and Abū Dharr]. The latter version contains additional benefits to which we shall refer later, *in shāʾ Allāh*. I did not see this ḥadīth narrated from Abū Hurayra except through this same Abū Zurʿa ibn ʿAmr ibn Jarīr, and al-Bukhārī did not document it except through Abū Ḥayyān from Abū Zurʿa.

[Muslim's Chains and the Variance of Their Texts]

Muslim outsets (*akhraja*)[290] the ḥadīth from the account of ʿUmar ibn al-Khaṭṭāb. That transmission also contains additional benefits. Al-Bukhārī did not cite it because there are some discrepancies in it according to some of its narrators. Its best known chain is the narration of Kahmas ibn al-Ḥasan: From ʿAbd Allāh ibn Burayda: From Yaḥyā ibn Yaʿmar: From ʿAbd Allāh ibn ʿUmar: From his father ʿUmar ibn al-Khaṭṭāb, which a large group of ḥadīth Masters have related. Following it up[291] is Maṭar al-Warrāq's narration from ʿAbd Allāh ibn Burayda; then Sulaymān [ibn Ṭarkhān] al-Taymī's from Yaḥyā ibn Yaʿmar. Likewise, ʿUthmān ibn Ghiyāth related it from ʿAbd Allāh ibn Burayda but said: From Yaḥyā ibn Yaʿmar and Ḥumayd ibn ʿAbd al-Raḥmān together: From ibn ʿUmar: From ʿUmar. Now Ḥumayd is mentioned in the best-known chain, but not as a narrator.[292]

Muslim forwarded these chains but did not convey from them other than the content (*matn*) of the first chain, assigning the remaining chains to that text. There is, however, much variance among them, and we shall point out some of it.

Maṭar's narration: Abū ʿAwāna in his *Ṣaḥīḥ* and others.

Sulaymān al-Taymī's narration: Ibn Khuzayma in his *Ṣaḥīḥ* and others.

ʿUthmān ibn Ghiyāth's narration: Aḥmad in his *Musnad*.

[290] The *makhraj* or outset of a chain or ḥadīth consists in its top two to five or more links from the Prophet ﷺ to one of the early (pre-fifth century) compilers.
[291] *I.e.* in descending order of strength in sister-chains.
[292] See above, §3. a-d ("I [Yaḥyā ibn Yaʿmar] went on pilgrimage with Ḥumayd ibn ʿAbd al-Raḥmān al-Ḥimyarī...").

At variance with the above three transmissions is that of Sulaymān ibn Burayda – ʿAbd Allāh's brother – who narrated it from Yaḥyā ibn Yaʿmar from ʿAbd Allāh ibn ʿUmar who said: "While we were with the Prophet ﷺ," thus classing it among Ibn ʿUmar's own narrations, not as his relation from his father. This chain is cited by Aḥmad also.

Also Abū Nuʿaym in the *Ḥilya* through ʿAṭāʾ al-Khurāsānī from Yaḥyā ibn Yaʿmar.

Also al-Ṭabarānī through ʿAṭāʾ ibn Abī Rabāḥ from ʿAbd Allāh ibn ʿUmar.

It is also narrated from Anas by al-Bazzār and al-Bukhārī in *Khalq Afʿāl al-ʿIbād* with a fair chain.

Also Abū ʿAwāna in his *Ṣaḥīḥ* from Jarīr [ibn ʿAbd Allāh] al-Bajalī, but his chain contains Khālid ibn Yazīd – this is al-ʿUmarī – who is unfit for the level of *ṣaḥīḥ*.

It is also narrated from Ibn ʿAbbās and Abū ʿĀmir al-Ashʿarī by Aḥmad with fair chains.

We shall mention the benefits of all these chains, *in shāʾ Allāh*, in the course of discussing the ḥadīth of this chapter. I only gathered the chains of this ḥadīth here and traced them to their compilers in order to facilitate future reference to them and avoid extended repetitions. Allāh grants all success.

The Prophet ﷺ was in full sight (*bārizan*) of the people one day It means that he was making himself seen to them, neither keeping himself away from them nor occupied with anyone in particular. "Exposure" (*burūz*) is visibility. The narration of Abū Farwa which we mentioned begins thus: "The Prophet ﷺ used to sit among his companions and if a stranger came he would not know who, among the people, was the Prophet ﷺ. So, we asked him if we could provide him a seat that would make him recognizable by visiting strangers, and we made him a clay seat on which he would sit."

Al-Qurṭubī[293] inferred from the above the ruling that it is desirable (*mustaḥabb*) for the person of knowledge to sit in a place special to him, and that it be raised if need be, for the necessity of teaching and the like.

when a man came to him[294] That is, an angel in the form of a man. Al-Bukhārī has in the Book of *Tafsīr*: "suddenly a man came to him on foot."[295] Abū Farwa has: "We were all sitting with him when suddenly a man came, the most handsome, most fragrant of people, and his clothes looked immaculate." Muslim – through Kahmas from ʿUmar's account – has:

> As we sat with the Messenger of Allāh ﷺ one day, lo and behold! a man came up to us. He wore exceedingly white clothes. His hair was jet-black. (Ibn Ḥibbān's narration here states: "His beard was jet-black.") There was no sign of travel on his person. Yet none of us knew him. He went to sit near the Prophet ﷺ, leaning his knees against his, and placing his hands on his thighs.

One narration through Sulaymān al-Taymī states: "There was no appearance of travel on him whatsoever, yet he was not from our parts. He stepped forward until he kneeled down in front of the

[293] This Qurṭubī is not the famous Qur'ānic commentator Muḥammad ibn Aḥmad ibn Abī Bakr ibn Farḥ, Abū ʿAbd Allāh al-Anṣārī al-Khazrajī al-Andalusī (d. 671) but his teacher the Imām Abū al-ʿAbbās Aḥmad ibn ʿUmar ibn Ibrāhīm al-Anṣārī al-Mālikī al-Iskandarī (d. 656) who authored a famed commentary of his own abridgment of *Ṣaḥīḥ Muslim* and whom Abū ʿAbd Allāh quotes most frequently in his *Tafsīr*.
[294] See p. 152 and note 274.
[295] See above, §2.

Prophet ﷺ as we do in the prayer, and he placed his hand on the Prophet's ﷺ knees."

Ibn ʿAbbās's ḥadīth has the same and so does Abū ʿĀmir al-Ashʿarī, with the wording "and he placed his hand on the Prophet's ﷺ knees." This narration tells us that the pronoun "his" in the phrase "on his thighs" refers to the Prophet ﷺ. That is al-Baghawī's and Ismāʿīl al-Taymī's categorical opinion on this version, while al-Ṭībī[296] merely favors it after discussing it, because he considers it the logical thread of the account. Al-Nawawī understands it categorically to the contrary – al-Tūribishtī agrees with him – on the grounds that Gibrīl sat like the student in front of his teacher. Even if this is evident from the context, nevertheless, the placing of his hands on the Prophet's ﷺ thighs serves to compel [the Prophet ﷺ] to listen to him.

There is in this detail an illustration of the requirements of modesty and tolerance for the one who is questioned by an apparently rude questioner. It appears that Gibrīl wanted by that to stress the commonality of his character so as to incline people to believe that he came from the coarsest of the Bedouins. Hence, he stepped over the people until he reached the Prophet ﷺ, as was said before. That is the reason the Companions considered his behavior strange,[297] and also because he was not from the region and came on foot, yet there was no trace of travel on him.

[296] The Ashʿarī Imām Sharaf al-Dīn al-Ḥusayn ibn Muḥammad ibn ʿAbd Allāh al-Ṭībī (d. 743) studied under Shaykh al-Islām Taqī al-Dīn al-Subkī and authored *al-Tibyān fil-Maʿānī wal-Bayān* as well as commentaries on *Maṣābīḥ al-Sunna*, the *Mishkāt*, and the *Kashshāf*. Ibn Ḥajar writes: "He was modest, excellent in his doctrine and tough in his rebuttal of philosophers and innovators. His love for Allāh and His Prophet ﷺ was very strong. He was a Sign of Allāh in the extraction of particulars from the Qur'ān and the *Sunan*." He quotes from him in abundance in *Fatḥ al-Bārī* as does al-Suyūṭī in his works.

[297] This can be gathered by the use of the expression "suddenly" in the accounts.

How did ʿUmar know that none of them knew him? He could have relied either on his viewpoint or on the explicit statement of those who were present at the time. The latter is more probable since it was mentioned to be the case in ʿUthmān ibn Ghiyāth's narration which has: "The folk looked at one another and said: We do not know this man!"

[**The Reason This Ḥadīth Took Place**]

Muslim reports, in ʿUmāra ibn al-Qaʿqāʿ's narration, the reason this ḥadīth occurred, since he begins it thus: "The Prophet ﷺ said: 'Ask me questions!' But they were too intimidated to ask him. Then a man came..."[298] Ibn Mandah's narration through Yazīd ibn Zurayʿ from Kahmas has: "As the Prophet ﷺ was giving a sermon (*yakhṭub*), a man came to him," as if his order to interrogate him was part of the *khuṭba*. It would seem that the man's arrival was during that sermon. Either it coincided with its end, or the Prophet ﷺ had mentioned that part while sitting and the narrator expressed it as a *khuṭba*.

and said: ["What is *īmān*?"] Al-Bukhārī here adds, in the version of the Book of *Tafsīr*: "Messenger of Allāh! What is *īmān*?" How could he initiate a question before giving *salām*? Perhaps to stress the commonality of his character, or to show that to give *salām* is not an obligation, unless he actually gave *salām* and the relater did not report it. The third scenario is the most authoritative since it is firmly established by Abū Farwa's relation which bears, after the words "as if his clothes were immaculate," the words

> and he gave *salām* from the edge of the carpet (*al-bisāṭ*), saying, "*al-Salāmu ʿalayka yā Muḥammad*!" and the Prophet ﷺ greeted him back. He said: "May I approach (*adnū*), O Muḥammad?" He replied: "Approach (*udnuh*)!" He kept asking again and

[298] See above, §5.

again, "May I approach?" and the Prophet ﷺ kept answering him, "Approach!"

There is something similar in ʿAṭā's relation from Ibn ʿUmar but ʿAṭā' has "*al-Salāmu ʿalayka yā Rasūl Allāh*!" whereas Maṭar al-Warrāq's relation has, "He said: *Yā Rasūl Allāh*, may I approach you? He replied: Approach," without mention of greetings.

So the versions differ as to whether Gibrīl said to the Prophet ﷺ "*yā Muḥammad*" or "*yā Rasūl Allāh*" in addition to whether he greeted him first.

As for the greeting, those who mention it take precedence over those who omit it. As for Gibrīl's omission of the greeting and his uttering "*yā Muḥammad*," al-Qurṭubī[299] said he wanted to show common manners, and so he did what the Bedouins do.

The two versions are reconciled if we consider that Gibrīl began by calling the Prophet ﷺ by name in the latter sense, then he addressed him with the words "O Messenger of Allāh." Al-Qurṭubī has: "He said, '*al-Salāmu ʿalaykum yā Rasūl Allāh*' and from this was inferred the desirability, for the newcomer, to give a collective greeting first, then specify whomever he wishes to specify after that." The versions I myself have seen, however, show that the only greeting given was an individual greeting, namely, "*al-Salāmu ʿalayka yā Rasūl Allāh*."

"What is *īmān*?" It was said the question about belief (*īmān*) came first because it is the foundation, then submission (*islām*) came second because it shows the veracity of the claim [of īmān], and excellence (*iḥsān*) comes third because it hangs upon the first two. In the relation of ʿUmāra ibn al-Qaʿqāʿ, he begins with *islām* because it relates to outward matters, and puts *īmān* second because it relates to inward matters. Al-Ṭībī preferred the latter because of its progressive development. There is no doubt that

[299] See note 293.

the original account is uniform and that those who related it differed in its conveyance by not keeping to a single sequence. This is proven by Maṭar al-Warrāq's relation, which has *islām* first, *iḥsān* second, and *īmān* third. So the truth is that the event is a single event and that the interchange in sequence is the doing of the narrators; and Allāh knows best.

He said: "*Īmān* is that you believe in Allāh, etc." The answer indicates that the Prophet ﷺ understood that he asked him about the correlatives (*muta'alliqāt*) of belief and not the meaning of the word itself, otherwise the answer would have been that belief is confirmation (*taṣdīq*).

Al-Ṭībī said: "The reply suggests tautology (*takrār*) but this is not the case, for his statement 'that you believe in Allāh' implies the meaning 'that you confess His existence,' hence the indirect transitive structure (*an tu'mina billāh*) which means 'that you confirm together with your acknowledgment of such-and-such.'" However, mere confirmation is also phrased with the indirect transitive, so there is no need to affirm such implication.

Al-Kirmānī (d. 668)[300] said: "The reply is not a tautological definition. Rather, what is meant by the thing defined (*al-maḥdūd, i.e. al-īmān*) is the legal dimension of belief, and what is meant by the definition (*al-ḥadd, i.e. an tu'mina billāh* etc.) is the lexical dimension.

In my view, he only repeated the word "belief" in order to address its importance and emphasize its matter. Of the same order is the saying of Allāh Most High {*Say: He will revive them Who produced them at the first*} (36:79) in reply to the question {*Who will revive these bones when they have rotted away?*} (36:78). In other words, belief is a constituent part of his statement "that you

[300] He authored *al-Kawākib al-Darārī fī Sharḥ Ṣaḥīḥ al-Bukhārī* in 25 volumes. Ibn Ḥajar relies on him heavily in the *Fatḥ*.

believe," as if he had said that belief in the legal sense is a specific form of confirmation.[301] Otherwise, the answer would have been that belief is confirmation and that belief in Allāh is confirmation of His existence and His being described with the Attributes of perfection, utterly exalted beyond any attribute of defect.

"and His angels" Belief in the angels is the confirmation that they exist and that they are just as Allāh Most High described them, {*honored servants*} (21:26). The angels come before the Books and the Messengers to reflect to factual sequence of events, since Allāh Most High has sent the angel with the Book to the Messenger. There is no support whatsoever in this sequence for someone who would rank the angel above the Messenger.

"and His Books" This is mentioned here by al-Aṣīlī[302] [alone] in the book of *Tafsīr*, but the narrators mention it one and all in the version of the Book of *Tafsīr*.

Belief in the Books of Allāh is the confirmation that they are indeed the Speech of Allāh and that what they contain is the truth.

"and His encounter" Thus in the present version, in between the Books and the Messengers, and so in Muslim through both chains, but not in the remainder of the narrations.

[301] The specific form of confirmation is to formally declare belief in Allāh, His angels, His Books, His Messengers, etc.

[302] The Qayrawānī Andalusian ḥadīth Master, qāḍī of Saraquṣṭa, and Mālikī jurist Abū Muḥammad 'Abd Allāh ibn Ibrāhīm ibn Muḥammad al-Aṣīlī (d. 392) was a student of Abū Bakr al-Shāfi'ī, Wahb ibn Maysara, Abū Ṭāhir al-Dhuhlī, and Abū Bakr al-Ājurrī. He taught al-Dāraquṭnī, who said "I never saw his like," and authored *al-Āthār wal-Dalā'il fil-Khilāf* and *Rubā'iyyat al-Asānīd lil-Bukhārī* ("al-Bukhārī's Four-Link Narrations") cf. *Ṭabaqāt al-Fuqahā'*, *Ṭabaqāt al-Ḥuffāẓ*, *Mu'jam al-Buldān*, *Shadharāt al-Dhahab*, *Kashf al-Ẓunūn*, etc. Ibn Ḥajar narrates the *Ṣaḥīḥ* through him, from Abū Zayd Muḥammad ibn Aḥmad al-Marwazī, from al-Bukhārī cf. his *Mu'jam al-Mufahras* (§1), as well as al-Tirmidhī's *'Ilal* (§584). He quotes him over 350 times in the *Fatḥ* but al-Kattānī overlooks him both in *al-Risāla al-Mustaṭrafa* and *Fahras al-Fahāris*!

It was said to be a repetition since it is inherent in the belief in resurrection, but the truth is that it is not a repetition since it was said that what is meant by resurrection is the rising from the graves, while what is meant by the meeting is what follows it.

It was also said that the meeting occurs with the passing away from the lower world followed by the resurrection. This is indicated by Maṭar al-Warraq's narration which has: "and death and resurrection after death." The ḥadīths of Anas and Ibn ʿAbbās have the same.

It was also said that what is meant by the meeting is the vision of Allāh. Al-Khaṭṭābī mentions it but al-Nawawī critiqued this on the grounds that no one may positively assert that he shall see Allāh Most High. For such sight is reserved for those who die believers, whereas one does not know for certain what one's end will be. How then can that [certainty] be one of the conditions of belief? It was replied that what is meant is belief in the reality of such sight in and of itself. This is one of the strong proof-texts for *Ahl al-Sunna* in affirming the vision of Allāh Most High in the hereafter, since it was listed among the foundations of belief.

"and His Messengers" (*wa-rusulih*). Al-Aṣīlī has "and in His Messengers" (*wa-bi-rusulih*) while the ḥadīths of Anas and Ibn ʿAbbās have "and the angels and the Book and the Prophets" (*wal-malā'ikati wal-kitābi wal-nabiyyīn*). Both phrasings are found in the Qur'ān, in Sūrat al-Baqara.[303] However, the expression "Prophets" includes the Messengers but not vice versa.

Belief in the Messengers is the confirmation that they are truthful in all that they related from Allāh Most High. The outlining (*ijmāl*) of the angels, the Books, and the Messengers indicates the sufficiency of that itemization in one's belief in them without

[303] Respectively {*Each one believes in Allāh and His angels and His scriptures and His Messengers*} (2:285) and {*but righteous is he who believes in Allāh and the Last Day and the angels and the Scripture and the Prophets*} (2:177).

elaboration, except inasmuch as one of them is named, in which case specific belief in him or it by name becomes obligatory.

This order of sequence conforms with the verse {*the Messenger believes in what has revealed unto him from his Lord*} (2:285). The aptness of such a sequence – although "and" does not determine sequence – or, rather, the meaning of precedence is that goodness and mercy come from Allāh, and of His greatest mercy He has revealed His Books unto His slaves; those who receive it among them are the Prophets, and the intermediary between Allāh and the Prophets are the angels.

"and that you believe in the Resurrection" The *Tafsīr* version has "the final Resurrection" while Muslim in ʿUmar's narration has "and the Last Day."

As for "the final Resurrection," it was said the mention of "last" is for emphasis, as in "yesterday which has passed" (*amsa al-dhāhib*). Another explanation is that the resurrection takes place twice: first, in being brought out into the lower world from non-existence into existence, or from the wombs of mothers, after having been a drop then a clot; second, in being resurrected from the bellies of the graves into the eternal abode.

"The Last Day" was thus named because it is the last of the days of the lower world or the last of the finite periods of time. The meaning of belief in it is the confirmation of what shall befall in it, such as the Reckoning, the Balance, Paradise, and Hellfire. These four are explicitly mentioned after the Resurrection in the narration of Sulaymān al-Taymī and also in the ḥadīth of Ibn ʿAbbās.

A Note of Benefit

Al-Isma'īlī in his *Mustakhraj* added at this point: "and that you believe in the foreordained Decree (*al-qadar*). This is also in Abū Farwa's narration and that of Muslim from 'Umāra ibn al-Qa'qā'. The later adds the word "entirely" (*kullih*) for emphasis. The narration of Kahmas and Sulaymān al-Taymī has "and that you believe in the foreordained Decree, both its good and its evil" (*khayrihi wa-sharrih*). This is also found in the ḥadīth of Ibn 'Abbās and the narration of 'Aṭā' from Ibn 'Umar with the addition "and its sweet and its bitter, [all] from Allāh." It is as if the wisdom of reiterating the words "and that you believe" (*wa-tu'mina*) at the mention of the Resurrection is to signal that it is another kind of article of faith, because it is experienced later, whereas whatever came before is already at hand, and also to stress the Resurrection for its own sake in view of its denial by the disbelievers. This is the reason for its frequent mention in the Qur'ān. The same wisdom dictates the repetition of "and that you believe" at the mention of the foreordained Decree, as if to allude to the differences of opinion concerning it. Hence, it is accentuated through the reiteration of "you believe," then it is resolved with the appositions "its good and its evil, its sweet and its bitter." Finally, it is emphasized even more by his saying "as coming from Allāh" in the last narration.

The word *qadar* is a verbal noun or substantive (*maṣdar*). You say "I measured or measure the thing" (*qadartu al-shay'*, *uqdiruhu*, *aqdaruhu*) "by its measurement" (*qadr*, *qadar*), when thoroughly assessing its extent. It means that Allāh Most High knows the extent of all things and their timing before they are brought into existence, then He brings into existence whatever He knew would exist in the first place. Thus, every new creation originates (*ṣādir*) in His Knowledge, His Power, and His Will.

This is known in the Religion through categorical and incontrovertible proofs. Such was the belief of the Predecessors among the Companions and the elite of the Successors until the innovation pertaining to *qadar* emerged toward the end of the time of the Companions. Muslim chronicled it through Kahmas, from Ibn Burayda, from Yaḥyā ibn Ya'mar who said: "The first one to speak about *qadar* in al-Baṣra was Ma'bad al-Juhanī, so I departed with Ḥumayd al-Ḥimyarī," then he mentioned their meeting with 'Abd Allāh ibn 'Umar, how he questioned him about that, the latter's disavowal of whoever made such claims, and his affirmation that Allāh would not accept the deeds of whoever did not believe in *qadar*.

The heresiographers related from many Qadarī groups their denial of the Creator's foreknowledge of any of the actions of creatures prior to their enacting them. He only knows of these actions, they say, after they come to be. Al-Qurṭubī[304] and others said: "This school is now extinct and we know of none among later Muslims to whom such a position is attributed. Today's *Qadariyya* agree one and all that Allāh knows the actions of creatures before their occurrence. They contradict the Predecessors only in claiming that the actions of creatures are actually ordained by them and performed by them independently. Although this school is also falsehood, nevertheless, it is less deviant than the first one."

As for its later representatives, they deny the linkage (*ta'alluq*) of the Divine Will to the acts of creatures lest they link up what is pre-existent with what is originated. Their position is defeated from the start as indicated by al-Shāfi'ī's statement: "If a Qadarī concedes the Divine foreknowledge, he is refuted."[305] He means

[304] See note 293.

[305] This concise statement shows al-Shāfi'ī's mastery of the science of *kalām*. See on this the chapter devoted to him in our *Four Imāms and Their Schools* as well as the chapter on Imām Aḥmad, Allāh be well-pleased with them.

that he is immediately asked: "Can something exist contrary to what is in the Divine knowledge?" If he say no, he conforms to the position of *Ahl al-Sunna*; if he says yes, he attributes ignorance [to Allāh], exalted is He far beyond that!

A Warning

The context suggests that belief is attributed only to someone who confirms (*ṣaddaqa*) all that precedes, whereas the jurists are content to attribute belief to whoever believes in Allāh and His Messenger. There is no difference between the two positions: by "belief in the Messenger of Allāh" is meant belief in the Messenger's existence and what he brought from his Lord; thus, all the foregoing enters into this definition, and Allāh knows best.

[**"Submission (*al-islām*) is**] **that you worship Allāh,"** Al-Nawawī said: "'Worship' here could mean the knowledge of Allāh (*maʿrifat Allāh*), so that its coordination with prayer (*ṣalāt*) and the rest is to make it part of *islām*. It is also possible that what is meant by 'worship' is obedience in absolute terms, as a heading which regroups all the religious duties. In the second sense, the coordination of prayer and so forth with it is like coordinating the particular to the general."

In my opinion, the first alternative is far-fetched because knowledge of Allāh is among the concerns of belief while submission consists of verbal and physical acts. The wording of Umar's narration here is, "that you bear witness that there is no God but Allāh and that Muḥammad is the Messenger of Allāh." This wording indicates that what is meant by "worship" in the ḥadīth under study is the utterance of the two testimonies. This shows that the second alternative must be rejected also.

When the narrator expressed [the sense of] worship, he needed to clarify it by adding "and that you associate nothing with Him." He needed no such clarification in ʿUmar's version because it included it by necessity.

If it is said that the question was general and the answer specific – he asked what *islām* was, and the reply was "to worship or testify, etc.;" what *īmān* was, and the reply was "to believe, etc.;" what *iḥsān* was, "to worship [as if you were seeing], etc." – the answer is: it is a subtle point, namely, the difference between the verbal noun [*islām, īmān, iḥsān*] and the conjunction "that" (*an*) followed by a verb [the noun clause "that you + verb"]. For the conjunction and the verb "that you do" point to something future, whereas the verbal noun is timeless.

Nevertheless, some of the narrators did express [the replies] here as verbal nouns. ʿUthmān ibn Ghiyāth's narration has: "He said, 'the testimony that there is no God but Allāh.'" Likewise, Anas's narration.

The fact that the questioner is addressed with the singular of the second person does not mean that the reply concerns him exclusively. Rather, the reply is meant to teach all the listeners the proper ruling concerning them and all those who, like them, are legally responsible. This is made plain in the end by the phrase "[he came] to teach the people their Religion."

The question arises: why was pilgrimage not mentioned? Someone said it may have not been a categorical obligation at the time, but this is disproved by Ibn Mandah's narration in *al-Īmān* with his chain of transmission per Muslim's criterion, through Sulaymān at Taymī, as narrated by ʿUmar and beginning with the words: "Toward the end of the Prophet's ﷺ life a man came to him [...]"[306] then he cited the narration in full. "The end of the

[306] Narrated by Ibn Mandah in *al-Īmān* (1:144-145) and Abū Nuʿaym in *al-Musnad al-Mustakhraj ʿalā Ṣaḥīḥ Muslim* (1:102 §83).

Prophet's life" may mean that the event took place after the Farewell Pilgrimage, since that was his last trip, shortly after which, less than three months later, he passed away. It is as if the event described came after all the rulings of the religion had been revealed, to establish and confirm, in a single sitting, all the matters of the religion which the Prophet ﷺ had declared seperately, so that they would be established as canon (*li-tanḍabiṭ*). Also inferred from this is the permissibility, for one who already knows the answer, to ask the learned for the benefit of the listener.

As for the Pilgrimage it is definitely mentioned, but some of the transmitters have either overlooked it or forgotten it. This is proven by the discrepancies among them in mentioning certain acts and omitting others. For example:

- In Kahmas's narration, we have "and that you perform pilgrimage to the House if you are able to find a way." The same is found in Anas's ḥadīth.
- In ʿAṭā' al-Khurāsānī's narration, there is no mention of the fast.
- Abū ʿĀmir's ḥadīth stops after listing prayer and the poor-due.
- Ibn ʿAbbās's ḥadīth adds nothing to the two testimonies.
- Sulaymān al-Taymī mentions everything in his narration and, after mentioning "and that you perform pilgrimage," even adds "and the lesser Pilgrimage, and that you wash in case of major impurity, and make your ablution perfect."
- Finally, Maṭar al-Warrāq has in his narration: "'And that you establish the prayer and pay the poor-due,' then he mentioned the bonds (*ʿurā*) of Islām."[307]

It is clear from all that we mentioned that some narrators rendered with precision what others did not.

[307] Narrated by Abū ʿAwāna in his *Musnad* (4:194).

"establish the prayer," Muslim added "prescribed" (*al-maktūba*), that is, compulsory (*al-mafrūḍa*). This expression is only for stylistic beauty since the same term was used in relation to the poor-due, and also in keeping with the saying of Allāh Almighty: {*The Prayer is enjoined on the Believers at stated times*} (4:103).

"and fast Ramaḍān." This clause was used as proof that one may say "Ramaḍān" without having to say "the month of." This question will be discussed in the Book of Fasting, Allāh willing.

"Excellence (*iḥsān*) [is that you worship Allāh as if you were seeing Him]." *Iḥsān* is a verbal noun (*maṣdar*). You say, "He has excelled (*aḥsana*), he excels (*yuḥsinu*) with excellence (*iḥsānan*)." The verb is used absolutely or transitively. You say: "You have excelled in this" (*aḥsanta kadhā*) to mean that you did it thoroughly; and "you have excelled toward so-and-so" (*aḥsanta ilā fulān*) to mean you brought him benefit. We are concerned here with the first meaning, since the purport is thorough worship. The second meaning can also be borne in mind since a sincere worshipper, for example, excels toward himself because of his sincerity. Excellence in worship consists in sincerity in worship, humility and awe, full attention from the moment one enters worship, and contemplation of the One Who is worshipped.

He referred to two states in his reply, the highest being that the witnessing of *al-Ḥaqq* in the heart overwhelms one to the point that one seems to see Him with one's very eyes. Hence he said: "as if you were seeing Him," that is, as if you were seeing Him seeing you. The second state is that one recollects (*yastaḥḍir*) that *al-Ḥaqq* is watching him and sees everything he does, as in the words: "He certainly sees you."

These two states are brought to fruition by knowledge of Allāh and fear of Him. The expression used in the narration of ʿUmāra ibn al-Qaʿqāʿ is, "that you fear (*takhshā*) Allāh as if you were seeing Him" and also in Anas's narration.

Al-Nawawī said:[308]

> Its meaning is that you would observe the aforementioned manners only when you see Allāh and He sees you, not because you see Him, but because He sees you; and He always sees you, therefore, excel in your worship of Him even if you do not see Him. The gist of the narration, therefore, is that even if you do not see Allāh, persevere in excellent worship because He is seeing you.
>
> This passage of the ḥadīth is a sublime principle among the principles of the Religion and a paramount foundation for Muslims. It is the reliance of the most truthful ones, the focus of wayfarers, the treasure of knowers, and the rule of the righteous. It is one of the pithy expressions encompassing the widest meanings (*jawāmiʿ al-kalim*) which were given to the Prophet ﷺ. The people of spiritual realization (*ahl al-taḥqīq*) have exhorted us to sit in the company of the righteous and recommended that such be devoid of even the slightest blemish out of respect for them and shame before them. What about one whom Allāh never ceases watching, privately and publicly?

Al-Qāḍī ʿIyāḍ and others spoke about this principle before him. More on this in the commentary on Sūrat Luqmān, Allāh willing.

A Warning

The context of the narration indicates that there is no visual sight of Allāh in this world. (The Prophet's ﷺ sight [of Allāh ﷻ] is supported by another proof-text.) Muslim explicitly mentioned in his narration from Abū Umāma that the Prophet ﷺ said: "And you must know that you cannot see your Lord until you die."

[308] Perhaps in his commentary on al-Bukhārī.

[**Critique of Ibn ʿArabī's Interpretation**]

One of the extreme Sufis (*baʿḍu ghulāt al-ṣūfiyya*) ventured to interpret the ḥadīth without knowledge, saying:

> It contains an allusion (*ishāra*) to the station of self-effacement and extinction (*maqām al-maḥwi wal-fanā'*) and the gist of it is, "if you are not" (*fa-in lam takun*), that is, if you become nothing and extinguish your self to the point that you no longer exist, then "at that time you shall see Him" (*fa-innaka ḥīna'idhin tarāh*).[309]

Whoever said this erred carelessly due to ignorance of the Arabic language, for if the meaning was as he claimed, it would not say *tarāh* but *tarah* without a long *alif* but a short vowel, the verb being – according to that interpretation – the apodosis of a conditional sentence. Yet, in none of the different versions of this narration does the verb occur with a shortened vowel. Whosoever claims that it is kept long even if the verb is in the apocopate genitive form (*majzūm*) contrary to the norm, we reply there is no need here for such an exception.[310] Moreover, if the inter-

[309] Cf. Shaykh Muḥyī al-Dīn Ibn ʿArabī toward the end of his very brief *Kitāb al-Fanā' fil-Mushāhada*, trans. Stephen Hirtenstein and Layla Shamash, *Journal of the Muhyiddin Ibn ʿArabi Society* IX (1991) p. 1-17.

[310] Al-Shaykh al-Akbar undoubtedly possessed mastery of the language and it would have been fair to mention the continuation of his text at this point, since it pre-empts the grammatical objections through a typically Akbarī argument: "It is established that the *alif* in '*tarāhu*' is for the sake of His manifestation, because of the vision's dependence upon it. If he had eliminated it and said '*tarahu*,' the vision would not occur because the pronoun *ha* in the word '*tarāhu*' denotes the one who is absent, and the absent one cannot be seen, and if the *alif* had been eliminated, then He would be seen without vision, and that cannot occur. So that is why the *alif* was mentioned. As for the wisdom of maintaining the pronoun *ha*, the meaning given is that the words 'if you are not, you see Him' point to the fact that while you see by the existence of the *alif*, you do not say 'I have encompassed,' for He, the Most High, is too majestic and glorious to be encompassed, and such a thing would not be possible. So the *ha* exists as the pronoun of that which is ab-

pretation he claimed were sound, then the words, "verily He sees you" would make no sense, as they would remain suspended without connection to what precedes them.[311]

Another weakness in this interpretation is that the narration of Kahmas has the wording "For, if you see Him not, verily He sees you" (*fa-innaka in lā tarāh, fa-innahu yarāk*) – likewise that of Sulaymān al-Taymī – where negation unequivocally governs the seeing, not the being, contrary to what the contrived interpretation claims. Also, Abū Farwa's narration has "for if you see Him not, verily He sees you" (*fa-in lam tarah, fa-innahu yarāk*); and there is something similar in the ḥadīths of Anas and Ibn ʿAbbās. All of this invalidates the foregoing interpretation, and Allāh knows best.

A Note of Benefit

Muslim adds, in ʿUmāra ibn al-Qaʿqāʿ's narration, the questioner's comment "what you say is true" (*ṣadaqta*) following each of the three answers. Abū Farwa added in his narration: "When we heard the man saying 'what you say is true,' we disapproved of him," while Kahmas has: "We wondered about him – first he questioned the Prophet ﷺ then he confirmed him?" and Maṭar: "Look at him questioning him and then confirming him!" Anas has in his ḥadīth: "Look at him questioning him and confirming him as if he knew more than him!" In Sulaymān ibn Burayda's

sent from you during the vision of the Reality of the Truth *(ḥaqīqat al-ḥaqq)*, which acts like a witness for you of the impossibility of encompassment." *Kitāb al-Fanā'* (p. 14).

[311] Because the text of the ḥadīth has been altered to read "for if you are not, you will see Him" *(fa-in lam takun, tarah)* by which the sense is complete, instead of the original "for if you are not seeing Him" *(fa-in lam takun tarāh)*, which requires a conclusion. Nevertheless, the Sufi interpretation simply adds the remaining clause as a new proposition, thus: "For if you are not, you will see Him, and He sees you in any case."

narration: "The people said, 'We never saw a man such as this (*mā ra'aynā rajulan mithla hādhā*),[312] he seemed to be teaching the Prophet ﷺ, telling him: *ṣadaqt, ṣadaqt*!"

Al-Qurṭubī[313] said: "They were astonished at this only because what the Prophet ﷺ brought could not be known except by himself, whereas this questioner was not recognized as someone who had met the Prophet ﷺ or heard from him. Yet, there he was, asking questions like one who is already an expert in what he is asking, since he was informing the Prophet ﷺ that what he said was true. Hence, they were astonished at this as they never expected it." And Allāh knows best.

"When is the Final Hour?" Meaning: "When will the Final Hour begin?" as was explicitly stated in ʿUmāra ibn al-Qaʿqāʿ's narration. The definite article "the" points to a specific sense (*lil-ʿahd*) and what is meant is the Day of Resurrection.

"The one who is questioned about it is no" (*mā al-mas'ūlū ʿanhā*): "*mā*" is a negating particle here. Abū Farwa's narration adds: "He bent his head and did not answer him. Then the man repeated his question but, again, he did not answer him, and so three times. Then he raised his head and said: 'The one who is questioned is no…'"

"more informed at all" (*bi-aʿlama*): the letter "*ba*" here is redundant (*zā'ida*) for the emphasis of negation. Although this [reply] implies parity of knowledge (*al-tasāwī fīl-ʿilm*), what is actually meant is parity in the [specific] knowledge that Allāh Almighty has reserved the knowledge of the Final Hour for Himself, since

[312] I could not trace the wording *rajulan mithla hādhā*. Ibn Burayda's narration in Aḥmad's *Musnad* actually has, "We never saw a man treat the Messenger of Allāh with greater reverence than this man" *(mā ra'aynā rajulan ashadda tawqīran li-Rasūl Allāh min hādhā)*.

[313] See note 293.

the Prophet ﷺ follows up by saying: "There are five things known only to Allāh." This phrasing reoccurs toward the end of our discussion of this ḥadīth when he says "I knew no more at all about it than any one of you," where parity in being uninformed about it is also meant. Likewise, in the ḥadīth of Ibn ʿAbbās, he said: "Glory to Allāh! There are five things from the unseen which no one knows except He." Then he recited the verse [{*Lo! Allah! With Him is knowledge of the Hour. He sends down the rain, and knows that which is in the wombs. No soul knows what it will earn tomorrow, and no soul knows in what land it will die. Lo! Allah is Knower, Aware*} (31:34)]."[314]

Al-Nawawī said: "From this [reply] it can be inferred that when a scholar is asked about what he does not know, he declares that he does not know it without it detracting from his rank. On the contrary, such an answer shows his Godfearing scrupulousness.

Al-Qurṭubī[315] said: " The purpose of this question is to stop the listeners once and for all from asking about the time of the Final Hour. They had asked about it a great deal, as shown in many verses and ḥadīths. When the answer was obtained in its aforementioned form, they finally despaired of knowing it [in advance]. The previous questions, on the other hand, were intended to elicit answers for the listeners to learn and act upon. Those answers highlighted the distinction between what can be known and what cannot."

"than the questioner;" Rather than saying, "I know nothing more about it than you do," he used an expression with universal implications to draw in all listeners. That is, every possible person to be questioned and every possible questioner are also meant.

[314] Narrated from Ibn ʿAbbās by Aḥmad and al-Bazzār cf. al-Haythamī (1:39).
[315] See note 293.

A Note of Benefit

This question-and-answer exchange took place between ʿĪsā ibn Maryam and Gibrīl, upon them peace, but ʿĪsā was the questioner and Gibrīl the one being questioned. Al-Ḥumaydī said in his Nawādir: "Sufyān narrated to us: Mālik ibn Mighwal narrated to us, from Ismāʿīl ibn Rajā', from al-Shaʿbī: "ʿĪsā ibn Maryam asked Gibrīl about the Final Hour. Gibrīl's wings shuddered and he said: 'The one who is questioned about it is no more informed at all than the questioner.'"[316]

"and I shall inform you about its preconditions." In the [Book of] *Tafsīr*, [al-Bukhārī has] "but I shall tell you." Abū Farwa's narration has "but it has signs (*ʿalāmāt*) by which it can be known" and Kahmas's "He said: 'Then inform me of its portent (*amāra*),'" whereupon he informed him.

At this point it is not clear whether he initiated the mention of the portents or whether the questioner asked him about the portents first. This [difficulty] is resolved if we consider that he first said, "and I shall inform you," then the questioner replied, "do inform me." The wording in Sulaymān al-Taymī's narration supports this: "But if you wish, I shall appraise you of its preconditions. He said: Yes (*ajal*)." Something similar is found in the ḥadīth of Ibn ʿAbbās, with the addition: "Do tell me (*fa-ḥaddithnī*)."

The detailing of these preconditions (*ashrāṭ*) was given in the other narration where it is made clear that they are the signs [of the Day of Judgment]. The variances in the narrations suggest that "telling" (*taḥdīth*), "informing" (*ikhbār*), and "appraising" (*inbā'*) are all one and the same meaning. The ḥadīth scholars differentiated between them only in ḥadīth nomenclature.[317]

[316] Narrated by Ibn al-Mubārak in *al-Zuhd* (p. 77 §228).
[317] *Ḥaddathanā* means the students heard the narration(s) from the mouth of the

Al-Qurṭubī[318] said: "The signs of the Final Hour are two types: what is customary and what is not. The type mentioned here is the first type. As for extraordinary things such as the rising of the sun from where it sets, the customary signs precede them closely or accompany them. So, what is meant here is the first kind of signs." And Allāh knows best.

"When she gives birth" The term "when" impresses upon us the certainty of the event. The clause comes as an elucidation (*bayānan*) for the preconditions of the Final Hour with regard to the meaning, namely, [that the preconditions of the Day of Judgment are] the slave girl's giving birth and the over-reaching of shepherds.

It may be asked why the conditions are in the plural, which requires three items at least according to the most correct usage, while only two are mentioned. Al-Kirmānī answered: "The term for the few can be borrowed to denote the many and vice versa." Another answer is that the differentiation between the few and the many is only for indefinites (*al-nakirāt*), not specifics (*al-ma'ārif*), or because the word "condition" (*sharṭ*) does not have a plural of multitude. All these answers leave something to be desired.

The most satisfying answer is that there are in fact three preconditions being mentiond but some of the narrators mentioned only two, such as here (birth-giving and over-reaching) and in

shaykh, *akhbaranā* means (in late usage) the students read the narration(s) back to the shaykh, and *anba'anā* means (in late usage) the narrations are narrated by permission of the shaykh without audition. In early usage they are all mostly one and the same meaning. See the "ways of conveyance" *(ṭuruq al-adā')* in Ibn Hajar, *Nuzhat al-Naẓar* ('Itr 3rd ed. p. 123-125), al-Qārī, *Sharḥ Sharḥ Nukhbat al-Fikar* (Tamīm ed. p. 661-673), 'Itr, *Manhaj al-Naqd fī 'Ulūm al-Ḥadīth* (3rd ed. p. 224-225), etc.

[318] See note 293.

the Book of *Tafsīr* (birth-giving and the usurpation of leadership by the unshod rabble). However, the narration of Muḥammad ibn Bishr whose chain Muslim narrated – and whose wording Ibn Khuzayma cited – from Abū Ḥayyān [al-Tamīmī] mentions three things. So does the narration in al-Ismāʿīlī's *Mustakhraj* through Ibn ʿUlayya. Thus did ʿUmāra ibn al-Qaʿqāʿ also mention it and, likewise, ʿUmar's ḥadīth, while Kahmas's narration mentions only the birth-giving and the over-reaching, as does ʿUthmān ibn Ghiyāth's. Sulaymān al-Taymī's narration mentions three items and ʿAṭā' al-Khurāsānī agrees with him. The same three items are also mentioned in the ḥadīth of Ibn ʿAbbās and that of Abū ʿĀmir.

"When the slave girl gives birth to her master" The Book of *Tafsīr* has: "her mistress" in the feminine as does ʿUmar's narration. Muḥammad ibn Bishr has the same but adds "meaning, concubines (*al-sarārī*)." ʿUmāra ibn al-Qaʿqāʿ's narration has: "When you see a woman giving birth to her master" while Abū Farwa has something similar. ʿUthmān ibn Ghiyāth's narration has: "When slave girls give birth to their masters" in the plural. "Master" (*al-rabb*) means the owner (*al-mālik*) or lord (*al-sayyid*).

The scholars have long differed over the meaning of this passage. Ibn al-Tīn said there were seven different interpretations of it and he mentioned them but they overlap. I have summed them up without overlapping and reduced them to four views:

I. Al-Khaṭṭābī said it means the expansion of Islām and the Muslims' empowerment over heathendom (*bilād al-shirk*) and capture of its offsprings for use as concubines. Then, when a man who owned a slave girl had a child by her, her child was like her lord because it was her master's child. Al-Nawawī and others said this was the opinion of the majority of the scholars. Nevertheless, the claim that this is what is meant here leaves something to be desired. Taking possession of slave women existed at the time of this saying, while empowerment over the lands of disbelievers, the capture of their offspring, and their use as concubines took place in the early stages of Islām for the most part. The context has to allude to something unprecedented that will happen near the rising of the Final Hour.

Wakīʿ [ibn al-Jarrāḥ] explained it even more specifically – with regard to Ibn Mājah's narration – as the non-Arabs giving birth to the Arabs. Someone said it signifies a slave giving birth to a king, the mother becoming part of his subjects and the king being master over them. This is what Ibrāhīm al-Ḥarbī said. He defended it by pointing out that the early leaders generally stayed away from the beds of slave women and, instead, vied in marrying free women; then the matter was reversed, especially in the Abbāsid period. However, the narration of "her mistress" (*rabbatahā*) in the feminine does nothing to help this explanation.

Someone said that the term "master" for the slave's child is figurative. Because her child is the cause of her emancipation after the master's death, that was called her master.

Someone put it in the specific context that when captives abound, the child might initially be among the captives in his childhood, then he is emancipated, grows up, and becomes a leader or even a king. Then his mother might be made captive later and he becomes in a position to buy her, either knowing her to be his mother or unaware of the fact, and he uses her as his servant or for his sexual gratification (*aw yattakhidhuhā mawṭū'atan*), or he might free her and marry her. Indeed, one of the narrations has: "When the slave woman gives birth to her husband (*baʿlahā*)." This is in Muslim, and it is understood according to that scenario. However, it was also said that the term *baʿl* here meant the owner, which is more indicated so that the narrations are all in agreement.

II. It means that the masters will sell the mothers of their children and this kind of practice will abound. Owners will keep buying and selling the mother until her own son buys her unawares. In this sense, the precondition of the Hour which is meant is pervasive ignorance of the prohibition against selling child-bearing slaves (*ummahāt al-awlād*), or contempt for the rule of law.

If it is objected that the fact there is disagreement over the issue invalidates such an interpretation, since the one who holds that it is permitted is neither ignorant nor contemptuous of the Law, my answer is that it is possible to interpret it in a sense agreed upon by all sides, for example selling the mother while she is pregnant, which is unanimously forbidden.

III. In the same vein as the preceding view, al-Nawawī said: "The scenario of the child buying his or her mother is not exclusive to the case of child-bearing slaves. It is conceivable, also, for a slave woman to give birth to a free child from other than her master through intercourse in which there is doubt as to the identity of the father, or for her to give birth to a bond child from another slave either through marriage or adultery. In both cases she is then sold in valid fashion. Then she roams from hand to hand until her own son or daughter buys her." This view is not impaired by Muḥammad ibn Bishr's interpretation that what is meant is concubines, since there is no proof that it is exclusively so.

IV. It means that there will be much filial impiety (*'uqūq al-awlād*) and a son will treat his mother the way a master treats his slave, demeaning her through insults, blows, and servitude. Hence, he is called her lord metaphorically; or, if "master" (*rabb*) here means "tutor" (*murabbī*), then literally. The latter is the soundest explanation in my opinion because it encompasses the most meanings and because the context indicates that what is meant is a strange state of affairs in addition to general depravity.

To sum up, the passage indicates that the rising of the Final Hour will become imminent when matters are reversed, such that the cub will become the tutor and the underling will become lofty. This concurs with his statement regarding the next sign, "the rabble shall become the kings of the earth."

Two Warnings

Al-Nawawī said: "This passage neither constitutes a proof that it is forbidden to sell child-bearing slaves nor does it consitute a proof that it is permissible. Whoever held either view was mistaken, for taking something as a sign for something else indicates neither prohibition nor permissibility." Second, what reconciles the use of "lord" (*rabb*) in the sense of master and owner in this ḥadīth with [its prohibition in] another authentic ḥadīth, "Let none of you say 'feed your lord' (*aṭʿim rabbak*), 'cleanse your Lord' (*waḍḍiʾ rabbak*), or 'bring your lord something to drink' (*isqi rabbak*), but let him say 'my master and patron' (*sayyidī wa-mawlāy*)," is that the wording here serves the purpose of exaggeration, or that "lord" here signifies "tutor," while in the ḥadīth of prohibition it means "master." Another two possibilities are that the prohibition post-dates the ḥadīth under study or that it applies to other than the Messenger of Allāh ﷺ.

"and when the destitute camelherds (*ruʿātu al-ibili al-buhmu*) / the herders of jet-black camels (*ruʿātu al-ibili al-buhami*) compete [in building tall structures]" It means they pride themselves and compete in building tall structures and doing so in abundance.

The word *buhm* is cited as *bahm* in al-Aṣīlī's[319] narration; this is incompatible with the mention of the camels but is compatible

[319] See note 302.

with sheep or goats, as in the version without the camel construct in Muslim: "the sheperds of little lambs" (*riʿāʾ al-bahmi*). *Buhm* in al-Bukhārī's version can either be a nominative attribute of the camelherds (*buhmu*), or a genitive attribute of the camels (*buhumi*) in the sense of the jet-black camel. It is said that they consider black the worst color for camels while red is the proverbial best, as in the expression "better than red livestock."

The herders were described as destitute either because they are of unknown lineage, whence we say "he is obscure" (*huwa abhamu al-amr*) and "anonymous" (*mubham*) when one is unable to ascertain his actual identity. Al-Qurṭubī[320] said: "It is best understood as meaning the black color because this is their complexion in most cases. It is also said they are destitute, as in the ḥadīth 'People will be gathered barefoot, naked, and destitute' (*ḥufātan ʿurātan buhman*),[321] but this leaves something to be desired, as they are said to have camels, so how could they be said to own nothing?" My answer is that expression can be understood as an annexation of function (*iḍāfat ikhtiṣāṣ*), not ownership. In the majority of cases, herders graze the herd for someone else in exchange for a wage and seldom does the owner graze his own herd himself.

In the Book of *Tafsīr*: **"And when the barefoot and naked"** to which al-Ismāʿīlī's narration [following *Ṣaḥīḥ Muslim*] adds "the

[320] See note 293.

[321] Narrated from ʿAbd Allāh ibn Unays al-Anṣārī by Aḥmad, al-Bukhārī in *al-Adab al-Mufrad* (2:433) and his *Ṣaḥīḥ* without chain *(taʿlīqan)* but with categorical attribution *(bi-ṣīghat al-jazm)*, al-Ḥākim (2:427-428, 4:574-575), and others cf. *Fatḥ al-Bārī* (1:127). This is the first of the "single ḥadīths for the sake of which one of the Companions undertook travel" which al-Khaṭīb narrated in his *Riḥla fī Ṭalab al-Ḥadīth* (p. 109-118 §31-33 *ṣaḥīḥ*) and we heard it from the latter's editor, our teacher Nūr al-Dīn ʿItr, all of which in the wording "naked, uncircumcized, and destitute" *(ʿurātan ghurlan buhman)*. As for the wording "barefoot, naked, and uncircumcized" *(ḥufātan ʿurātan ghurlan)*, it is narrated from Ibn ʿAbbās and ʿĀʾisha by al-Bukhārī, Muslim, al-Tirmidhī, al-Nasāʾī, al-Dārimī, and Aḥmad.

deaf and dumb." They were given these attributes as a hyperbole for their ignorance, since they did not use their hearing or eyesight to discern any of their religious obligations although their senses were sound.

"are the top leaders of the people" This means the kings of the earth as explicitly stated in al-Ismā'īlī's and Abū Farwa's narrations. Those meant are the people of the desert, as explicitly stated in Sulaymān al-Taymī's and other narrations: "Who are 'the barefoot and naked?'" He replied: "The little Arabs (*al-'urayb*)."

Al-Ṭabarānī narrates through Abū Ḥamza, from Ibn 'Abbās, from the Prophet ﷺ: "Part of the overthrow (*inqilāb*) of the Religion is the affectation of eloquence by the boors (*al-nabaṭ*) and their betaking to palaces in big cities." Al-Qurṭubī said: "What is meant here is the prediction of a reversal in society whereby the people of the desert will take over and hold sway over every region by force. They will become very rich and their primary concern will be to erect tall buildings and take pride in them. We have witnessed this in our time." Of identical import are the ḥadīths "The Hour will not rise until the happiest man in the world will be the depraved son of a depraved father (*luka' ibn luka'*)" and "If leadership is entrusted to those unfit for it, expect the Hour," both of them in the *Ṣaḥīḥ*.

"Among five things" That is: the knowledge of the Hour is numbered among five things. It is allowed to suppress the subject of the governing word (*muta'allaq al-jārr*), as when Allāh Most High said {*Among nine signs*} (27:12), meaning: "Go to Pharaoh with this sign which is one of nine signs in all." 'Aṭā' al-Khurāsānī's narration has: "He said, 'Then when is the Hour?' He replied, "It is among five things of the unseen which Allāh alone knows."

Al-Qurṭubī said:

> No one whatsoever may aspire to know anything about these five things as stipulated in this ḥadīth. In addition, the Prophet ﷺ explained that the verse {*And He has with Him the keys to the unseen, which no one knows except He*} (6:59) means these five things. This explanation is in the *Ṣaḥīḥ*. Therefore, whoever claims to know any of them independently of the Messenger of Allāh ﷺ, that person is a liar in what they claim. As for conjecture about the unseen, such is possible on the part of the astrologer (*al-munajjim*) and others[322] since it is a matter of custom, not knowledge, and Ibn ʿAbd al-Barr cited Consensus over the prohibition of taking, stipulating, or giving any kind of compensation in exchange for such information.

It is narrated that Ibn Masʿūd said: "Your Prophet was given the knowledge of all things except these five."[323] There is a similar narration from Ibn ʿUmar from the Prophet ﷺ[324] and Aḥmad related both of them. Ḥumayd ibn Zanjūyah related from one of the Companions ؓ that someone mentioned [by way of objection] the knowledge of the times of solar eclipses before their occurrence, whereupon he rebuked him and said: "The unseen consists in five things," and he recited this verse. "As for the rest, it is a kind of unseen known to some people and unknown to others."

A Warning

The reply not only addressed the question but also comprised additional guidance of importance for the *Umma* due to the general benefits derived therefrom.

[322] Such as the various types of fortune-tellers.
[323] Narrated from Ibn Masʿūd by Aḥmad through the narrators of the *Ṣaḥīḥ* according to al-Haythamī (8:263).
[324] Narrated from Ibn ʿUmar by Aḥmad through the narrators of the *Ṣaḥīḥ* according to al-Haythamī (8:263).

If it is said: "There is no preposition of exclusion in the verse ['except'] as there is in the ḥadīth," al-Ṭībī replied:

> When a verb is of tremendous significance[325] and what is based upon it is a lofty matter,[326] the verb is tantamount to exclusive (*fuhima minhu al-ḥaṣru ʿalā sabīl al-kināya*), especially if one recalls what was mentioned among the causes of revelation (*asbāb al-nuzūl*), concerning the Arabs' claim that they possessed knowledge of [predicting] rainfalls. All this suggests that what is meant by the verse is to refute their claim and to restrict such knowledge to Allāh alone.

A Note of Benefit

[Al-Ṭībī continued:]

> The play on words which consists in switching from affirmation to negation in the saying of Allāh Most High: {*No soul knows what it will earn tomorrow*}[327] and the formal mention of cognizance devoid of knowledge (*al-dirāyatu dūna al-ʿilm*) are for hyperbole and universalization. For cognizance is the obtainment of the knowledge of something through some device. The fact is that such knowledge is precluded from every soul, although cognizance is among the soul's qualifications, yet it can never know this. It follows that the soul's unacquaintance with what lies beyond such knowledge is even more certain.

Here ends the summarized excerpt from al-Ṭībī.

"the verse." It means he recited the verse to the end of the Sūra as explicited by al-Ismāʿīlī and in ʿUmāra's narration. Muslim has

[325] *I.e.* to know the unseen.
[326] *I.e.* the five things in which the unseen consists.
[327] {*Lo! Allāh! With Him is knowledge of the Hour. He sends down the rain, and knows that which is in the wombs. No soul knows what it will earn tomorrow, and no soul knows in what land it will die. Lo! Allāh is Knower, Aware*}(31:34).

"until the word {*Aware*}," likewise in Abū Farwa's narration. As for what is found in al-Bukhārī's version in the *Tafsīr* where he says "until the phrase {*in the wombs*}," it is a shortcoming on the part of one of the narrators. The context tells us loud and clear that he recited the entire verse.

Then He [Gibrīl] turned around and left. Then the Prophet ﷺ said: "Bring him back!" Al-Bukhārī added in the book of *Tafsīr*: "They went to bring him back but saw nothing." It shows that it is possible for the angel to take a visible form for other than the Prophet ﷺ, be seen by them, and speak audibly in their presence. It is established that ʿImrān ibn Ḥuṣayn used to hear the speech of the angels. And Allāh knows best.

"He came teaching (*jā'a yuʿallimu*) the people" The *Tafsīr* version has "to teach" (*li-yuʿallima*). In al-Ismāʿīlī: "He wanted you to learn because you did not ask." ʿUmāra has something similar. Abū Farwa's narration has "By the One Who sent Muḥammad with the truth, I knew no more than any one of you who he was! Truly, that was Gibrīl." Abū ʿĀmir's ḥadīth has: "Then he went away, and when we did not see which way he went, the Prophet said: 'Glory to Allāh! This was Gibrīl, he came to teach the people their Religion. By the One in Whose hand is Muḥammad's soul! He never came to me before save I recognized him, but for this time.'"

Al-Taymī's narration has: "Then he got up and left, after which the Messenger of Allāh ﷺ said: "Bring that man back to me!" We looked for him everywhere but could not find him. The Prophet ﷺ said: "Do you know who that was? That was Gibrīl, he came to teach you your religion, so take what he said from him. By the One in Whose hand is my soul! he was never unrecognizable to me since he first came to me except this once. I did not recognize him until after he left."

Ibn Ḥibbān said Sulaymān al-Taymī alone has the words "take what he said from him." Nevertheless, he is among the highly trustworthy narrators. There is an allusion to those additional words in the Prophet's ﷺ phrase: "He came to teach the people their Religion." In other words, Sulaymān only singled himself out by making it explicit. The attribution of teaching to Gibrīl is metaphorical. He was the reason for which the answer came, hence they were told to learn from him.

All these narrations concur in that the Prophet ﷺ told the Companions about his identity after they looked for him and could not find him. As for the ḥadīth of ʿUmar through the narration of Kahmas as found in Muslim and others:

> Then he departed. ʿUmar said: "A long time passed then he [the Prophet ﷺ] said to me: 'ʿUmar, do you know who that questioner was?' I said, 'Allāh and His Prophet know best.' He said: 'Truly, that was Gibrīl.'"

One of the commentators combined the meanings of the two versions in making ʿUmar's words "a long time passed" (*fa-labithtu maliyyan*) mean a certain period of time after Gibrīl left, as if the Prophet ﷺ revealed his identity to them after some time, but in that same sitting. However, the fact that the narration of al-Nasāʾī and al-Tirmidhī says "three nights passed" makes this agreement flawed. Someone claimed misspelling (*taṣḥīf*) here and said that the *mīm* of *maliyyan* مليا was minimized so that the word resembled *thalāthan* which can be written ثلثا without *alif*. This claim is wrong for Abū ʿAwāna's narration has "several nights passed. The Prophet ﷺ met me after three nights" while Ibn Ḥibbān has "after three" and Ibn Mandah "after three days."

Al-Nawawī reconciled the two ḥadīths in the sense that ʿUmar was not present in the gathering at the time the Prophet ﷺ spoke but was only among those who were up and about, either with those who were searching for the man or for some other task, and he did not return with those who returned for some reason he had, so the Prophet ﷺ informed those who were present on the spot and he did not happen to inform ʿUmar until three days later. This scenario is supported by the wordings "he met me" and "He said to me, ''Umar...'" addressing him alone, contrary to his first disclosure. This is a nice reconciliation.

Abū ʿAbd Allāh said, that is, the author [al-Bukhārī].

"He made all this part of belief" that is, perfect belief, which comprises all those matters.[328]

Warnings

First, the narrations we mentioned showed that the Prophet ﷺ did not know that it was Gibrīl except after the fact and that Gibrīl came to him in the form of a man of handsome appearance but whom they did not know. As for what appears in al-Nasāʾī's narration through Abū Farwa at the end of the ḥadīth: "Truly, it was Gibrīl who came down in the form of Diḥya al-Kalbī," the last clause is a misapprehension, as Diḥya was known among them whereas ʿUmar said: "None of us knew him." Muḥammad ibn Naṣr al-Marwazī narrated it in his book *al-Īmān* through the same path of transmission as al-Nasāʾī and he said in the end: "Truly, it was Gibrīl who came to teach you your Religion," and no more. The latter is the version that is retained since it concurs with the rest of the narrations.

Second, Ibn al-Munayyir[329] said: "His statement 'teaching you your Religion' indicates that an excellent question can be called

[328] Ibn Ḥajar apparently defuses al-Bukhārī's intention which was to refute the Ḥanafī view that deeds are not part of belief at the root but only as its perfection.
[329] Sharaf al-Dīn ʿAbd al-Wāḥid ibn al-Munayyir al-Mālikī (d. 733) was a scholar of Qur'ān commentary and ḥadīth whom Ibn Ḥajar quotes hundreds of times in *Fatḥ al-Bārī*.

knowledge and teaching, since Gibrīl did nothing other than ask questions, yet the Prophet ﷺ called him a teacher. The scholars are famous for saying 'An excellent question is half of knowledge' and it is possible to glean it from this ḥadīth, since benefit grew out of the question and the answer together."

Third, al-Qurṭubī said: "This ḥadīth is fit to be called the Mother of the Sunna in light of all the guidelines in the knowledge of the Sunna it contains." Al-Ṭībī said: "This is the wisdom behind the fact that al-Baghawī began both his *Maṣābīḥ al-Sunna* and *Sharḥ al-Sunna* with this ḥadīth, following the lead of the Qur'ān which began with the Fātiḥa since the latter contains the generality of the teachings of the Qur'ān." Qāḍī 'Iyāḍ said: "This ḥadīth contains all the outward and inward duties of the profession of faith, its inception, its state, and its ultimate point as well as the works of the limbs, the sincerity of inward disposition, and how to guard oneself from defective deeds. Even the sciences of the Law as a whole all go back to that ḥadīth and are supplied by it."

This is why I discussed this ḥadīth at length, and yet, even if what I mentioned is abundant, it is still little in relation to what the ḥadīth contains, so I did not forsake concision. Allāh is the Grantor of success!

Indexes

Index of Qur'ānic Verses

1:6 142
2:2 32
2:43 17, 135
2:83 135
2:110 135
2:143 85
2:151 70
2:177 176
2:285 176
2:196 136
2:231 70
3:31 5, 80
3:32 72
3:85 165
3:132 72
3:150 116
3:164 70
4:13-14 79
4:43 59
4:58 74
4:59 37, 73-78
4:60 80
4:61 64
4:64 14, 78
4:65 5, 32, 41, 67-69, 102
4:69 78
4:79-80 79
4:80 14
4:101 56
4:103 183
4:113 70, 84
4:136 62
5:3 50, 85, 165
5:38 137
5:44 37
5:48-49 83
5:67 83
5:92 37, 72
6:57 37
6:59 197
6:65 119
6:82 137
6:106 83
7:156-157 81
7:157 84
7:158 62
8:4 164
8:13 79
8:20-21 72
8:24 55
8:40 116
8:46 72
9:24 81
9:32 34
9:34 136
9:91 63
11:73 110-114
11:114 121
12:40 37
12:67 37
12:108 84
16:44 14, 70, 134
16:64 70
17:78 65, 140
21:26 175
21:107 85

22:77 135
22:78 116
23:73 84
24:47-54 66
24:54 121
24:56 17, 135
24:62 63
24:63 79, 102
27:12 196
27:79 85
30:17 135
31:34 155, 156, 160, 162, 188, 198-199
33:1-2 82
33:6 80, 116
33:21 80
33:28-34 109
33:32 113
33:33 109-115
33:34 70
33:36 66, 74, 101
33:37 82
33:45-46 85
33:56 136
33:64-66 79
33:70-71 78
36:1-5 84
36:78 174
36:79 174
42:52-53 84
45:18 83
47:32 80
47:33 72
48:8-9 62
48:10 78
48:13 62
49:7 165
49:14 165
49:15 62
59:7 14, 38, 78
62:2 70
64:8 62
64:12 72
66:2 116
68:1-4 85
68:4 82
68:4-7 81
69:38-47 84
73:20 17, 135
99:7-8 134

Index of Narrations

Allah brighten the face of him among His servants who hears my words, remembers them… 129, 130
Allah curses women who tattoo others… 38
Allah has made pilgrimage obligatory upon you… 126
Allah never gave any learned person knowledge except He took from them a covenant 94
Allah is He Who sets the market prices… 92
Allah revealed His Book to His Prophet and made the latter the indicator… (Aḥmad) 149
Allah sent forth Muḥammad and we knew nothing (Ibn ʿUmar) 145
Allah will not ask me of any Sunna I innovated among you… 92
Angels came to the Prophet while he was sleeping… 98
Anyone whose patron I am, this [ʿAlī] is his patron 108, 116, 117
Are you all going to fall into the same chaos into which fell the Jews and Christians? 104
Argue with them by means of the *Sunan*… (ʿAlī) 142-143
Ask for your sustenance through obedience to Allah 47, 93
Avoid relating my words except what you know for sure 130
[The] believer is no different than the docile camel… 49
[The] best of all discourse is the Book of Allah and the best of all guidance is the guidance of Muḥammad 104
Beware of Allah and ask Him gracefully… 46
Beware of narrating something about me except what you know for sure 94
Beware of those who put forward opinions… (ʿUmar) 141
[The] black seed is a remedy for every disease except death 21, 23
Can you tell me about the *ṣalāt*, what it contains… (ʿImrān) 43
Certain people shall appear who will dispute with you concerning the Qur'ān… (ʿUmar) 142
[The] claimant must produce clear proof… 47
Do not argue by means of the Qur'ān, but argue by means of the Sunna (ʿAlī) 142

Do not, when I narrate to you from the Messenger, claim a contradiction with the Book (Sa'īd ibn Jubayr) 146
Do not sit in the roadways 17
Do you not bear witness that Allah is your Lord? 116
Does any of you think that Allah prohibited nothing except what is in this Qur'ān? 91
Every newfangled matter is an innovation, and every innovation is misguidance 49, 104, 125
Every servant of Allah goes through a phase of eagerness... 102
Fast three days of the months... 102
[The] first thing you will lose from your Religion is humility and the last, prayer 121
[A] *fitna* is coming which shall not leave one house of the Arabs intact except it shall enter it 118
Follow the largest mass... 120
Follow us [Companions] or, by Allah! you shall go astray ('Imrān) 143
For every forty sheep or goats, one head... 17
Four dissensions shall appear... 119
[The] Hand of Allah is with the *Jamā'a* 120
Have I conveyed the Message? 50
Here is Gibrīl, the Messenger of the Lord of the worlds... 46
Hold in the highest suspicion any personal opinion... ('Umar) 141-142
How will you [Mu'ādh] pass judgment if judgment is asked of you? 54
I am leaving among you the two weighty matters... 107, 116
I am leaving you on a path that is clear as day... 49, 50
I am only a human being... 126
I am the most knowledgeable of Allah among them, and the most intense of them in fear of Him 127
I do not command you anything except what Allah has commanded 92
I do not fear for this Community a believer whose faith holds him in check... ('Umar) 141
I do not prohibit you anything except what Allah has prohibited 47, 92
I exhort you to beware of Allah... 48, 125
I fear two things for my *Umma*: the Qur'ān and milk... 95

I have left among you something which, if you cling to it, you shall never be led astray: the Book of Allah and the Sunna... 48
I have left among you that which if you hold to it you shall never go astray: the Book of Allah and the People of my House 108, 116
I have left among you two matters... 107, 116
I myself sleep and pray; I fast and break my fast... 103
I only fear for you two matters... (ʿUmar) 141
I remind you by Allah of the People of my House! 107
I seem to be called back [by my Lord], therefore I am responding... 116
I used to write down everything that I heard from the Messenger (ʿAbd Allah ibn ʿAmr) 104
I was given the Qur'ān and something like it 90
I was given the Qur'ān and something very near it... 45
I was not sent except as an opener and a sealer 105
I was ordered to fight people until ... 100
If a fly falls into one of your containers [of food or drink]... 28
If I order you to do something, do it to the extent that you can... 126
If Mūsā were alive, he would have no alternative but to follow me! 104, 105
If the Religion went according to personal opinion, wiping the bottom of the *khuff* would have been more appropriate (ʿAlī) 142
If one's eagerness wanes toward the Sunna he has succeeded 102
If you are able to rise in the morning and retire at night without the least spite in your heart for anyone, then do so 102
If you find yourself in difficulty because of some need... 47, 93
Islam began as a stranger and shall again be considered a stranger 98
Islam is built on five things 47
Islam shall coil back between the Two Mosques... 98
[The] Israelites divided into seventy-one sects... 120
It is a charity given to you by Allah, so accept His charity 56
Jihād in the path of Allah, together with belief, is the best of all deeds 91
[The] keeper of my Sunna...receive the reward of a hundred martyrs 98
Knowledge consists in three matters, whatever else is superfluous 123
Let every witness among you tell the one who is absent... 129
Let him take her back and keep her until after her menses 56

Let him wash his organ and make ablution 56
Let none pray ʿ*aṣr* before you reach the Banū Qurayẓa 57
Let not those who are in chaos induce you into chaos 105
[A] man assuredly does the deeds of the people of Paradise... 164
[A] man stands more in need of the Sunna than he stands in need of food and drink (Ibn Mahdī) 149
May Allah increase you [ʿAbd Allah ibn Rawaḥa] in obedience 53
[The] meat of the domestic ass is prohibited to you... 45, 90
[The] Messenger imposed upon us such-and-such in *zakāt* (ʿImrān) 43, 144
[The] Messenger prayed among us then turned to face us and admonished us so that the eyes wept and the hearts trembled 48, 125
[The] Messenger was among us while the Qur'ān was being revealed... (Jābir) 145, 149
Muḥammad is the separator between the people (Angels) 99
My Community shall divide into seventy-three sects... 117, 118, 120
My Community shall never concur on error... 119, 120
My sayings are difficult and a burden to anyone that hates them... 96
My similitude and that of the message Allah sent me with is... 122
Neither am I a swindler, nor can a swindler deceive me (ʿUmar) 34
None of you believes until his likes and dislikes are in conformity with what I have brought 101
Nothing but truth ever comes out of this (indicating his mouth) 104
Nothing is begun on a Wednesday except it is completed 19-20
O Allah! Bless my Community in its mornings 13
O Allah, my Lord! These are my Family 109
One does not obtain what He [Allah] has except through obedience 46
Only three types of persons give *fatwās* to people... (Ḥudhayfa) 146
Part of obedience to Allah is obedience to me... 96
Perhaps the one who is conveyed to shall understand better than the one who heard in the first place 129
Pollination of the datepalm-trees 87, 125
Praise to Allah Who has sent me as a mercy to the worlds... 105
Praise to Allah Who has graced the messenger of the Messenger... 54
Pray as you see me pray 47

[The] Prophet began to wear a gold ring... 52
[The] Prophet called Abū Sa'īd as the latter was praying... 55
[The] Prophet had prayed two *rak'as* when he was ordered to face the Holy Sanctuary... 53
[The] Prophet liked to set forth on Thursday, 13, 19
[The] Prophet passed (during his Ascension) by Prophets followed by their nations 121
[The] Prophet suddenly removed his sandals... 52
[The] Prophet turned around [in the prayer]... 53
[The] Prophet visited 'Ā'isha and said: "*As-Salāmu 'alaykum Ahl al-Bayt! wa raḥmatullah* 113
[The] Prophet was delivering his sermon and said: "Sit all of you!" 53
[The] Prophet went out on the campaign of Tabūk on a Thursday 13
[This] Qur'ān is difficult and felt as a burden to anyone who hates it 96
Rarely did the Messenger set forth other than on Thursday 13
Revelation would descend upon the Messenger and Gibrīl would also tell him the Sunna that expounded it (Ḥassān ibn 'Aṭiyya) 146
[The] rule(r) of Allah on earth is the Qur'ān and Sunna (Musaddad) 99
[A] ruling is one of two kinds... (Mālik) 124
Satan has despaired of ever being worshipped in your land... 48
Say: O Allah! Inspire me with right guidance and protect me from the evil of my *nafs* 101
Soon a man will say, leaning on his couch: "Follow this Qur'ān..." 45, 90
[The] Sunna in our definition consists in the reports transmitted from the Messenger (Aḥmad) 149
[The] sustenance of each one of you shall surely come to him... 47
Tactical advice in the battle of Badr 88
Take your pilgrimage rites [from me]... 48
That is the waiting period (*'idda*) which Allah has commanded 56
There are six types whom I have cursed and whom Allah has cursed as well as every Prophet... 122
There shall come out of my Community people in whom unspeakable lusts run amok... 118
There shall dawn upon my Community exactly what dawned upon the Israelites 117

This morning I am a real believer 164
Truly Allah is my Patron and I am the patron of every believer 108
Truly I do not command you except what Allah has commanded 47, 92
Truly Religion is nothing but absolute good faith (*al-naṣīḥa*) 64, 103
Truly the most delusive misguidance is for a man to read the Qur'ān without understanding (Mu'āwiya) 143
Truly the People of the Book divided into seventy-two sects 117-120
Truly this Qur'ān has been torn to tatters...(Maymūn ibn Mahrān) 147
Two men went on a trip and decided to pray but found no water 58
'Umar and Mu'ādh woke up in need of *ghusl* but found no water 59
'Umar brought the Prophet a book he had taken from one of the People of the Book 104-106
'Umar forbade the copying or keeping of Biblical material 106
We alighted in Khaybar with the Prophet... 90
We are well-pleased with Allah for our Lord and Islam for our Religion and Muḥammad for our Messenger! ('Umar) 106
What earth would carry me... if I narrated from the Messenger something but did not adhere to it? (al-Shāfi'ī) 141
What heaven will shade me... if I say about the Book of Allah something of which I have no knowledge? (Abū Bakr) 141
What I most fear for my Community is the silver-tongued hypocrite 95
What I most fear for my Community is three things... 95
What if it is not in the Sunna...? 54
[Most of] what is abrogated in the Book of Allah is known only through the indications of the *Sunan* (al-Shāfi'ī) 146
What is the matter with certain people who disdain to avail themselves of something which I practice? 127
What prevented you [Abū Sa'īd] from answering me? 55
Whatever the Messenger has declared prohibited... 45, 90
When innovations appear in my Community... 130
Who are the strangers? Those far away from their tribes 98
Whoever deliberately lies about me, let him take his seat in the Fire 94
Whoever denigrates the rule(r) of Allah on earth... 99-100
Whoever desires other than my Sunna has nothing to do with me... 103
Whoever dismisses my sayings dismisses the Qur'ān... 97

Whoever disobeys me certainly disobeys Allah... 96
Whoever eats seven *'ujwa* dates in the morning... 21, 25
Whoever eats wholesome food, puts a Sunna into practice... 97
Whoever follows my example is part of me... 103
Whoever gives life to my Sunna certainly loves me... 97, 102
Whoever gives life to one of my Sunnas... 97
Whoever hears of a ḥadīth of mine then belies it... 100
Whoever hears my saying and preserves it, putting it into practice... 96
Whoever innovates in this matter of ours... 48, 124
Whoever innovates something new or abets someone who does... 130
Whoever is asked about knowledge he possesses but conceals it... 93
Whoever is wailed over shall be punished 130
Whoever lies about me willfully, let him take now his seat in the Fire 130
Whoever loves me is with me in Paradise 97
Whoever marches against the rule(r) of Allah on earth... 99
Whoever obeys me certainly obeys Allah... 96
Whoever obeys Muḥammad, obeys Allah... (Angels) 99
Whoever obeys my leader (*amīrī*), certainly obeys me... 96
Whoever of you lives shall live to see great divisions... 48, 50, 125
Whoever speaks about the Qur'ān without knowledge... 93
Why should I not curse whom the Messenger cursed? (Ibn Mas'ūd) 38
You and your friends all read the Qur'ān: can you tell me... ('Imrān) 43, 144
You have followed the Sunna faithfully, and your prayer is complete 58
You have twice the reward 58
You know best about your mundane matters 126
You must follow my Sunna and the Sunna of the Rightly-Guided Successors 49, 118, 125
You must hold fast to knowledge [*i.e.*, Sunna] before it is taken away (Ibn Mas'ūd) 143
You must stick with the largest mass (Abū Umāma) 120
You shall adopt the practices of the People of the Book before you... 119
You shall tread the path of those that came before you as closely as the arrow-feather... 121

Bibliography

ʿAbd ibn Ḥumayd. *Musnad*. Eds. Subḥī al-Badrī al-Sāmarrāʾī and Maḥmūd al-Saʿīdī. Cairo: Maktabat al-Sunna, 1988.

ʿAbd al-Khāliq, ʿAbd al-Ghanī. *Ḥujjiyyat al-Sunna*. Herndon, VA: Dār al-Wafā', 1993.

ʿAbd al-Razzāq. *Al-Muṣannaf*. 11 vols. Ed. Ḥabīb al-Raḥmān al-Aʿẓamī. Beirut: al-Maktab al-Islāmī, 1983. With Maʿmar ibn Rāshid al-Azdī's *Kitāb al-Jāmiʿ* as the last two volumes.

Abū ʿAwāna. *Musnad*. 2 vols. in 1. Hyderabad al-Dakn: Dā'irat al-Maʿārif al-ʿUthmāniyya, 1943-1944.

Abū Dāwūd. *Sunan*. 3 vols. Ed. Muḥammad Fu'ād ʿAbd al-Bāqī. Beirut: Dār al-Kutub al-ʿIlmiyya, 1996. See also al-ʿAẓīm Ābādī, *ʿAwn al-Maʿbūd*.

Abū Nuʿaym al-Aṣfahānī. *Al-Arbaʿīn ʿalā Madhhab al-Mutaḥaqqiqīn min al-Ṣūfiyya*. With Sharaf al-Dīn al-Maqdisī's *al-Arbaʿīn fī Fal al-Duʿā' wal-Dāʿīn: al-Juz' al-Khāmis*. Ed. Badr ibn ʿAbd Allāh al-Badr. Beirut: Dār Ibn Ḥazm, 1993.

———. *Dhikr Akhbār Aṣbahān*. 2 vols. Ed. Sven Dedering. Leiden: Brill, 1931-1934.

———. *Ḥilyat al-Awliyā' wa-Ṭabaqāt al-Aṣfiyā'*. 12 vols. Ed. Muṣṭafā ʿAbd al-Qādir ʿAṭā. Beirut: Dār al-Kutub al-ʿIlmiyya, 1997.

———. *Maʿrifat al-Ṣaḥāba*. 6 vols. Ed. ʿĀdil ibn Yūsuf al-ʿAzāzī. Ryadh: Dār al-Waṭan, 1998.

Abū al-Shaykh [Ibn Ḥayyān al-Aṣbahānī]. *Al-ʿAẓama*. 5 vols. Ed. Riḍā' Allāh al-Mubārakfūrī. Ryad: Dār al-ʿĀṣima, 1988.

———. *Ṭabaqāt al-Muḥaddithīn fī Aṣbahān wal-Wāridīn ʿalayhā*. 4 vols. Ed. ʿAbd al-Ghafūr al-Balūshī. Beirut: Mu'assasat al-Risāla, 1992.

Abū al-Suʿūd. *Irshād al-ʿAql al-Salīm ilā Mazāyā al-Qur'ān al-Karīm*. 9 vols. Beirut: Dār Iḥyā' al-Turāth al-ʿArabī, n.d. Reprint.

Abū Yaʿlā al-Mawṣilī. *Musnad*. 13 vols. Ed. Ḥusayn Salīm Asad. Damascus: Dār al-Ma'mūn līl-Turāth, 1984.

Al-Aḥdab, Khaldūn. *Zawā'id Tārīkh Baghdād ʿalā al-Kutub al-Sitta*. 10 vols. Damascus: Dār al-Qalam, 1996.

Aḥmad ibn Ḥanbal. *Faḍā'il al-Ṣaḥāba*. 2 vols. Ed. Waṣī Allāh Muḥammad ʿAbbās. Beirut: Mu'assasat al-Risāla, 1983.

———. *Al-Musnad*. 20 vols. Ed. Aḥmad Shākir and Ḥamza Aḥmad al-Zayn. Cairo: Dār al-Ḥadīth, 1995.

———. *Al-Musnad*. 50 vols. Ed. Shuʿayb al-Arnaʾūṭ. Beirut: Muʾassasat al-Risāla, 2000-2001.

Al-ʿAjlūnī. *Kashf al-Khafā*. 2nd ed. 2 vols. Beirut: Dār Iḥyāʾ al-Turāth al-ʿArabī, 1932.

Al-Ājurrī. *Al-Sharīʿa*. Ed. ʿAbd al-Razzāq al-Mahdī. Beirut: Dār al-Kitāb al-ʿArabī, 1996.

Al-Arnaʾūṭ, Shuʿayb and Bashshār ʿAwwād Maʿrūf. *Taḥrīr Taqrīb al-Tahdhīb*. 4 vols. Beirut: Muʾassasat al-Risāla, 1997.

Al-ʿAẓīm Ābādī, Muḥammad Shams al-Ḥaqq. *ʿAwn al-Maʿbūd Sharḥ Sunan Abī Dāwūd*. 14 vols. in 7. Beirut: Dār al-Kutub al-ʿIlmiyya, n.d. Includes Abū Dāwūd's *Sunan*.

Al-Baghawī. *Maʿālim al-Tanzīl*. 5 vols. Ed. ʿAbd al-Razzāq al-Mahdī. Beirut: Dār Iḥyāʾ al-Turāth al-ʿArabī, 2000.

———. *Sharḥ al-Sunna*. 8 vols. Eds. Shuʿayb al-Arnaʾūṭ and Zuhayr al-Shāwīsh. Beirut: al-Maktab al-Islāmī, 1971..

Al-Bayḍāwī. *Anwār al-Tanzīl*. 5 vols. Ed. ʿAbd al-Qādir ʿArafāt Ḥassūna. Beirut: Dār al-Fikr, 1996.

Al-Bayhaqī. *Al-Asmāʾ wal-Ṣifāt*. 2 vols. Ed. ʿAbd Allāh al-Ḥāshidī. Riyad: Maktabat al-Sawādī, 1993.

———. *Dalāʾil al-Nubuwwa wa-Maʿrifat Aḥwāl Ṣāḥib al-Sharīʿa*. 7 vols. Ed. ʿAbd al-Muʿṭī Qalʿajī. Beirut: Dār al-Kutub al-ʿIlmiyya, 1985.

———. *Al-Iʿtiqād ʿalā Madhhab al-Salaf Ahl al-Sunna wal-Jamāʿa*. Beirut: Dār al-Afāq al-Jadīda, 1981; 2nd ed. Dār al-Kutub al-ʿIlmiyya, 1986.

———. *Al-Madkhal ilā al-Sunan al-Kubrā*. Ed. Muḥammad Ḍiyāʾ al-Raḥmān al-Aʿẓamī. Al-Kuwait: Dār al-Khulafāʾ līl-Kitāb al-Islāmī, 1984. 2nd ed. 2 vols. Riyadh: Maktabat Aḍwāʾ al-Salaf, 1990.

———. *Maʿrifat al-Sunan wal-Āthār*. 15 vols. Ed. ʿAbd al-Muʿṭī Amīn Qalʿajī. Aleppo and Cairo: Dār al-Waʿī, 1991.

———. *Shuʿab al-Īmān*. 8 vols. Ed. Muḥammad Zaghlūl. Beirut: Dār al-Kutub al-ʿIlmiyya, 1990.

———. *Al-Sunan al-Kubrā*. 10 vols. Ed. Muḥammad ʿAbd al-Qādir ʿAta. Makka: Maktaba Dār al-Baz, 1994.

Al-Bazzār. *Al-Musnad.* [*Al-Baḥr al-Zakhkhār.*] 9 vols. Ed. Maḥfūẓ al-Raḥmān Zayn Allāh. Beirut and Madīna: Mu'assasat 'Ulūm al-Qur'ān & Maktabat al-'Ulūm wal-Ḥikam, 1989.

———. *Mukhtaṣar al-Musnad.* See Ibn Ḥajar, *Mukhtaṣar Zawā'id Musnad al-Bazzār.*

Al-Bukhārī. *Khalq Af'āl al-'Ibād.* Ed. 'Abd al-Raḥmān 'Umayra. Beirut: Mu'assasat al-Risāla, 1990. Ryad: Dār al-Ma'ārif al-Sa'ūdiyya, 1978.

———. *Ṣaḥīḥ.* 8 vols. in 3rd Ed. Muḥammad al-Zuhrī al-Ghamrāwī. Bulāq: al-Maṭba'at al-Kubrā al-Amīriyya, 1314/1896. Repr. Cairo: al-Maṭba'at al-Maymūniyya [Muṣṭafā Bābā al-Ḥalabī *et al.*], 1323/1905.

———. *Ṣaḥīḥ.* See Ibn Ḥajar, *Fatḥ al-Bārī.*

———. *Al-Tārīkh al-Kabīr.* 8 vols. Ed. al-Sayyid Hāshim al-Nadwī. Beirut: Dār al-Fikr, n.d.

Al-Būṣīrī. *Miṣbāḥ al-Zujāja fī Zawā'id Ibn Mājah.* 2nd ed. 4 vols. Ed. Muḥammad al-Muntaqā al-Kashnawī. Beirut: Dār al-'Arabiyya, 1983.

Al-Dānī. *Al-Sunan al-Wārida fil-Fitan.* 6 vols. in 3. Ed. Riḍā' Allāh al-Mubārakfūrī. Ryadh: Dār al-'Āṣima, 1995.

Al-Dāraquṭnī. *Al-'Ilal.* 9 vols. Ed. Maḥfūẓ al-Raḥmān Zayn Allāh al-Salafī. Ryad: Dār Tiba, 1985.

———. *Sunan.* 4 vols. in 2. Together with Muḥammad Shams al-Ḥaqq al-'Aẓīm Ābādī's *al-Ta'līq al-Mughnī.* Ed. Al-Sayyid 'Abd Allāh Hashim Yamānī al-Madanī. Beirut: Dār al-Ma'rifa, 1966. Repr. Beirut: Dār Ihyā al-Turāth al-'Arabī, 1993.

Al-Dārimī. [*Al-Musnad al-Jāmi'.*] *Fatḥ al-Mannān Sharḥ wa-Taḥqīq Kitāb al-Dārimī al-Musammā bil-Musnad al-Jāmi'.* 10 vols. Ed. Abū 'Āṣim Nabīl Hāshim al-Ghamrī. Makka and Beirut: al-Maktba al-Makkiyya and Dār al-Bashā'ir al-Islāmiyya, 1999.

———. *Musnad* [*Sunan*]. 2 vols. Ed. Fu'ād Aḥmad Zamarlī and Khālid al-Sab' al-'Ilmī. Beirut: Dār al-Kitāb al-'Arabī, 1987.

Al-Daylamī, Shīrūyah ibn Shahradār. *Firdaws al-Akhbār bi-Ma'thūr al-Khiṭāb 'alā Kitāb al-Shihāb.* Ed. Fawwāz Aḥmad al-Zayralī and Muḥammad al-Mu'taṣim Billāh al-Baghdādī. Beirut: Dār al-Kitāb al-'Arabī, 1987.

Al-Dhahabī. *Mīzān al-I'tidāl.* 4 vols. Ed. 'Alī Muḥammad al-Bajawī. Beirut: Dār al-Ma'rifa, 1963.

———. *Mīzān al-Iʿtidāl.* 8 vols. Eds. ʿAlī Muḥammad Muʿawwaḍ and ʿĀdil ʿAbd al-Mawjūd. Beirut: Dār al-Kutub al-ʿIlmiyya, 1995

———. *Siyar Aʿlām al-Nubalā'.* 19 vols. Ed. Muḥibb al-Dīn al-ʿAmrāwī. Beirut: Dār al-Fikr, 1996.

———. *Siyar Aʿlām al-Nubalā'.* 23 vols. Ed. Shuʿayb al-Arna'ūṭ and Muḥammad Naʿīm al-ʿAraqsusī. Beirut: Mu'assasat al-Risāla, 1992-1993.

———. *Tadhkirat al-Ḥuffāẓ.* 4 vols. in 2. Ed. ʿAbd al-Raḥmān ibn Yaḥyā al-Muʿallimī. A fifth volume, titled *Dhayl Tadhkirat al-Ḥuffāẓ*, consists in al-Ḥusaynī's *Dhayl Tadhkirat al-Ḥuffāẓ*, Muḥammad ibn Fahd al-Makkī's *Lahẓ al-Alḥāẓ bi-Dhayl Tadhkirat al-Ḥuffāẓ*, and al-Suyūṭī's *Dhayl Ṭabaqāt al-Ḥuffāẓ*. Ed. Muḥammad Zāhid al-Kawtharī. Beirut: Dār Iḥyā' al-Turāth al-ʿArabī and Dār al-Kutub al-ʿIlmiyya, n.d. Reprint of the 1968 Hyderabad edition.

Al-Ghumārī, ʿAbd Allāh ibn Muḥammad ibn al-Ṣiddīq. *Al-Ibtihāj bi-Takhrīj Aḥādīth al-Minhāj.* With al-Bayḍāwī's *Minhāj al-Wuṣūl fī Maʿrifat ʿIlm al-Uṣūl.* Ed. Samīr Ṭaha al-Majdhūb. Beirut: ʿĀlam al-Kutub, 1985.

Al-Ghumārī, Aḥmad ibn Muḥammad ibn al-Ṣiddīq. *Al-Mudāwī li-ʿIlal al-Jāmiʿ al-Ṣaghīr wa-Sharḥay al-Munāwī.* 6 vols. Ed. Muṣṭafā Ṣabrī. Cairo al-Maktaba al-Makkiyya, 1996.

Al-Ḥākim. *Maʿrifat ʿUlūm al-Ḥadīth*, ed. Sayyid Muʿaẓẓam Ḥusayn. Dacca: n.p. 1935. Reprint Beirut: Dār al-Kutub al-ʿIlmiyya, 1977.

———. *Al-Mustadrak ʿalā al-Ṣaḥīḥayn.* With al-Dhahabī's *Talkhīṣ al-Mustadrak.* 5 vols. Indexes by Yūsuf ʿAbd al-Raḥmān al-Marʿashlī. Beirut: Dār al-Maʿrifa, 1986. Reprint of the 1334/1916 Hyderabad edition.

———. *Al-Mustadrak ʿala al-Ṣaḥīḥayn.* With al-Dhahabī's *Talkhīṣ al-Mustadrak.* 4 vols. Annotations by Muṣṭafā ʿAbd al-Qādir ʿAṭā'. Beirut: Dār al-Kutub al-ʿIlmiyya, 1990.

Al-Ḥakīm al-Tirmidhī. *Nawādir al-Uṣūl.* Beirut: Dār Sadir, n.d. Repr. of Istanbul ed.

Al-Harawī al-Anṣārī. *Dhamm al-Kalām wa-Ahlih.* 5 vols. Ed. ʿAbd Allāh ibn Muḥammad al-Anṣārī. Madīna: Maktabat al-Ghurabā', 1998.

Al-Ḥārith ibn Abī Usāma. *Musnad.* [*Bughyat al-Bāḥith 'an Zawā'id Musnad al-Ḥārith*]. 2 vols. Ed. Ḥusayn Aḥmad Ṣāliḥ al-Bakirī. Madīna: Markaz Khidmat al-Sunna wal-Sīra al-Nabawiyya, 1992.

———. *Musnad.* [*Bughyat al-Bāḥith 'an Zawā'id Musnad al-Ḥārith*]. Ed. Mus'ad 'Abd al-Ḥamīd Muḥammad al-Sa'dānī. Beirut: Dār al-Ṭalā'i', n.d

Al-Haythamī. *Majma' al-Zawā'id wa-Manba' al-Fawā'id.* 10 vols. in 5. Cairo: Maktabat al-Qudsī, 1932-1934. Repr. Beirut: Dār al-Kitāb al-'Arabī, 1967, 1982, and 1987.

Al-Ḥumaydī. *Musnad.* 2 vols. Ed. Ḥabīb al-Raḥmān al-A'ẓamī. Beirut: Dār al-Kutub al-'Ilmiyya, n.d.

Ibn 'Abd al-Barr. *Al-Intiqā' fī Faḍā'il al-A'immati al-Thalāthati al-Fuqahā': Mālik wal-Shāfi'ī wa-Abī Ḥanīfa.* Ed. 'Abd al-Fattāḥ Abū Ghudda. Beirut: Dār al-Bashā'ir al-Islāmiyya, 1997.

———. *Jāmi' Bayān al-'Ilm wa-Faḍlih.* 2 vols. Ed. Abū al-Ashbal al-Zuhayrī. Dammam: Dār Ibn al-Jawzī, 1994.

———. *Al-Tamhīd limā fīl-Muwaṭṭa' min al-Ma'ānī wal-Asānīd.* 22 vols. Eds. Muṣṭafā ibn Aḥmad al-'Alawī, Muḥammad 'Abd al-Kabīr al-Bakrī. Morocco: Wizārat 'Umūm al-Awqāf wal-Shu'ūn al-Islāmiyya, 1967-1968.

Ibn 'Abd al-Salām. *Al-Fatāwā al-Mawṣiliyya.* Ed. Iyād Khālid al-Ṭabbā'. Beirut and Damascus: Dār al-Fikr, 1999.

Ibn Abī 'Āṣim. *Al-Sunna.* Ed. Nāṣir al-Albānī. Beirut and Damascus: Al-Maktab al-Islāmī, 1993.

Ibn Abī Shayba. *Al-Muṣannaf.* 7 vols. Ed. Kamāl al-Ḥūt. Ryadh: Maktabat al-Rushd, 1989.

Ibn 'Adī. *Al-Kāmil fī Ḍu'afā' al-Rijāl.* 7 vols. Ed. Yaḥyā Mukhtār Ghazawī. Beirut: Dār al-Fikr, 1988.

Ibn al-'Arabī, Abū Bakr. *'Āriḍat al-Aḥwadhī Sharḥ Sunan al-Tirmidhī.* 13 vols. Beirut, Dār al-Kutub al-'Ilmiyya, n.d.

Ibn 'Asākir, Abū al-Qāsim. *Al-Arba'īn al-Buldāniyya.* Ed. Muḥammad Muṭī' al-Ḥāfiẓ. Beirut and Damascus: Dār al-Fikr, 1992.

———. *Tabyīn Kadhib al-Muftarī fīmā Nasaba ilā al-Imām Abī al-Ḥasan al-Ash'arī.* Ed. Muḥammad Zāhid al-Kawtharī. Damascus: al-Qudsī, 1347/1929. Repr. Dār al-Fikr, 1979.

———. *Tabyīn Kadhib al-Muftarī fīmā Nasaba ilā al-Imām Abī al-Ḥasan al-Ash'arī*. Ed. Muḥammad Zāhid al-Kawtharī. Damascus: al-Qudsī, 1347/1929. Repr. Dār al-Fikr, 1979.

———. *Tārīkh Dimashq*. 70 vols. Damascus: Dār al-Fikr, 2000.

Ibn al-Athīr al-Jazarī. *Jāmi' al-Uṣūl fī Aḥādīth al-Rasūl*. 2nd ed. 12 vols. Ed. Muḥammad Ḥāmid al-Fiqqī. Beirut: Dār Iḥyā' al-Turāth al-'Arabī, 1980.

———. *Jāmi' al-Uṣūl fī Aḥādīth al-Rasūl*. 11 vols. Ed. 'Abd al-Qādir al-Arna'ūṭ. Damascus: Ḥalwānī, 1973.

———. *Al-Nihāya fī Gharīb al-Athar*. 5 vols. Eds. Ṭāhir Aḥmad al-Zāwī and Maḥmūd Muḥammad al-Ṭabbākhī. Beirut: Dār al-Fikr, 1979.

Ibn Ḥajar. *Al-Amālī al-Ḥalabiyya*. Ed. 'Awwād al-Khalaf. Beirut: Mu'assasat al-Rayyān, 1996.

———. *Fatḥ al-Bārī Sharḥ Ṣaḥīḥ al-Bukhārī*. 13 vols. Ed. Muḥammad Fu'ād 'Abd al-Bāqī and Muḥibb al-Dīn al-Khaṭīb. Beirut: Dār al-Ma'rifa, 1959-1960.

———. *Fatḥ al-Bārī Sharḥ Ṣaḥīḥ al-Bukhārī*. Cairo: al-Maṭba'at al-Bahiyya, 1348/1929-1930.

———. *Hadī al-Sāri Muqaddimat Fatḥ al-Bārī*. Ed. Muḥammad Fu'ād 'Abd al-Bāqī and Muḥibb al-Dīn al-Khaṭīb. Beirut: Dār al-Ma'rifa, 1959-1960. [1st vol. of *Fatḥ al-Bārī*].

———. *Al-Iṣāba fī Tamyīz al-Ṣaḥāba*. 8 vols in 4. Ed. 'Alī Muḥammad al-Bajawī. Beirut: Dār al-Jīl, 1992.

———. *Lisān al-Mīzān*. 7 vols. Hyderabad: Dā'irat al-Ma'ārif al-Niẓāmiyya, 1329/1911. Repr. Beirut: Mu'assassat al-A'lamī, 1986.

———. *Al-Maṭālib al-'Āliya*. 4 vols. Kuwait, 1973.

———. *Mukhtaṣar Zawā'id Musnad al-Bazzār*. 2 vols. Ed. Ṣabrī 'Abd al-Khāliq Abū Dharr. Beirut: Mu'assasat al-Kutub al-Thaqāfiyya, 1993.

———. *Al-Qawl al-Musaddad fīl-Dhabb 'an Musnad al-Imām Aḥmad*. In the 1st volume of Shākir's edition of the *Musnad*.

———. *Tahdhīb al-Tahdhīb*. 14 vols. Hyderabad: Dā'irat al-Ma'ārif al-Niẓāmiyya, 1327/1909. Repr. Beirut: Dār al-Fikr, 1984.

———. *Talkhīṣ al-Ḥabīr*. 4 vols. Ed. Sayyid 'Abd Allāh Hāshim al-Yamānī. Madīna, 1964. Repr. 4 vols. in 2, Cairo: Maktabat al-Kulliyāt al-Azhariyya, 1979.

———. *Taqrīb al-Tahdhīb*. Ed. Muḥammad ʿAwwāma. Aleppo: Dār al-Rashid, 1997.

Ibn Ḥazm. *Al-Iḥkām fī Uṣūl al-Aḥkām*. 8 vols. Cairo: Dār al-Ḥadīth, 1984.

———. *Marātib al-Ijmāʿ*. With Ibn Taymiyya's *Naqd Marātib al-Ijmāʿ*. 3rd ed. Beirut: Dār al-Āfāq al-Jadīda, 1982.

———. *Al-Muḥallā*. 11 vols. Beirut: Dār al-Āfāq al-Jadīda, n.d.

Ibn Ḥibbān. *Ṣaḥīḥ Ibn Ḥibbān bi-Tartīb Ibn Balbān*. 18 vols. Ed. Shuʿayb al-Arna'ūṭ. Beirut: Mu'assasat al-Risāla, 1993.

Ibn al-Jawzī. *Al-ʿIlal al-Mutanāhiya fīl-Aḥādīth al-Wāhiya*. 2 vols. Ed. Shaykh Khalīl al-Mays. Beirut: Dār al-Kutub al-ʿIlmiyya, 1983.

———. *Zād al-Masīr fī ʿIlm al-Tafsīr*. 3rd ed. 10 vols. Beirut: al-Maktab al-Islāmī, 1984.

Ibn Juzayy. [*Tafsīr*] *al-Tas-hīl li-ʿUlūm al-Tanzīl*. 4 vols. Cairo: Dār al-Kutub al- Ḥadītha, 1973.

———. *Tafsīr Ibn Juzayy*. Beirut: Dār al-Kitāb al-ʿArabī, 1983.

Ibn Kathīr. *Tafsīr al-Qur'ān al-ʿAẓīm*. 4 vols. Beirut: Dār al-Fikr, 1981.

Ibn Khuzayma. *Al-Ṣaḥīḥ*. 4 vols. Ed. Muḥammad Muṣṭafā al-Aʿẓamī. Beirut: Al-Maktab al-Islāmī, 1970.

Ibn Mājah. *Sunan*. See al-Suyūṭī *et al.*, *Sharḥ Sunan Ibn Mājah*.

Ibn al-Mubārak. *Al-Zuhd*. Ed. Ḥabīb al-Raḥmān al-Aʿẓamī. Beirut: Dār al-Kutub al-ʿIlmiyya, n.d.

Ibn Naṣr al-Marwazī. *Al-Sunna*. Ed. Sālim ibn Aḥmad al-Salafī. Beirut: Mu'assasat al-Kutub al-Thaqāfiyya, 1988.

Ibn Qayyim al-Jawziyya. *Iʿlām al-Muwaqqiʿīn ʿan Rabb al-ʿAlamīn*. 3 vols. Eds. Yūsuf Aḥmad al-Bakrī, Shākir Tawfīq al-ʿArūrī. Beirut: Dār Ibn Ḥazm, 1997.

———. *Iʿlām al-Muwaqqiʿīn ʿan Rabb al-ʿĀlamīn*. 4 vols. Ed. Ṭaha ʿAbd al-Ra'ūf Saʿd. Beirut: Dār al-Jīl, 1973

Ibn Qudāma, Muwaffaq al-Dīn. *Al-Mughnī fī Fiqh al-Imām Aḥmad ibn Ḥanbal al-Shaybānī*. 10 vols. Beirut: Dār al-Fikr, 1985; Dār al-Kitāb al-ʿArabī, 1994.

Ibn Rajab. *Dhayl Ṭabaqāt al-Ḥanābila*. 2 vols. Ed. Muḥammad Ḥāmid al-Fiqqī. Cairo: Dār Iḥyā' al-Kutub al-ʿArabiyya, n.d.

———. *Jāmiʿ al-ʿUlūm wal-Ḥikam*. 2 vols. Ed. Wahba al-Zuḥaylī. 2nd ed. Beirut: Dār al-Khayr, 1996.

———. *Jāmi' al-'Ulūm wal-Ḥikam*. Ed. Shu'ayb al-Arna'ūṭ. Beirut: Mu'assasat al-Risāla, 1998[7].

Ibn Sa'd. *Al-Ṭabaqāt al-Kubrā*. 8 vols. Beirut: Dār Sadir, n.d.

Al-'Irāqī, Zayn al-Dīn. *Al-Mughnī 'an Ḥaml al-Asfar*. 3 vols. Ed. Abū Muḥammad Ashraf ibn 'Abd al-Maqṣūd. Riyadh: Maktabat Dār Ṭabariyya, 1995.

'Iyāḍ. *Al-Shifā bi-Ta'rīf Ḥuqūq al-Muṣṭafā*. Ed. 'Abduh 'Alī Kawshak. Damascus and Beirut: Maktabat al-Ghazālī and Dār al-Fayḥā', 2000. Abridged by 'Abd Allāh al-Talīdī, *Itḥḥāf Ahl al-Wafā' bi-Tahdhīb Kitāb al-Shifā*. Beirut: Dār al-Bashā'ir al-Islāmiyya, 2000. See also al-Qārī's *Sharḥ al-Shifā'*.

Al-Jaṣṣāṣ. *Aḥkām al-Qur'ān*. 5 vols. Ed. Muḥammad al-Ṣādiq Qamḥāwī. Beirut: Dār Iḥyā' al-Turāth al-'Arabī, 1985. Reprint.

Kabbani, Hisham. *Encyclopedia of Islamic Doctrine*. Ed. G. F. Haddad. 7 vols. Moutain View: Al-Sunna Foundation of America, 1998.

Al-Kattānī, Muḥammad ibn Ja'far. *Naẓm al-Mutanāthir fil-Ḥadīth al-Mutawātir*. Ed. Sharaf Ḥijāzī. Cairo: Dār al-Kutub al-Salafiyya, n.d. and Beirut: Dār al-Kutub al-'Ilmiyya, 1980.

Al-Kawtharī, Muḥammad Zāhid. *Fiqh Ahl al-'Iraq*. Ed. 'Abd al-Fattaḥ Abū Ghudda. Aleppo: Maktab al-Maṭbū'āt al-Islāmiyya, 1970.

———. *Maqālāt*. Ryad and Beirut: Dār al-Aḥnāf, 1993.

———. *Maqālāt*. 2nd ed. Cairo: al-Maktabat al-Azhariyya līl-Turāth, 1994.

Al-Khallāl. *Al-Sunna*. 3 vols. Ed. 'Aṭiyya al-Zahrānī. Ryad: Dār al-Rāya, 1990.

Al-Khaṭīb al-Baghdādī. *Al-Faqīh wal-Mutafaqqih*. 2 vols. Ed. 'Ādil al-'Azāzī. Dammām: Dār Ibn al-Jawzī, 1997.

———. *Al-Faqīh wal-Mutafaqqih*. Ed. Ismā'īl al-Anṣārī. Beirut: Dār al-Kutub al-'Ilmiyya, 1980.

———. *Al-Jāmi' li-Akhlāq al-Rāwī wa-Adab al-Sāmi'*. 2 vols. Ed. Muḥammad 'Ajāj al-Khaṭīb. Beirut: Mu'assasat al-Risāla, 1991.

———. *Al-Jāmi' li-Akhlāq al-Rāwī wa-Adab al-Sāmi'*. 2 vols. Ed. Maḥmūd al-Ṭaḥḥān. Ryad: Maktabat al-Ma'ārif, 1983.

———. *Al-Kifāya fī 'Ilm al-Riwāya*. 2nd ed. Ed. Aḥmad 'Umar Hāshim. Beirut: Dār al-Kitāb al-'Arabī, 1986.

———. *Al-Kifāya fī ʿIlm al-Riwāya*. Eds. Abū ʿAbd Allāh al-Ṣawraqī and Ibrāhīm Ḥamdī al-Madanī. Madīna: al-Maktabat al-ʿIlmiyya, n.d.

———. *Sharaf Aṣḥab al-Ḥadīth*. Ed. Muḥammad Saʿīd Hatīboğlu. Ankara: University Publications, 1972. Repr. Dār Iḥyā' al-Sunna al-Nabawiyya.

———. *Tārīkh Baghdād*. 14 vols. Madīna: al-Maktabat al-Salafiyya, n.d. See also al-Aḥdab, *Zawā'id Tārīkh Baghdād*.

Al-Khāzin. *Lubāb al-Ta'wīl fī Maʿānī al-Tanzīl*. 4 vols. Beirut: Dār al-Maʿrifa, 197?.

Al-Lacknawī. *Al-Ajwibat al-Fāḍila lil-As'ilat al-ʿAshrat al-Kāmila*. Ed. ʿAbd al-Fattāḥ Abū Ghudda. Followed by *al-Taʿlīqāt al-Ḥāfila ʿalā al-Ajwibat al-ʿAshra* by Abū Ghudda. 3rd ed. Aleppo: Maktab al-Maṭbūʿāt al-Islāmiyya, 1994.

———. *Tuḥfat al-Akhyār bi-Iḥyā' Sunnati Sayyid al-Abrār* ﷺ with its commentary *Nukhbat al-Anẓār ʿalā Tuḥfat al-Akhyār*. Ed. ʿAbd al-Fattāḥ Abū Ghudda. Contains the latter's *Bayān Madlūl Lafẓ al-Sunna* and *Bayān Ḥāl Sunan al-Dāraquṭnī*. Aleppo: Maktab al-Maṭbūʿāt al-Islāmiyya, 1992.

Al-Lālikā'ī. *Sharḥ Uṣūl Iʿtiqād Ahl al-Sunna*. 4 vols. Ed. Aḥmad Saʿd Ḥamdān. Ryad: Dār Ṭayba, 1982.

Mālik ibn Anas. *Al-Muwaṭṭa'*. 2 vols. Ed. Muḥammad Fouad ʿAbd al-Bāqī. Beirut: Dār al-Kutub al-ʿIlmiyya, n.d.

Al-Maqdisī. *Al-Aḥādīth al-Mukhtāra*. 10 vols. Ed. ʿAbd al-Mālik ibn ʿAbd Allāh ibn Duhaysh. Makka: Maktabat al-Nahḍat al-Ḥadītha, 1990.

Maʿrūf, Bashshār ʿAwwād and Shuʿayb al-Arna'ūṭ. *Taḥrīr Taqrīb al-Tahdhīb*. 4 vols. Beirut: Mu'assasat al-Risāla, 1997.

Al-Mubārakfūrī. *Tuḥfat al-Aḥwadhī bi-Sharḥ Jāmiʿ al-Tirmidhī*. 10 vols. Beirut: Dār al-Kutub al-ʿIlmiyya, 1990. Includes al-Tirmidhī's *Sunan*.

Al-Munāwī. *Fayḍ al-Qadīr Sharḥ al-Jāmiʿ al-Ṣaghīr*. 6 vols. Cairo: al-Maktabat al-Tijāriyya al-Kubrā, 1356/1937. Repr. Beirut: Dār al Maʿrifa, 1972.

Al-Mundhirī. *Al-Targhīb wal-Tarhīb*. 4 vols. Ed. Ibrāhīm Shams al-Dīn. Beirut: Dār al-Kutub al-ʿIlmiyya, 1997.

———. *Al-Targhīb wal-Tarhīb*. 4 vols. Ed. Ibrāhīm Shams al-Dīn. Beirut: Dār al-Kutub al-ʿIlmiyya, 1997.

Muslim. *Ṣaḥīḥ*. 5 vols. Ed. M. Fu'ād 'Abd al-Bāqī. Beirut: Dār Iḥyā' al-Turāth al-'Arabī, 1954. Also see al-Nawawī, *Sharḥ Ṣaḥīḥ Muslim*.

Al-Naḥḥās. *Ma'ānī al-Qur'ān al-Karīm*. Ed. Muḥammad 'Alī al-Ṣābūnī. Makka: Jāmi'at Umm al-Qurā, 1989.

Al-Nasafī. *Madārik al-Tanzīl wa-Ḥaqā'iq al-Ta'wīl*. 5 vols. Beirut: al-Maktabat al-Umawiyya, 1973.

———. *Madārik al-Tanzīl wa-Ḥaqā'iq al-Ta'wīl*. 4 vols. Ed. Marwān Muḥammad al-Sha''ār. Beirut: Dār al-Nafā'is, 1996.

———. *Madārik al-Tanzīl wa-Ḥaqā'iq al-Ta'wīl*. 3 vols. Ed. Yūsuf 'Alī Badyawī and Muḥyī al-Dīn Mustū. Beirut: Dār Ibn Kathīr, 1998.

Al-Nasā'ī. *'Amal al-Yawm wal-Layla*. 2nd ed. Ed. Fārūq Ḥammāda. Beirut: Mu'assasat al-Risāla, 1986.

———. *Sunan*. See al-Suyūṭī, *Sharḥ Sunan al-Nasā'ī*.

———. *Al-Sunan al-Kubrā*. 6 vols. Eds. 'Abd al-Ghaffār Sulaymān al-Bandārī and Sayyid Kusrawī Ḥasan. Beirut: Dār al-Kutub al-'Ilmiyya, 1991.

Al-Nawawī. *Fatāwā*. Ed. Muḥammad al-Ḥajjār. Ḥalab: al-Maṭba'at al-'Arabiyya, 1971.

———. *Matn al-Arba'īn al-Nawawiyya*. Eds. 'Abd al-Qādir and Maḥmūd al-Arna'ūṭ. Kuwait: Dār al-'Urūba, 1989.

———. *Sharḥ Ṣaḥīḥ Muslim*. 18 vols. Ed. Khalīl al-Mays. Beirut: Dār al-Kutub al-'Ilmiyya, n.d. Includes Muslim's *Ṣaḥīḥ*.

Nu'aym ibn Ḥammād. *Al-Fitan*. 2 vols. Ed. Samīr Amīn al-Zuhrī. Cairo: Maktabat al-Tawḥīd, 1992.

Al-Qāsimī. *Al-Masḥ 'alā al-Jawrabayn*. Ed. Nāṣir al-Albānī. Beirut: al-Maktab al-Islāmī, 1986[5].

Al-Quḍā'ī. *Musnad al-Shihāb*. 2 vols. Ed. Ḥamdī ibn 'Abd al-Majīd al-Salafī. Beirut: Mu'assasat al-Risāla, 1986.

Al-Qurṭubī. [*Tafsīr*] *Al-Jāmi' li-Aḥkām al-Qur'ān*. 2nd ed. 20 vols. Ed. Aḥmad 'Abd al-'Alīm al-Bardūnī. Cairo: Dār al-Sha'b and Beirut: Dār Iḥyā' al-Turāth al- 'Arabī, 1952-1953. Reprint.

Al-Qushayrī. [*Tafsīr*] *Laṭā'if al-Ishārāt*. 6 vols. Ed. Ibrāhīm Basyūnī. Cairo: Dār al-Kitāb al-'Arabī, 1969.

Al-Rāmahurmuzī. *Al-Muḥaddith al-Fāṣil*. Ed. Muḥammad al-Khaṭīb. Beirut: Dār al-Fikr, 3rd ed. 1984.

Al-Rāzī, Fakhr al-Dīn. *Mafātīḥ al-Ghayb* [*al-Tafsīr al-Kabīr*] with Abū al-Su'ūd's *Tafsīr*. 7 vols. Cairo: al-Maṭba'at al-'Āmira, 1308/1891.

Al-Rāzī, Tammām. *Al-Fawā'id*. 2 vols. Ed. Ḥamdī 'Abd al-Majīd al-Salafī. Ryadh: Maktabat al-Rushd, 1992.

Al-Sakhāwī. *Al-Maqāṣid al-Ḥasana*. Ed. Muḥammad 'Uthmān al-Khisht. Beirut: Dār al-Kitāb al-'Arabī, 1985.

Al-Ṣan'ānī. *Subul al-Salām Sharḥ Bulūgh al-Marām*. 4th ed. Ed. Muḥammad 'Abd al-'Azīz al-Khawlī. Beirut: Dār Iḥyā' al-Turāth al-'Arabī, 1960.

Al-Shāfi'ī. [*Musnad*] *Tartīb Musnad al-Imām al-A'ẓam wal-Mujtahid al-Muqaddam Abī 'Abd Allāh Muḥammad ibn Idrīs al-Shāfi'ī*. 2 vols. Eds. Yūsuf 'Alī al-Zawlawī al-Ḥasanī and 'Izzat 'Aṭṭār al-Ḥusaynī. Cairo: n.p., 1951. Repr. Beirut: Dār al-Kutub al-'Ilmiyya, n.d.

———. *Al-Risāla*. Ed. Aḥmad Muḥammad Shākir. Cairo: n.p., 1939.

———. *Al-Umm*. 8 vols. Ed. Muḥammad Zahrī al-Najjār. Beirut: Dār al-Ma'rifa, 1973.

Al-Shawkānī. *Fatḥ al-Qadīr al-Jāmi' Bayna Fannay al-Riwāya wal-Dirāya min 'Ilm al-Tafsīr*. 5 vols. Beirut: Dār al-Fikr, n.d.

Al-Sindī. *Sharḥ Sunan Ibn Mājah*. See under al-Suyūṭī.

Al-Suyūṭī, Jalāl al-Dīn. *Al-Durr al-Manthūr fil-Tafsīr al-Ma'thūr*. 8 vols. Beirut: Dār al-Fikr, 1994.

———. *Iḥyā' al-Mayt bi-Faḍā'il Ahl al-Bayt*. Ed. Kazim Fatali. Beirut: Dār al-Thaqalayn, 1995.

———. *Al-Jāmi' al-Ṣaghīr min Ḥadīth al-Bashīr al-Nadhīr* ρ. 2 vols. Ed. Muḥammad Muḥyī al-Dīn 'Abd al-Ḥamīd. Damascus: Maktabat al-Ḥalbūnī, 1983.

———. *Al-Khaṣā'iṣ al-Kubrā aw Kifāyat al-Ṭālib al-Labīb fī Khaṣā'iṣ al-Ḥabīb* ﷺ. 2 vols. Hyderabad al-Dakn: Dā'irat al-Ma'ārif al-Niẓāmiyya, 1901-1903. Beirut: Dār al-Kutub al-'Ilmiyya, 1985. See also below, *Tahdhīb al-Khaṣā'iṣ*.

———. *Miftāḥ al-Janna fil-I'tiṣām bil-Sunna*. Ed. Badr ibn 'Abd Allāh al-Badr. Beirut and Kuwait: Mu'assasat al-Rayyān and Dār al-Nafā'is, 1993.

———. *Sharḥ Sunan ibn Mājah*. Eds. Raḥmat Allāh al-Sindī, 'Abd al-Ghanī al-Dihlawī, and Fakhr al-Ḥasan al-Gangohi. Karachi: Qadimi Kutub Khana, n.d. Includes Ibn Mājah's *Sunan*.

———. *Tahdhīb al-Khaṣā'iṣ al-Nabawiyya al-Kubrā*. 2nd ed. By ʿAbd Allāh al-Talīdī. Beirut: Dār al-Bashā'ir al-Islāmiyya, 1990.

Al-Ṭabarānī. *Al-Muʿjam al-Awsaṭ*. 10 vols. Eds. Ṭāriq ibn ʿAwaḍ Allāh and ʿAbd al-Muḥsin ibn Ibrāhīm al-Ḥusaynī. Cairo: Dār al-Ḥaramayn, 1995.

———. *Al-Muʿjam al-Kabīr*. 20 vols. Ed. Ḥamdī ibn ʿAbd al-Majīd al-Salafī. Mosul: Maktabat al-ʿUlūm wal-Ḥikam, 1983.

———. *Al-Muʿjam al-Ṣaghīr*. 2 vols. Ed. Muḥammad Shakūr Maḥmūd. Beirut and Amman: Al-Maktab al-Islāmī, Dār ʿAmmār, 1985.

———. *Musnad al-Shāmiyyīn*. 2 vols. Ed. Ḥamdī ibn ʿAbd al-Majīd al-Salafī. Beirut: Mu'assasat al-Risāla, 1984.

Al-Ṭabarī, Muḥammad ibn Jarīr. *Jāmiʿ al-Bayān fī Tafsīr al-Qur'ān*. 30 vols. Beirut: Dār al-Maʿārif, 1980; Dār al-Fikr, 1985.

Al-Ṭabarī, Muḥibb al-Dīn. *Al-Riyāḍ al-Naḍira fī Manāqib al-ʿAshara*. 2 vols. Ed. ʿĪsā al-Ḥimayrī. Beirut: Dār al-Gharb al-Islāmī, 1996.

Al-Tahānawī. *Iʿlā' al-Sunan*. 21 vols. Ed. Muḥammad Taqī ʿUthmānī. Karachi: Idārat al-Qur'ān wal-ʿUlūm al-Islamiyya, 1995. First two introductory volumes contain [1] al-Tahānawī's *Qawāʿid fī ʿUlūm al-Ḥadīth*, ed. ʿAbd al-Fattāḥ Abū Ghudda; [2] al-Kirānawī's *Fawā'id fī ʿUlūm al-Fiqh* and al-Tahānawī's *Abū Ḥanīfa wa-Aṣḥābuhu al-Muḥaddithūn*.

Al-Ṭaḥāwī. *Mushkil al-Āthār*. 4 vols. Hyderabad: Dā'irat al-Maʿārif al-ʿUthmāniyya, 1915. Repr. Beirut: Dār Sadir, n.d.

———. *Sharḥ Maʿānī al-Āthār*. 4 vols. Ed. Muḥammad Zuhrī al-Najjār. Beirut: Dār al-Kutub al-ʿIlmiyya, 1979.

———. *Sharḥ Mushkil al-Āthār*. 16 vols. Ed. Shuʿayb al-Arna'ūṭ. Beirut: Mu'assasat al-Risāla, 1994.

Al-Ṭayālisī, Abū Dāwūd. *Musnad*. Beirut: Dār al-Kitāb al-Lubnānī; Dār al-Maʿrifa; Dār al-Tawfīq, n.d. All three are offset reprints of the 1321/1903 edition of Dā'irat al-Maʿārif al-ʿUthmāniyya in Hyderabad.

Al-Tirmidhī. *Al-Sunan*. See al-Mubārakfūrī, *Tuḥfat al-Aḥwadhī*. Al-Zaylaʿī. *Naṣb al-Rāya li-Aḥādīth al-Hidāya*. 4 vols. Ed. Muḥammad Yūsuf al-Binūrī. Cairo: Dār al-Ḥadīth, 1357/1938.

Al-Wāḥidī. *Asbāb al-Nuzūl*. Ed. Ayman Ṣāliḥ Shaʿbān. Cairo: Dār al-Ḥadīth, 1996.

———. *Al-Wajīz fī Tafsīr al-Kitāb al-ʿAzīz*. 2 vols. Ed. Ṣafwān ʿAdnan Dāwūdī. Damascus and Beirut: Dār al-Qalam and al-Dār al-Shamiyya, 1995.

Al-Zamakhsharī. *Al-Kashshāf ʿan Ḥaqāʾiq al-Tanzīl wa-ʿUyūn al-Aqāwīl fī Wujūh al-Taʾwīl*. 4 vols. Cairo: Maṭbaʿat Dār al-Kitāb al-ʿArabī, 1965.

———. *Al-Kashshāf ʿan Ḥaqāʾiq al-Tanzīl wa-ʿUyūn al-Aqāwīl fī Wujūh al-Taʾwīl*. 4 vols. Cairo: al-Ḥalabī, 1966-1968.

Al-Zarkashī. *Al-Burhān fī ʿUlūm al-Qurʾān*. 3 vols. Ed. Muḥammad Abū al-Faḍl Ibrāhīm. Beirut: Dār al-Maʿrifa, 1971.

www.ingramcontent.com/pod-product-compliance
Lightning Source LLC
Chambersburg PA
CBHW030518080526
44586CB00011B/237
9781938058806